WINNERS AND LOSERS

The 1988 Race for the Presidency—
One Candidate's Perspective

Also by Paul Simon

The Politics of World Hunger
(with Arthur Simon)

Lincoln's Preparation for Greatness

The Tongue-Tied American:
Confronting the Foreign Language Crisis

The Once and Future Democrats:
Strategies for Change

The Glass House: Politics and
Morality in the Nation's Capital

Let's Put America Back to Work

Beginnings: Senator Paul Simon
Speaks to Young Americans

WINNERS AND LOSERS

The 1988 Race for the Presidency—
One Candidate's Perspective

Senator
PAUL SIMON

CONTINUUM | NEW YORK

1989

The Continuum Publishing Company
370 Lexington Avenue
New York, NY 10017

Printed in the United States of America

Library of Congress Cataloging-in-Publication Data

Simon, Paul, 1928–
    Winners and losers.

    1. Presidents—United States—Election—1988.
2. United States—Politics and government—1981–
I. Title.
E880.S65   1989   324.973'0927   88-34015
ISBN 0-8264-0428-6

Dedicated to those marvelous,
incredible volunteers who make our
system of government work

Contents

PREFACE

After the Cuban missile crisis, President John F. Kennedy recited a poem to some of his key people:

> Bullfight critics ranked in rows
> Crowd the enormous plaza full,
> But only one there is who knows,
> And he's the man who fights the bull.[1]

This book is an account by one who was in the fight on the floor of the arena, not a spectator or critic. It is a look at the fight, at the winners and losers, and more significantly, the process. As the process changes or fails to change, the public themselves become the winners or losers.

Books will be written giving insights into the presidential campaign. "Teddy" White pioneered in this field with his dramatically successful, *The Making of the President, 1960*. But this is a candidate's story. This book tells what the campaign looks like from one candidate's perspective.

I am grateful to more people than I can recount in any brief preface. Among those who read the rough draft of the manuscript were my wife Jeanne, my daughter Sheila and her husband Perry Knop, and my son Martin. All four had ringside seats at these events. Others who read my rough draft and made suggestions include my brother Rev. Arthur Simon, Jim Broadway, Gene Callahan, Dave Carle, Arthur Greles, Pam Huey, State Senator John Marty, Jim

Pyrros, Bernard Rapoport, Christopher Ryan, Jerry Sinclair, and Judy Wagner.

My secretary, Jackie Williams, has once again typed my manuscript, deciphered my virtually illegible notes, and has been patient.

And the president of the publishing company, Michael Leach, who has worked with me on some of my earlier books, again encouraged me and made helpful suggestions.

The usual disclaimer applies: None of them bears the responsibility for my views or my errors. Because so many books by public officials are in fact written by others, I should add: These are my words, my thoughts, written on an old manual typewriter. There is no ghost writer.

Paul Simon

☆ 1 ☆

PRELUDE TO A CANDIDACY

My mother has been quoted as saying that I wanted to be president when I achieved the advanced age of eight.

Congressman Dick Gephardt's mother has been quoted as saying that Dick first mentioned that he wanted to be president at the age of eight.

My guess is that hundreds of thousands—if not millions—of young Americans say at age eight they would like to become president, and their mothers are the only ones who remember those sacred moments, and only if you become a candidate.

The days when you said you wanted to become a policeman or fireman or teacher or football player or whatever are lost to posterity—only those crucial words uttered at age eight, "I want to become president."

Perhaps no one entering political life totally dismisses that possibility, even though he or she might never admit the thought to anyone. Just as reporters may say to themselves, "If I became publisher here, I'd run things differently."

My tortuous path to a presidential candidacy probably began with my father's interest in politics. He grew up in Wisconsin and believed to his dying day that the two greatest Americans who ever lived were Abraham Lincoln and "Old Bob" LaFollette, the Wisconsin Progressive governor and senator. My father, a Lutheran minister, took an unusual interest in public affairs for that period when members of the Lutheran clergy particularly were reluctant to par-

1

ticipate. The pervasive attitude among the Lutheran clergy in the United States (and unfortunately also in Germany) was that "politics" should be avoided. Few sensed that faith must be applied to life and social conduct beyond avoiding burglary, adultery, murder, and other forms of antisocial conduct. That attitude of aloofness from political life was not reserved to Lutherans. However, aloofness from social problems became more of a trait for Lutherans and Catholics in the United States, than for Presbyterians, Methodists, Episcopalians, Quakers, and other groups, in part because many Lutherans and Catholics spoke in a foreign language. Political isolation usually followed language isolation. When succeeding generations spoke English, they often did not change the pattern of political isolation. For those not familiar with the tragic deficiencies of political aloofness—not just for Lutherans and Catholics—a good jolt is provided in David Wyman's book, *The Abandonment of the Jews*. It is not pleasant reading for either Christians or Jews.

My father rejected nonparticipation. He served on the board for rural Dunn School near Eugene, Oregon, a grade school that no longer exists. One of my first political memories is of my father writing a letter to the editor of the *Eugene Register-Guard* defending the right of retail clerks to strike at a local store. He led in civil rights before the phrase became widely used; in the 1930s and 1940s, the phrase was "race relations" or "human relations." I can remember when Rev. Marmaduke Carter, a black Lutheran minister, came to preach at my father's church and stayed overnight as a guest in our home. It was unusual for a white family to have black overnight guests in the mid-1930s. My parents were among the first members of the Lutheran Human Relations Association of America, formed to promote a more open church and a more just society. In one of the most cruel actions in U.S. history, 130,000 Japanese-Americans and their relatives were taken in 1942 from the Pacific Coast states and placed in camps in Utah and elsewhere. I vividly recall my father standing in front of an old papercutter in a small printshop he had acquired to publish religious materials, explaining to my brother and me why the action taken against the Japanese-Americans was wrong. Then on radio station KORE, where he periodically delivered sermons, he spoke in his usual plain and clear-cut fashion, explaining to the listening audience why what had happened to the Japanese-Americans was wrong, just as he had explained it to my brother and me.

What seemed like a storm erupted. The Japanese attack on Pearl Harbor had evoked a patriotic fervor like nothing I have known in my lifetime. Even the American Civil Liberties Union did not stand up initially for the rights of these American citizens, nor, tragically, did Franklin D. Roosevelt or the United States Supreme Court. (Ironically, one of the few to advise the president against taking the action was J. Edgar Hoover, head of the FBI, not noted for his concerns for minorities.) The storm of controversy I remember may have been only a few phone calls and a few unhappy parishioners. Time distorts memory. I do remember taking a little verbal abuse from my friends for a short period. I wish I could record that I stood up for my father and defended the cause of justice. Thirteen years old at the time, I felt what my father had done was right on the basis of his explanation to me, but I also felt embarrassed and wished mightily that he had not done it. Now as I look back on my father's life, it is one of the things for which I am proudest of him.

Despite his concern about public issues, I do not remember my father going to political meetings, though he considered himself a Republican in those years. After the death of their movement, most LaFollette Progressives shifted over to become Republicans and in Oregon, the Republican party had leaders like Senator Wayne Morse. To this day, Oregon retains that progressive Republican heritage with Senators Mark Hatfield and Robert Packwood. Despite my father's orientation, I can recall the Roosevelt stickers on our old Model A, which my parents bought new in 1929 and kept until 1946. I also remember my father taking me at age nine to hear Eleanor Roosevelt speak shortly after the 1936 election. I read political stories almost as avidly as I did sports stories. Since sports did not interest my parents, the two major topics for discussion around our dinner table were politics and religion.

My mother shared my father's concerns but was the more pragmatic of the two. These were lean years financially. I never felt poor, though I remember my father making $65 a month, having clothes not as good as most others in my class at school, and my mother working part-time at the local cannery when fruit and vegetables ripened. I also remember the thrill of a rare ice cream cone—at a cost of five cents—at Christensen's store, and the first time I tasted a strawberry shortcake at my Uncle Rudy's and Aunt Emma's, a luxury beyond my dreams. My mother kept the family together financially, keeping my father's instincts for generosity in tow.

I acquired my mother's instincts for practicality, my father's idealism and interest in public life.

My political instincts were undoubtedly whetted when, in my junior year at Dana College in Blair, Nebraska, my peers elected me student body president. I had the opportunity to lead on a few things, including the effort to integrate an all-white student body. Toward the end of my junior year in 1949, I received the opportunity to become publisher of a small weekly newspaper in Troy, Illinois, population 1,200. My career goal at that time was to become a journalist in the tradition of two of my heroes, William Allen White and Walter Lippmann. Both were journalists who, in different ways, also played an active political role. The chance to take over a small newspaper sounded better than starting somewhere writing obituaries. I already had fourteen months as a sports writer, working about thirty hours a week at the *Eugene Register-Guard*, and I had acquired some knowledge of printing from my father's small printshop. At the time of this offer, I was nineteen. It is amazing as I look back, that with no security, people extended loans and credit for more than $3,500—a sizable sum then—to a nineteen-year-old starting in the newspaper business.

I anticipated going to this small community, writing thoughtful and thought-provoking editorials that newspapers around the nation would reprint, and gradually my influence would rise. But reality set in. My writings were rarely picked up by other newspapers, and I am sure they were not as thoughtful and thought-provoking as I intended. Local issues came to dominate my horizon, and fighting for a sewer system for a community that had none suddenly grew in importance. More significantly, illegal commercialized gambling and prostitution were obviously being winked at by Madison County officials who were in office at the behest and tolerance of some underworld figures. I did not buy this small newspaper with any intent to start what some later called a crusade; I did not have the faintest inkling of anything untoward going on in the county when I acquired the newspaper.

But I soon learned. One day at a small cafe in Troy, seated on a stool at the counter I asked the owner, Charlie Struckhoff, how much he made on the punchboards on the counter. A punchboard is a relic of the past. You would pay ten cents or a quarter to push out a small roll of compressed paper from a board. When you opened the piece of paper, you won nothing, one dollar, five dollars, or some small prize. When I asked Charlie about the punchboards, I did not know that they were illegal. He told me that ordinarily business owners would pay three dollars for a punchboard, take in about $90, and give out about $30 in prizes for a net gain of about $57. But in Madison County, he told me, unless you bought your punchboards from a man named Carl Davis, someone from the sheriff's office would come around warning that punchboards were illegal. Carl Davis charged $30, rather than three dollars, for his punchboards, so Charlie's small restaurant netted $30 rather than $57. "But $30 is better than nothing, so I go along," Charlie told me. I checked around our community of 1,200 and found thirteen businesses that had punchboards in a county with close to 200,000 in population. I got the same story about buying them all over the county.

After I wrote about that, I was inundated with reports about other illegal activities in which the sheriff and prosecuting attorney were involved, many turning out to be accurate. I eventually signed a warrant for the arrest of the sheriff for malfeasance in office and asked the Illinois Bar Association to disbar the prosecuting attorney for bringing disrespect to the law. My stories and actions resulted in my being called before U.S. Senator Estes Kefauver's committee studying organized crime. The hearings were the first televised proceedings of that type, and they captured the public's imagination. My appearance resulted in some small degree of attention in our area, much more attention than I received as a small-town newspaper publisher.

During this activity, I tried to get someone of unquestioned integrity to run for either sheriff or prosecuting attorney, but there were no takers. People were either frightened or indifferent or both.

In the midst of all this I entered the army for two years, serving in Germany. It gave me a chance to reflect on what had happened and what could happen.

I decided that after my discharge I would try to prove that you could win without the benediction of the underworld. I became a candidate for state representative at age twenty-five. The executive committee of the Democratic party in Madison County met the following evening and unanimously went on record against me. It did not seem a propitious way to start a political career. I quietly went around knocking on doors and talking to people, and on election day I won—and won big—to everyone's surprise.

That launched my political career.

I served eight years in the Illinois House of Representatives, four years in the Illinois State Senate, then four years as Lieutenant Governor. I ran for governor in 1972 and lost in a primary contest by the narrowest of margins. Two years later I successfully ran for the U.S. House of Representatives from Illinois's southernmost district. In 1984, after ten years in the U.S. House, I sought the Senate seat against three-term incumbent Charles Percy and in a major upset I defeated him.

During my campaign for governor in 1972, *Chicago Tribune* reporter Michael Kilian wrote a feature story in which he mentioned that if I were elected governor, inevitably there would be speculation about my becoming a presidential candidate. I believe that was the first time any journal of general circulation mentioned that remote possibility.

The first speculation from a public official came early in 1985, after my Senate victory. Congressman William Lehman of Florida, interviewed on Cable News Network, responded to a question about the 1988 presidential race and said that the Democratic nominee should be Paul Simon.

A few other extremely isolated items appeared in print or on television and radio, but the possibility of my becoming a candidate for President had not become household conversation—not even in my own household.

But on June 30, 1986, fifteen members of the House sent me a letter:

> Dear Paul:
>   We urge you to consider becoming a candidate for the Democratic Party nomination for the Presidency.
>   Those of us who have signed this letter are from all parts of the Nation and from all viewpoints of the Democratic Party. We are united, however, in wanting strong, effective leadership in the White House and a Democratic candidate who can win.

We believe that you have such qualities. You have the combination our Nation wants and our party needs.

We need a candidate with a proven record of attracting all parts of our society, not just the hard core Democratic base. You have shown that ability dramatically. We need a candidate who understands economic policies and has demonstrated the courage to stand up for the hard choices, even to members of our own party. We need a candidate of compassion, common sense, and vision.

You have these qualities. We hope you will seriously consider our appeal.[1]

About the same time, three members of the Senate, separately, talked to me of the possibility. Then columnist Richard Reeves wrote in his nationally syndicated column:

"If you had the power to make any Democrat president, which one would you pick?" a friend asked me over dinner the other night.

I didn't want to get into an argument. He wanted me to pick his favorite, Mario Cuomo, but he thought I might say Gary Hart. Instead, I said, half-meaning it: "Paul Simon."

"No, no," he said. "I don't mean who's the best. I mean, which of the ones running would you pick?"

. . . .

Lincolnesque is not Simon's style, except for seriousness of purpose. He misses by about 8 inches in height, miles of rhetoric and a lot of brooding. At 57, he looks like he must have in his high-school yearbook. A nerd, my kids would say. He has not done it on looks, I would say.

But, he has done it. He is a symbol of the decency and dedication that representative democracy can produce.

Simon describes himself as a "pay-as-you-go Democrat." He is fiscally quite conservative, voting for Gramm-Rudman-Hollings and sponsoring a balanced-budget amendment, but he is a solid liberal vote on most ideological issues.

"I don't want to become too acceptable to country clubs and corporate boards," he told me one day. "There's no future in being a carbon copy of the Republicans. If people have a choice, they'll pick the real thing. Ronald Reagan got elected because he projected conviction.

There's a lesson in that: You have to stand for something."

"And you have to give them a dream," he added. His dream,

constructed of a greatly increased commitment to education, tougher trade legislation and public service programs, is to "guarantee a job for every American."

"Planting trees, teaching reading, working in day-care centers," he said. "There has to be something for every American." And for himself?

"I think if anything developed on the presidency, it would have to be a self-generated thing," he said. "I have to say I think it is unlikely that a self-generated thing is going to develop."

If he means that, and he probably does, it's too bad for the dialogue of 1988.[2]

That column stirred a small—the right word—amount of interest and speculation. The state Democratic chair of California called and urged me to become a candidate, as did a handful of other leaders around the nation, all caused by the Reeves column. I had not hit any serious list of possible Democratic nominees or even dark horses. But the newspaper stories and questions from reporters were becoming more frequent. Even conservative TV talk-show host John McLaughlin had a semifavorable column in *The National Review* about the possibility of my becoming a candidate.[3]

I had genuine ambivalence about becoming a candidate. As a newcomer to the Senate, it seemed a bit hasty and presumptuous to suddenly jump into the race, even though in total years of experience in government I outranked the other possible candidates. I also really enjoyed working in the Senate. My colleagues of both political parties were good to me. Spending the rest of my public service years in the Senate did not sound like a bad option. Those factors were balanced by the reality that there really was a void in the field. I did not want to go into the next decade with the United States passing up its opportunities to meet our problems and achieve our potential.

As I mulled this over, Senator Dale Bumpers of Arkansas and I had a discussion in which he indicated serious interest in the presidential race.

Dale Bumpers, it seemed to me, had three attributes essential for an effective presidency: First, he does not listen to the polls to make up his mind. Second, he is willing to use the tools of government to solve our problems. Third, he has a deep commitment to moving away from the arms race. Those three qualities are essential if the United States is going to become the nation we wish for.

The other person whose candidacy would have kept me out of the race was New York Governor Mario Cuomo. That represented more of a gamble on my part. I did not know him that well and his knowledge of the federal government and foreign affairs is somewhat limited. But he more than compensates for whatever deficiencies he may have with a strong sense of intellectual curiosity that I find refreshing, and with a clear sense of purpose and direction. Those characteristics combined with an above average dose of courage made me feel I could comfortably and enthusiastically support his candidacy. But on February 20, as a guest on a radio call-in show, he said he would not become a candidate for president.

On February 25, 1987, I called a press conference and said I would not be running for president, that I would support Senator Dale Bumpers.

The Arkansas Senator indicated privately also to others that he would be running, but the date for the announcement kept being postponed—all for legitimate reasons—but postponed nevertheless. On Friday, March 20, Bumpers announced he would not be a candidate.

That night our home phone rang until 1:30 in the morning. And for the next few days it kept ringing. Among the callers, for example, was Berkley Bedell, who had just retired as a member of the House from Iowa and is a respected figure in that state. Berkley said that if I would be willing to run, he would donate the next year of his life to seeing that I carried Iowa. No small offer. Bernard Rapoport, an insurance executive in Texas, called and said he would help raise money if I would run; but more than that, I sensed genuine enthusiasm on his part. A nationally recognized pollster, Lou Harris, who does no polling for political candidates, called and said he had done a poll of 1,638 Democrats across the nation—a large poll—and Gary Hart came in first, Mario Cuomo second, Bill Bradley third, and far down, tied at 3 percent each, were Sam Nunn and Paul Simon, followed by the others. "But," he added, "two things are of real significance. First, we have never polled where a front-runner had as many negatives as Gary Hart. He will not be your nominee. Second, while your numbers are small, there is a surprising amount of in-depth support. I believe you have a good chance to become the Democratic nominee and the next president."

Advice—pro and con—came in by the truckload. I sought the

advice of people I respect, whose judgment I should weigh. That included, among others, Lane Kirkland, Tom Donohue, John Perkins and Ken Young of the AFL-CIO. I did not seek an endorsement from them, but I wanted to know if there was some scenario in the works that I did not know. And I wanted their advice. My soundings included people from all walks of life. My wife Jeanne and I talked it over with our children, Sheila and Martin; and then Jeanne and I spent a weekend in Florida to consider the whole matter.

The negatives were the personal things. If we were to be successful, never again could we just get in a car and travel across the country, enjoy a meal, and go to a movie without anyone recognizing us. In Illinois we can't do that today, but when we drive from Washington to Illinois across Virginia, West Virginia, Kentucky, and Indiana, we can. It could mean a year and a half out of our lives. It would certainly mean less time in the Senate during this candidacy period. It frequently would mean having what you say or do twisted and distorted. While we are somewhat accustomed to that as a senator and senator's wife, the additional dimension that comes with a presidential candidacy and the presidency is much greater.

There was a positive side too.

And the positive side differs from person to person. I would not do it because the presidency represented a political Mt. Everest, not because I wanted to live in a big white house and hear the band play "Hail to the Chief" and hear the crowds cheer. I have been in politics long enough to know how empty those things can be.

But the opportunity to lead and inspire and give the nation a vision of the kind of tomorrow we can build for future generations is exciting. That outweighed the negative considerations. I had won a U.S. Senate seat in 1984, a Reagan landslide year, saying what I believed and what I felt could be done nationally. Jeanne and I had one other thing going for us that not all candidates have: We like meeting people, and we like campaigning. I cannot imagine the agony of candidates who do not enjoy getting out and meeting people. As we talked it over, the scales started tipping in the direction of running, and I remember well that point at which Jeanne suddenly said to me, "Go for it."

☆ 2 ☆

THE RACE (I)

I decided that as soon as I knew my decision, we should let others know.

I did not formally announce until May 18, but on April 9, 1987, in the Mansfield Room in the Capitol I held a press conference in which I said:

> I dream of an America at work in a world at peace. This is not some distant dream impossible to achieve. It can happen if we have leadership that cares, that is willing to bring out the best in us, leadership that has vision, leadership rooted in the traditional values of our party.
>
> I am not a neo-anything. I am a Democrat.
>
> As I weighed this decision, I saw three children walking along hand in hand, perhaps three to eight years of age. I wondered about their future. Are we doing what we should to create a better tomorrow for them? For their parents and grandparents? To ask the questions is to answer them.
>
> To Americans who yearn for leadership that will build, that will care, that will dream, I offer my candidacy.

The reaction of our friends was strongly supportive, but the media reacted skeptically. It varied from "long shot" to "extremely long shot" to the fact that "he doesn't have a presidential appearance" to the assumption that I "would have very little appeal to young people."

11

The *Baltimore Sun* editorialized: "His candidacy seems forlorn to us today. He probably cannot do in Iowa and New Hampshire, much less on Super Tuesday, what he did in Illinois. But it is a possibility."[1]

Floyd Fithian, a former member of the House who had done a superb job as my Chief of Staff in the Senate, took a temporary leave from Senate duties to get things launched in the presidential race. Jim Rosapepe came aboard as our campaign treasurer, and Vic Fingerhut helped as campaign consultant.

An embryonic staff started to take shape.

At the time I announced, the official and unofficial candidates were former Senator Gary Hart, Rev. Jesse Jackson, Senator Albert Gore, Jr., Governor Michael Dukakis, Senator Joseph Biden, former Governor Bruce Babbitt, and Representative Richard Gephardt.

Big names talked about but not announced were Governor Mario Cuomo of New York who weeks earlier said he would not be a candidate; Senator Bill Bradley of New Jersey, who encouraged me to become a candidate and gave no indication that he would enter the fray; and Senator Sam Nunn of Georgia.

A campaign in its infancy is a pitiable thing to behold, like a newborn calf struggling to walk. It takes some stumbling and falling before the legs seem to coordinate properly and actual movement can take place.

And the first *Des Moines Register* poll in Iowa gave no encouragement to the struggling campaign or candidate; it showed me at 1 percent. The poll seemed to confirm the conventional wisdom: Simon is going nowhere. *Roll Call,* a weekly circulated in the capital area, placed my odds at 70–1.

The *St. Louis Post-Dispatch* called my entrance into the race "refreshing" and added: "His chances in a crowded field may be slim. But win or lose, Paul Simon is a thoughtful man with serious ideas that can contribute much to the party's debate on what to offer the American people in 1988."[2] The *Peoria Journal-Star* commented, "If his candidacy causes us to strengthen our focus on such issues as employment, Star Wars, budget balancing and education, then Paul Simon's very presence in the race will be worthwhile."[3] A few other journals and columnists around the nation joined in that sentiment, but *Chicago Tribune* writer Jon Margolis typified much more of the commentary: "Most people probably will have these two reactions: laughter and wonder about what Simon is smoking."4

A candidate does not need polls to tell himself that he has a long way to go. The message delivered sounds reasonably good to your own ears, but you know it needs to be polished and tuned, that it is not good enough, and that improvement will come only with time, time that is essential to get a basic message down. Those sparse "crowds"—attendance would be a much more accurate word—tell you that the public still does not consider you a serious candidate. And the lack of news coverage signals that the media still has great skepticism.

Gradually that picture changed.

Part of the change came four weeks after I announced, when Gary Hart withdrew from the race after massive national attention focused on his private life.

For at least two weeks the Hart news and withdrawal dominated all questions to me from the media. My standard reply: "I'm not a candidate for sainthood. I'm a candidate for the presidency. I believe the public can trust me. That's the fundamental issue here."

The unexpected development dramatically altered the race. The revelations about Hart came May 3, the same day a *Des Moines Register* poll showed him increasing his lead in Iowa from 59 percent to 65 percent. That same poll showed me seventh in a field of eight, at 1 percent. On June 4, the Associated Press carried this story:

WASHINGTON—The Rev. Jesse Jackson and Senator Paul Simon of Illinois have been the biggest beneficiaries so far from Gary Hart's decision to withdraw from the race for the Democratic presidential nomination, according to a [national] poll released today.

The ABC News-Washington Post poll says Jackson's support has doubled and Simon's has tripled since Hart's front-running campaign was derailed by questions about his relationship with a Miami woman.

Jackson had the highest name recognition among seven announced or expected Democratic presidential candidates, and was the first choice of 25 percent of Democrats and Democratic-leaning independents, according to the poll. That was up 13 percentage points from a poll conducted a few days before Hart's withdrawal in May, the sponsors said.

Simon ran second in the latest poll and was the choice of 13 percent, up from 4 percent in the earlier survey.

Massachusetts Gov. Michael Dukakis was third, with 11 percent, followed by Rep. Richard Gephardt of Missouri, 10 percent; Sen. Albert Gore of Tennessee, 5 percent; former Arizona Gov. Bruce Babbitt, 4 percent; and Sen. Joe Biden of Delaware, 3 percent. Fourteen percent were undecided.

But national polls at this point had limited meaning except for fund-raising. The significant polls at this point were in Iowa, where all the candidates were spending as much time as possible. Gephardt, Babbitt, and Biden were ahead of the rest of us, having devoted a good portion of two years to building a base in Iowa.

Iowa, the neighbor state to both Gephardt's state of Missouri and my state of Illinois, gave neither of us the kind of media base that Dukakis had in New Hampshire. When Mike had a Boston press conference, it reached 82 percent of the people of New Hampshire. There is only limited media overlap from either Missouri or Illinois into Iowa.

Dick and I had a slight advantage in understanding the area. Gephardt had built a base, including the rural areas, and I played catch-up. But there was a real sense that my candidacy had started to move. The crowds gradually grew, and we had a staff in Iowa, slowly growing.

A typical Iowa campaign day started with a 7:00 A.M. breakfast— early, so that the farmers would attend and so that teachers and others who had regular-hour jobs could be present. Breakfast usually would be in a small-town restaurant, with attendance rarely more than ten to twelve people when the campaign started.

Then came a series of stops at radio stations, newspaper offices, coffee hours in homes, and on to the next stop, where this would be repeated. Frequently a reporter would travel with me doing an interview between stops. Later in the campaign, the one or two reporters increased to anywhere from six to twenty, depending on the time in the political calendar and depending on how "hot" I happened to be as a candidate.

Between stops I worked in telephone calls to reporters and potential fund-raisers, dictated letters, and handled Senate matters, both in Washington and Illinois. I tried to keep on top of my Senate work as the campaign progressed. I had worked out an arrangement with the Democratic leader, Senator Robert Byrd, so that he would let me know if there were going to be key votes that might be close. On those occasions I canceled the campaign schedule and flew to Washington.

Joe Biden had not emerged as a major figure in the national polls. I regarded him as a much more significant factor in the race than most political writers did. Joe had three things going for him: a strong treasury, extensive efforts in Iowa that had developed an organization base stronger than the polls indicated, and a good mind coupled with Senate experience. I felt Biden would be one of the finalists for top honors in Iowa. He had been running for president for several years, making appearances in every corner of the nation, assisting local candidates, collecting political "due bills." Joe is a much above average speaker.

He made speeches quoting Robert Kennedy and British Labor leader Neal Kinnock and others. Perhaps because he switched to "automatic pilot" he didn't always mention the source of the lines, though he clearly had done so in some of his speeches. That mistake occurred in one of our Iowa debates in which he quoted the British leader extensively on family background and the generational change, a theme Joe had developed early in his campaign. Kinnock's lines became Biden's lines.

This televised debate tape made national news when Joe's message appeared alongside the tape of the British leader, much of it word-for-word the same. The disclosure caused an uproar.

Those who were campaign activists immediately assumed that one of Biden's opponents had made the tape available to Cable News Network, the first to report the comparison, and rumors spread as to who it might be.

In the midst of the political storm—on September 13, I remember the day well, the day after my daughter married—Biden called relating that a Delaware newspaper had quoted Dick Gephardt's campaign manager as saying I was responsible for providing the tape comparisons. Joe told me, "You're going to hear about it, and I simply want you to know in advance that I know you didn't do it. I don't know who did do it, but I know who didn't do it." A class act by a class person.

Before and after that phone call I had responded to the media by saying that Joe "had made a mistake, but I did not question his basic integrity." I did not and I do not.

Day after day the political storm clouds stayed. Biden served as chair of the Senate Judiciary Committee, and shortly after the quotation problems erupted, hearings commenced on the controversial nomination of Judge Robert Bork to the U.S. Supreme Court. What had been anticipated as the time for the Biden star to rise instead complicated his life even more. It threw him into the limelight at a time when he would have preferred to let things quiet down. Joe could have changed the dates for the hearing, but that would have caused even more furor. He took what became the only realistic option. He withdrew from the race.[5]

It turned out that Dukakis's campaign manager and close friend, John Sasso, circulated the tapes. The full story we do not know. But the surreptitious distribution and the timing—just before the Judiciary Committee hearings—gave it an unpleasant aroma. If either Dukakis or Sasso had called a press conference and taken the action openly, there would have been far less criticism of their actions. Sasso resigned as the Dukakis campaign manager. It slowed the Dukakis campaign temporarily. Dukakis had moved into the lead in some of the Iowa polls and seemed to be gathering momentum. He had a strong staff and by far the most money. For a time he looked like the person who would carry Iowa. The Biden episode changed that.

In the meantime, my campaign made slow but steady progress. Particularly encouraging from the perspective of a fall campaign were the large numbers of Republicans turning out for my Iowa meetings. Repeatedly the Democratic county chairs said they had not seen that many Republicans showing up for a Democratic meeting before. It helped to shatter the myth that someone with my views could not appeal to Republicans, a myth my 1984 race for the Senate should have demolished with the massive crossover of Republicans to support my Senate candidacy. In a poll conducted by a Republican organization in Illinois, I received 126 votes, Bush 74, and Dole 56.[6] A survey conducted by pollster Peter Hart, among favorite sons in their home states pitted against George Bush, showed:

| In New York: | Cuomo 62% | In Florida: | Graham 41% |
| | Bush 30% | | Bush 44% |

In California: Cranston 40%   In Texas: Bentsen 39%
                   Bush 50%   Bush 48%

          In Illinois: Simon 52%
                     Bush 33%

In the four states that have not gone Democratic for the presidency since 1964—California, Florida, Texas, and Illinois— I was the only winner against Bush.[7]

In Texas a conservative former Republican congressman, Jim Collins, who ran against Lloyd Bentsen for the Senate in 1982, showed up at one of my fund-raising dinners and told the *Dallas Morning News*, "I hope the Democrats don't nominate him, because he's the best they've got."[8] He went on to praise a number of positions I have taken. Columnist David Broder wrote about a woman in New Hampshire who attended a high school assembly at which I spoke: "One of the few adults who dropped in to hear the speech was deeply impressed. 'It's so refreshing to hear a candidate who is not totally preoccupied with his own ambitions,' said the woman, who declined to give her name because, she said, 'I'm a Republican looking around for someone to support.' 'When do you think you will find him?' she was asked. 'I think,' she replied, 'I just did.'"[9] Moving Republicans to become sympathetic did not mean carrying the Democratic primary and caucuses, but it gave us encouragement for the general election.

A significant development beyond the polls were some quiet meetings taking place in Iowa between the Biden organization and the candidates remaining in the field. I felt good about the meetings. The rumors circulated that the Biden people were choosing between Al Gore and me. The last meeting I had with the Biden people, and probably the "clincher," took place at the home of Lowell Junkins in Montrose, Iowa. Lowell, former mayor of that community and former majority leader of the Iowa State Senate, ran unsuccessfully for governor in 1986, but ran a good race. More significant from my point of view, he had good political sensitivities and worked well with others.

Most of the Biden people decided to come with me. It gave me a major break. Not only did we get hard-working Lowell Junkins, but with him came most of the Biden key people, including Mike Lux, a quiet but sound political operator; Bruce Koeppl, who looked like a

Chicago Bears tackle; Larry Grizalano, Biden's field director; and eventually other key people around the state, like Betty Strong in Sioux City, who lived up to her name. Dave Wilhelm, a native of Ohio who headed the operation for Biden in Iowa, moved to Ohio to lead our efforts there.

We had good people in Iowa, headed by veteran campaigner Pat Mitchell, but the Biden people had been on the Iowa scene much longer and had both contacts and experience that only time can provide. And in Iowa we were picking up additional key supporters of substance, like Harold Hughes, former governor and senator; Mayor Thomas Hart of Davenport; Arthur Davis, former Democratic state chair; and Roxanne Conlin, 1982 Democratic candidate for governor.

Meanwhile, in New Hampshire, I had a friend from the 1976 Hubert Humphrey campaign, Bob Shaine, who had encouraged me to get into the race. A successful businessman who retained his commitment to the progressive traditions of the Democratic party, he helped launch and guide our efforts in that beautiful state. We recognized from the start that the Massachusetts governor would likely take the state. Boston radio and television coverage in New Hampshire gave him a tremendous advantage. But his support remained thin, and we felt that if we carried Iowa, we had a chance of a stunning upset in New Hampshire and at least would run a strong second.

Gary Galanis, a New Hampshire native and newsman by background, became our first full-time staff person and played a major role throughout our effort. Mike Marshall, a former Indiana state legislator, later headed our enlarged staff. And volunteers played a key role there as elsewhere. John Durkin, former United States Senator, endorsed me, as did other prominent citizens, including Steve McAuliffe, widower of the astronaut who died in the Challenger explosion; and John Broderick, attorney and influential citizen. Dan Callaghan, a Manchester lawyer, devoted a great amount of time to our effort. John Rassias, a nationally known foreign language teacher at Dartmouth and an old friend, helped in Hanover. Stalwarts of the campaign included former Massachusetts Governor Endicott "Chub" Peabody and his wife "Toni." Chub had moved to New Hampshire and ran once for the U.S. Senate from his new state and had great respect. But he brought more than respect. He worked tirelessly. And there was a host of others I should be naming.

Starting as a total unknown in the state, we worked it hard, and everyone knew we were gaining ground.

In the meantime the campaign took on growing momentum in other states. Volunteers were coming on board everywhere.

Members of congress were endorsing me, not in large numbers, but the quality of the endorsements was impressive. A few key national labor leaders, while not making formal endorsements, were not so quietly spreading the word that they felt I should be the candidate. And people like former U.S. House Speaker Carl Albert of Oklahoma endorsed me. From my state former Senator Adlai E. Stevenson and Senator Alan J. Dixon went to New Hampshire to speak for me. And little things seemed to start to break for us. Early in November, the *New York Times* ran this story:

> Governor Cuomo, who had for months hinted a preference for Gov. Michael Dukakis as the Democratic Presidential nominee, indicated today that he might not endorse Mr. Dukakis and expressed strong interest in Senator Paul Simon of Illinois.
> "He looks strong," the Governor said of Mr. Simon.
> Mr. Cuomo stopped short of an outright endorsement. "I'm not saying I'm committed," he said. But, a few seconds later, he added, "I feel great, great empathy with him."
> "I've been close to Simon—I don't know that people understand that," the Governor said. "I've been reading his papers. We exchanged books."[10]

The buildup took place not just in the grass roots of the nation and among political activists but also in the media, the attitude gradually changed from laughter and derision to a recognition that something was happening.

The initial announcement received serious comment from a few on the national scene, including George Will and James Kilpatrick. Local columnists like Molly Ivins of the *Dallas Times* (who also comments for National Public Radio) said: "This is the class act, the one with brains and grace and wit."[11] They were not typical, but gradually the observations changed.

In June, two months after my initial statement of candidacy, the widely circulated *Los Angeles Weekly* rated the candidates on our policies and our "ability to carry out those policies if elected." Their conclusion in a lengthy analysis: Paul Simon is Number 1.[12]

In August, an article by Jack Beatty, senior editor of the *Atlantic Monthly*, appeared in newspapers across the country, all but endorsing me. Though he cautioned: "Can a man who looks like Oscar Levant survive on Reagan's medium, television? . . . Paul Simon—who writes his own speeches, thinks his own thoughts, is his own man—is not just running against other candidates, he's taking on a culture."[13]

In early October my distorted features made the cover of *The New Republic*, and Fred Barnes concluded: "He has a shot."[14] *The Washington Times* noted that "his surprisingly strong popularity swells."[15] The *Los Angeles Times* noted, "Simon's candidacy is suddenly being taken seriously."[16] And in October, former President Jimmy Carter said he would endorse no one, but in talking about me he added, "The South is wide open now for an approach by a candidate who will tell the truth and who will be quite progressive on social issues, on environmental issues, on human rights, on arms control. . . . What the American people are going to be looking for is someone who will tell them the truth and be competent and compassionate. . . . Sen. Simon . . . certainly has these characteristics."[17]

By November, the favorable articles had developed into an avalanche. *Time* headed a two-page article: "Simon's Simple Sermon Catches Fire."[18] *Newsweek* observed, "Turn off the lights and let a room full of intense Democrats do what lust dictates, they will nominate Simon."[19] "Could Dukakis Be Simon-ized?" was the title of an editorial piece in the *Boston Globe*.[20] The author observed: "If the Illinois senator isn't exactly hot, he's now the warmest man in this tepid field." *Chicago Sun-Times* political editor Steve Neal headed his column: " 'Tortoise' Simon Overtakes Hares."[21] David Broder's column ran beneath the words: "Sen. Simon's Stock Suddenly Soaring," and in the column he observed: "The biggest story in presidential politics at the moment . . . is the emergence of the unglamorous, still largely unknown Simon."[22]

That same month, the *Wall Street Journal* called me "the hot candidate of the Democratic race."[23] *USA Today* noted: "Illinois

Sen. Paul Simon—once dismissed as a Democratic presidential impossibility—is on a roll."[24] And in November, Jimmy Carter commented: "If he can maintain this momentum and can come out number one in Iowa, this would be a very good launching pad for the primaries in New Hampshire and the South."[25]

In early December the *New York Times* described me as "the emerging candidate." The story added: "He projects a steadiness and a solidness that consultants dream of."[26] Columnist Robert Maynard noted, "The polls are now suggesting Simon's message is falling on increasingly receptive ears."[27] And the editorial page editor of the *Wichita Eagle-Beacon* wrote, "For what it's worth, I now think he will be the Democratic nominee."[28]

But the key to everything rested in Iowa.

Our strategy was relatively simple: Carry Iowa. Build a strong enough base in New Hampshire so that with the win in Iowa I could either carry New Hampshire or run such a strong second to Dukakis that he would emerge badly damaged as a candidate. If that happened, I would carry Minnesota and South Dakota and have significant momentum going my way into Super Tuesday. On Super Tuesday I would carry at least one-third of the delegates because of momentum and because of the base of support we had in many of these states. If the first four states delivered as planned, then the public support that would emerge from key figures in the South and around the nation would have a significant impact on Super Tuesday. And after Super Tuesday we moved to states where I was the natural candidate. Well before the June 7 primaries in California, New Jersey, New Mexico, and Montana, I should have it virtually wrapped up.

The plan looked achievable.

Gore's plan, relying almost entirely on Super Tuesday, seemed to me flawed because it failed to recognize Jackson's power in those Super Tuesday states and would flounder immediately after that date. Unimpressive totals from Super Tuesday would not garner votes from the electorate of the remaining states. It might guarantee consideration for the vice presidency, and some believe that was Al's goal, but I doubt that. The Gephardt plan had much more going for it, his scenario not dramatically different from mine. Babbitt, Biden, and Hart also had similar hopes and plans. Dukakis's were also similar except that he had enough of a financial base that unlike any other candidate, other than Jackson, he could continue to be a candidate until the end, if necessary, and do respectably well. He could run a weak third or fourth in a number of states and hold in, hoping the front-runner would stub his toe. But a decisive win for Dukakis in New Hampshire was the absolute essential. A weak win, or a second place there, and he would be out and he knew it. The Jackson strategy was to keep the black base but be more restrained than in 1984, show greater knowledge, appear more the statesman and in the process broaden the nonblack base appreciably. If that could be done before Super Tuesday, that day would give him a tremendous boost for the remaining primaries and caucuses. The conservatives who put together Super Tuesday handed Jesse a powerful weapon if he could demonstrate significant support in an early state.

The 100,000 Democrats who vote in the Iowa caucuses became the first and most important hurdle for all of us.

While political commentators still enjoyed talking about "the seven dwarfs," the Democratic and Republican candidates worked hard in Iowa and New Hampshire, and the *Des Moines Register* showed me gradually climbing with each of its polls.

I went from 1 percent to 6 percent—tied for fourth place—to a late-August poll that showed me in third place, but only 5 percentage points behind the leader, Dick Gephardt, and only 1 point behind second-place Michael Dukakis.

Finally a November 15 poll published by that newspaper showed me leading, with this breakdown:

Simon	24%
Dukakis	18%
Gephardt	14%
Jackson	11%
Babbitt	8%
Gore	3%

Confirming those polls were increasing attacks on me by my Democratic opponents and harsher ones from Republican candidates. An exception was Bob Dole, who told David Frost and others that if I ended up being the Democratic candidate, the Republicans would face a tough race. Early in the campaign, when few thought I had a chance, Dole told Larry King, "They have some excellent candidates, despite what you hear. And I agree with Senator Hart about all of their abilities. However, I think Senator Paul Simon of Illinois is going to surprise a lot of pundits. I've known Paul a long, long time, and he grows on people. He is a fighter. He is very, very smart. And he is tough."[29] More typical of the Republicans were the comments of George Bush: "I wouldn't mind if the Democrats nominated Paul Simon. Next to him, I look like Clint Eastwood."[30]

Our own polling confirmed the trend in Iowa. And in New Hampshire, under the leadership of Mike Marshall and Gary Galanis, we were gradually building the best organization of any of the Democratic candidates, with a tremendous assist from a host of local volunteers headed by my old friend Bob Shaine. Our New Hampshire polls showed our quiet and not-so-quiet efforts at grass roots building were paying off. Dukakis continued to show a significant but declining lead. But we were making enough headway so that we felt if I carried Iowa, we would at least come in a close second in New Hampshire; and there were some indications that if I won Iowa, I could win New Hampshire. Dukakis had said if he could not carry New Hampshire, he would be out of the contest.

The initial key remained Iowa.

In December the *Des Moines Register* poll showed:

Simon	35%
Dukakis	14%
Gephardt	11%
Jackson	9%
Babbitt	8%
Gore	0%

Then the roof fell in. Gary Hart announced his candidacy once again on December 15. Polls taken all over the nation immediately showed him in first place and, more significantly, the *Des Moines Register* poll showed this result for Iowa only a short time after polling had shown me with a commanding lead:

Hart	33%
Simon	17%
Gephardt	14%
Dukakis	14%
Jackson	4%
Babbitt	2%
Gore	1%

Hart's candidacy was not destined to last long. "Let the people decide," he called to the nation. And they did. But Hart's entrance into the race suddenly changed the dynamics of the entire campaign. Why a Hart candidacy should knock me into second place so dramatically is not clear, but it did. A less than stellar performance by me in the NBC debate probably played a small role, though a poll taken after that debate still showed me substantially ahead. The timing of our paid media may have played a small part. Whatever the cause, what appeared to be momentum propelling me to a decisive Iowa win suddenly stopped. Momentum is a huge factor in fundraising and in garnering support. Politicians rightfully call it "the big mo." The national and Iowa spotlight which had started to focus on me, suddenly and dramatically shifted away from me to Hart. For three weeks he dominated the political news. My momentum had been broken. "The Hart reentry stopped Simon in his tracks," wrote Fred Barnes in *The New Republic*. "It had the effect of starting the race all over again."[31]

Hart's reentrance brought a devastating press reaction. Political cartoonists were brutal. Johnny Carson, Mark Russell, and other comedians found themselves loaded with material, some of the jokes cruel. Jokes that didn't make the night shows were even worse, passed around in the bars and offices of the nation, including news offices and political headquarters. As a politician you can survive good-natured ribbing and must expect it. You can survive the bitterest of criticism because, by nature, those criticisms imply that you are to be taken seriously. But American politicians have a difficult if not impossible task escaping generally circulated humor that is derisive. Columnist Ellen Goodman typified press response: "Smart, but . . . still deeply flawed, [Hart] prefers ideas to people. A man whose own ambition—A for Arrogance—propelled him back into the race. Gary Hart is out for his political salvation. But this return is hardly the second coming."[32] *U.S. News & World Report* called Hart's move "a breath of stale air."[33]

The Hart reentrance into the race ultimately did not help Gary Hart, but it caused a fatal blow to my campaign. Prior to Hart's return, one of Iowa's key business and political figures who backed me, John Chrystal, advised me to start concentrating my efforts in other states, since I had a lock on Iowa. Prior to the Hart redeclaration of candidacy, that may have been sound advice.

Meanwhile Dick Gephardt, who banked heavily on Iowa, closed down virtually all of his national campaign effort, bringing his people into Iowa. If Dick did not carry Iowa, that ended his campaign. He knew that and we all knew that. He got forty House members to come in the weekend before the caucuses to campaign for him. And he put on a television blitz with effective spots. His actions started to pay off. A January 7 poll by the *New York Times* and CBS still showed me slightly ahead of Gephardt in Iowa, but after that all the polls showed him ahead narrowly, while Dukakis and I ran either second or third, depending on the poll. Four days before the Iowa caucuses, the *Los Angeles Times* summed it up:

> Several new polls show Simon—once the leader in Iowa—now running third to Missouri Rep. Richard A. Gephardt and Massachusetts Gov. Michael S. Dukakis.
>
> Simon is used to defying last-minute polls—all of them had him losing just before he won his 1984 U.S. Senate race in Illinois. . . .
>
> Simon, an unpretentious man with a consistent record of supporting social programs, appears to engender deep affection in his supporters.
>
> One hundred of them turned out to see him in a blizzard Wednesday night in Fort Madison. . . .
>
> Simon told the crowd . . . "If you will make that extra effort for me on Monday, I will do a job as President that you will never be ashamed of."
>
> He said the same thing Wednesday to a cheering, overflow crowd of 1,000 at the University of Iowa in Iowa City. By comparison, Gephardt drew 300 Tuesday at the same site.

The press, meanwhile, keeps talking about polls showing Simon far behind Gephardt.[34]

Adding some suspense to the apparent rise of Gephardt was a February 1 editorial in the *Des Moines Register* strongly endorsing Bob Dole on the Republican side and me on the Democratic side. The newspaper commented, "Simon's lifelong interests match the needs of the times. . . . He calls for shifting resources to education, jobs, the environment, peace—not a novel program but one offered by a candidate whose record shows unquestioned commitment to it. Once before in troubled times the nation turned to an unpretentious man from downstate Illinois. The times are not quite as troubled now, and perhaps the man is not as great, but he is good, honest and eager to turn the energies of government toward long-neglected needs."[35]

The last poll by the *Des Moines Register* on the Sunday before the caucuses showed:

Gephardt	25%
Simon	19
Dukakis	15
Babbitt	9
Jackson	9
Hart	7

The Iowa caucuses are unlike anything most Americans have experienced. People from the voting district, a precinct, gather in a home or hall or church basement and stage a miniconvention. Voters discuss the virtues and defects of the candidates, then they cast their votes, and any candidate receiving at least 15 percent of the votes gets part of the vote from that precinct. Persons supporting candidates receiving fewer than 15 percent can switch their votes to another candidate. Two people may show up for a caucus and sometimes do, and 200 may show up for a caucus and sometimes do. They select delegates for the county, which then select delegates for the state.

Caucuses are less predictable than primaries (which are less predictable than general elections) because the numbers voting are so small. Iowa is a state of six million people and about a hundred thousand show up for Democratic caucuses.

Adding to the unpredictability is the "wild card" of those supporting candidates who receive less than 15 percent. When that 14 percent or 10 percent switch to another candidate, to whom will they shift their support?

Despite polls showing Gephardt ahead, we knew we were gaining. I felt we had a chance to win. The Dukakis people sensed from their whirlwind tour around Iowa the day before the caucuses that they had a real chance to win. And the Gephardt people felt confident, buoyed by the polls.

Media coverage in Iowa is intense as the caucuses approach, particularly in Des Moines. On caucus day, I made several stops around the state to "rally the troops" and then did some door-to-door work in Des Moines. Jeanne and I stopped at the first house, and only three or four cameras were there. We were a little disappointed, but when we came out of the house, it became clear that most news persons had gone to the wrong home, and we saw a horde of camera people and reporters coming over the top of a small hill. I would guess there were forty cameras—from every point in the United States, as well as other countries, including the USSR.

From the first returns that night, Gephardt seemed to have the lead in the popular vote (used by the television networks to calculate a winner) as well as the caucus totals compiled by the Iowa Democratic Party. At one point in the evening, CBS declared Gephardt the winner, Dukakis second, and me third. That quickly appeared to be the wrong forecast. Before the networks went off the air, ABC and CBS both declared Gephardt the winner with me second, but NBC said it was too close to call between Gephardt and me. Even weeks later, there were still some discussions about who had won. But the newspapers and media across the nation the next day declared Gephardt the winner, with me a close second, and Dole the winner on the Republican side. Pat Robertson ran a stunning second, pushing George Bush to third place. Dukakis ran third on the Democratic side.

The "final" Iowa Democratic results:

Gephardt	31%
Simon	27%

Dukakis	22%
Jackson	9%
Babbitt	6%
Hart	0%
Gore	0%
Uncommitted	5%

I put "final" in quotes because at 1:00 A.M., when television went off the air, the popular vote total collection, done by the networks with no official standing, stopped. About 70 percent of the votes were in. Those not counted included one large county, which leaned heavily for me.

The Republican results:

Dole	37%
Robertson	24%
Bush	18%
Kemp	11%
DuPont	7%
Haig	1%

The big story was that Pat Robertson defeated George Bush for second place. It took the edge off the Dole victory, hurting him in New Hampshire, and the Robertson story meant that Gephardt received less momentum than might be expected. My second place finish received even less attention, and a third-place Dukakis finish became even less of a story. The Robertson victory over the Vice President became the stunning news of the evening, and the major cause for comment the next few days.

☆ **3** ☆

THE RACE (II)

T he day after the Iowa caucuses, Tom Brokaw reported on the NBC news that their projection, had all the votes been tallied, was that Gephardt won by "less than one-half of one percent."

Some believe I may have won the popular vote. It is probable that Gephardt did. In any event he won more headlines the next morning. Ultimately that is what really counts.

The Democratic caucus-goers elected delegates in the precincts who ultimately cast a majority of their votes for Dukakis.

While my family and I and our key campaign workers were depressed by the Iowa results, we quickly discovered that around the nation most people felt that running second in a seven-person race was a significant achievement; and everywhere I went for several days after that—primarily in New Hampshire—people congratulated me. My comments after the Iowa race should have reflected that upbeat mood of the electorate more than they did. We had no plans to look cheerful. The Dukakis team had planned to look excited about coming in third and pulled it off.

The next key state, New Hampshire, is nestled next to Massachusetts, where the governor dominates the media in both states, and this gave Dukakis a tremendous advantage. Prior to the Iowa caucuses, all the polls showed Dukakis's support eroding in New Hampshire—while keeping a commanding lead—and Paul Simon gaining.

The New Hampshire political scene is illustrated by this mid-

December news account: "Recent polls indicate that Dukakis's lead, while strong, is slipping slightly. A recent survey taken for WNEV-TV in Boston showed Dukakis's support at 37 percent, a drop of about 10 percent from two months ago. Sen. Paul Simon of Illinois is running second with 14 percent, followed by Rev. Jesse Jackson, 11 percent; Rep. Richard Gephardt of Missouri, 6 percent; and former Arizona Governor Bruce Babbitt and Sen. Albert Gore of Tennessee, 3 percent each. Who has the best shot at second? 'Whoever gets the nod in Iowa,' said Joseph Grandmaison, New Hampshire Democratic chairman."[1] An Iowa win could be expected to boost the victor 10 to 20 points in New Hampshire. If I could come at the top end of that range, that would make New Hampshire a close contest and maybe a victory for me. (Gephardt added 14 points after Iowa.)

Instead of striving to pull an upset win in New Hampshire after an Iowa victory, I found myself striving to upset the normal expectation of the Iowa winner coming in first or second in New Hampshire. If I could make second in New Hampshire, instead of the Iowa victor, Dick Gephardt, the media would focus on a Dukakis-Simon race.

We had a better organization in New Hampshire than Gephardt, but he had the advantage of all the media hype coming off of the Iowa caucuses. We thought we had a chance for taking second place.

The day of the primary, the exit polls coming in until about four in the afternoon showed me running second; but then, the after-work voters came in, and Gephardt had connected with them, particularly in the blue collar precincts of Manchester. I came in third. The New Hampshire results:

Dukakis	37%
Gephardt	20%
Simon	17%
Jackson	8%
Gore	7%
Babbitt	5%
Hart	4%

On the Republican side, Bush resuscitated his candidacy with these totals:

Bush	37%
Dole	28%
Kemp	12%
Robertson	9%
Others	12%

The New Hampshire totals probably would have been closer on the Democratic side if we had had more money to spend on media. I knew we were strapped for funds, and I had resolved not to get into debt. On the plane from Des Moines to New Hampshire the day after the Iowa caucuses, David Axelrod and our media people said that to have an impact in New Hampshire a minimum buy would be $100,000. I indicated reluctance to spend it. Bob Shaine of New Hampshire and John Schmidt, a Chicago lawyer who had been helpful on fund-raising, both said to go ahead. They would raise the $100,000. We did the media buy.

On the Thursday before the New Hampshire primary, I flew to Washington, and the general counsel for the campaign, Leslie Kerman, and the assistant executive director of the campaign, Barbara Pape, met me at the airport.

They told me that we were over $500,000 in debt and that some checks had been written with no funds to cover them. I was appalled. I had left strict instructions to run the campaign in such a way that if we had to get out at any point, there would be no debt. That night the fund-raising director of the campaign, former Congressman Bob Edgar, called me and confirmed what I had been told.

The next day I called Jerry Sinclair in Chicago, a longtime friend and former bank president who has been successful in a variety of investments. Jerry is one of those rare people who knows and understands the business field, remains a Democrat, is trustworthy, and has been a real friend and valued supporter for more than three decades. He also knows politics. I asked Jerry to fly to Washington immediately to determine what the financial situation was, and I ordered that no checks should be written without Jerry's approval. And under no circumstances should any further loans be taken out.

When I flew back to New Hampshire my morale was not high, and when I got there Dianne Terrell of ABC wanted to talk to me.

Alone. Was it true, she asked, that my campaign owed over one million dollars? We had some debt, I responded, but I did not believe it would be that great. It turned out later her source of information was more accurate than I knew at that time. (See chapter 13.)

The night of the New Hampshire primary, I met in my motel room with Bob Shaine; Mike Marshall, our New Hampshire campaign manager; Terry Michael, my campaign press secretary; Brian Lunde, the executive director; Paul Maslin, my pollster; and David Axelrod, my media consultant. I explained our financial problem and that I would not go into debt any further. We talked about just pulling out. We talked about picking one or two southern states, holding on through Illinois and Wisconsin, and then making our big comeback in New York. Any number of scenarios were discussed, but time was pressing. I knew I had to say something to the press the next morning, that any room with eight or ten people in it discussing an issue will have, at the most, three who will really not say anything to others. The human creature can hold a great deal of food, but holding a secret is difficult in the extreme. And the rumors that would spread about our discussion would inevitably be much worse than reality.

One other thing I knew: Unless we won somewhere, we would rapidly fade from the picture politically, and even more rapidly financially. People don't give to losers.

So I decided to announce to the press the next morning that you have to win to survive, that I had to win in either the Minnesota or South Dakota contests coming up, or I would withdraw.

The reaction to the announcement turned out to be good and bad. Bad in Minnesota and South Dakota and some other states around the nation, where many took it as a signal I was giving up, though "faltering" would be a more accurate description. But good also around the nation. People were writing, calling, sending telegrams urging me to stay in the race. A woman in St. Louis called and said her only income was Social Security, and she would send me part of her Social Security check if I would stay in the race.

Two days later in Sioux Falls, South Dakota, I announced that I would stay in the race. We received an avalanche of financial response. The Monday after that announcement we received $137,512 in the mail, the largest single day we experienced in the entire campaign.

In Minnesota, I had support from a number of key legislators; from Secretary of State and former Senate candidate Joan Growe; from Minneapolis Mayor Don Fraser and his wife, Arvonne; and from Hennepin County Commissioner Mark Andrews. In South Dakota, we had built a limited base early but had little follow-through until the days immediately following the New Hampshire caucus. In Minnesota I hoped to come in second to Dukakis, but I came in third—a close third, but third. Jesse Jackson came in second. The three of us were well ahead of the rest of the field. In South Dakota the endorsement of Dick Gephardt by Senator Tom Daschle combined with effective TV spots turned out to be decisive factors, though our financial situation also played a role. We spent no money on media in Minnesota and only $30,000 in South Dakota. In South Dakota Gephardt came in first and Dukakis second, well ahead of the rest of us. Gore came in third, I was fourth, with Jackson and Hart trailing us.

At this point perception was more important than delegates. If a clear winner had emerged from Iowa and New Hampshire, South Dakota and Minnesota would have virtually sealed the victory. As it turned out, the first four states produced more confusion than clarity, though Michael Dukakis held a lead both in delegates and in the perception of emerging as a winner.

My financial situation forced me to make a decision between borrowing about two million dollars needed to mount an effective campaign in the Super Tuesday states (primarily southern states), or bypassing those states, hoping to carry Illinois despite precedents that you don't win in your home state if you fail to carry other states. If I could carry Illinois, then I could hope to do well enough to survive in Wisconsin and be able to move into New York and succeeding states where I had a solid base.

I felt the only reasonable choice, though difficult, was to spend no money in the Super Tuesday states. That caused pain because in those states we had small groups of loyal supporters who had really extended themselves for me. I hated to let them down. But our calculation, which turned out to be accurate, suggested that Jesse Jackson, Michael Dukakis, Al Gore, and possibly Dick Gephardt would all claim victories because they carried some states. We felt that Dick Gephardt would do adequately but not well and would damage himself for the future. I had traveled enough in those states to have a reasonably good feel for what would happen, and we had some dependable sources for information there.

Jackson, Dukakis, and Gore each claimed Super Tuesday a night of victory and each with some justification. Dukakis carried Hawaii, Idaho, the State of Washington, American Samoa, Florida, Maryland, Massachusetts, Rhode Island, and Texas. Gephardt carried Missouri. Gore carried Nevada, Arkansas, Kentucky, North Carolina, Oklahoma, and Tennessee. Jackson carried Alabama, Georgia, Louisiana, Mississippi, Virginia, and the Texas county delegate conventions. The result: confusion.

My home state of Illinois was the next big one.

I had decided that if I could not carry Illinois—both in total popular vote and in delegate votes—I should get out of the race. To test whether I really still had a chance, I also made a decision with which some strongly disagreed, to spend no money on television or other advertising.

Their argument had much to commend it: If I did not do well in Illinois, I would not only be out of the presidential sweepstakes, I would hurt myself in my presumed race for reelection to the Senate in 1990. They argued that people do not ordinarily vote for a "favorite son" in a presidential race if he appears to be losing nationally, even though that person may be popular. They cited a series of examples including Senator Lloyd Bentsen of Texas who lost his state decisively to Jimmy Carter in 1976.

Buttressing that side of the argument, Mike Dukakis clearly was going to exceed $500,000 on television advertising in Illinois, and Al Gore had a television expenditure of around $200,000 in the state. Dick Gephardt had decided to skip Illinois and attempt a victory in the next state, Michigan, where a number of the leaders of the United Auto Workers were backing him, in part because of his foreign trade stance.

Because people in Illinois were seeing a lot of Dukakis and Gore commercials and none of mine, I used this line over and over in speaking around the state: "Thirty years of commitment and service should count for more than a thirty-second commercial." Applause greeted those words everywhere.

Among those who were particularly helpful in Illinois were Congressmen Dick Durbin and Lane Evans, State Democratic Chairman Vince Demuzio, Attorney General Neil Hartigan and Illinois House Speaker Mike Madigan.

Jesse Jackson, also an Illinois resident, had substantial support in the state. While early in the Illinois primary campaign a Dukakis sweep seemed possible, as election day approached it became clear that would not happen. He might carry part of the state, but Jesse and I had enough votes to prevent a sweep.

In the last few days of the campaign, it became increasingly a race between Jesse Jackson and me for the top spot. My lack of visibility on television, because I had no advertisements, led some to believe that Dukakis and Gore would siphon off enough of my votes so that Jesse would emerge the winner. The day before the primary, the *Chicago Sun-Times* ran a huge four-word heading that took almost half the page of the tabloid: "Simon Down, Jesse Up."[2] The same day, a *Chicago Tribune* poll showed me losing the race to Jackson. "Jackson Jumps Ahead of Simon in Poll," read the lead political story in the biggest downstate newspaper, the *Peoria Journal-Star*, the day before the Illinois primary.[3] "Simon Sagging on Eve of Vote in Home State," read the headline in the *Boston Globe*.[4]

But the people of Illinois came through decisively for one of the more gratifying moments of the campaign. I received 42 percent of the vote total, Jackson had 32 percent, Dukakis 16 percent, and Gore 5 percent.

"Simon Gets New Life," screamed a banner headline in the *Boston Herald*, and similar front-page stories appeared across the nation. The *Herald* story began: "Sen. Paul Simon popped from his political coffin last night to beat the Rev. Jesse Jackson and Gov. Michael Dukakis in both the delegate and popular vote contests in the Illinois primary."[5] Under a heading "Simon Cleans Duke's Clock," a columnist observed: "The Massachusetts governor pulled out all stops to come in second or even first in Illinois and he failed. . . . Of the 174 delegates at stake in Illinois, Dukakis got none."[6]

The Illinois results revived my flagging campaign. In the same primary, George Bush defeated Bob Dole, and that ended the Dole candidacy. The Republicans would nominate their vice president a person with less obvious ability to appeal to independents and Democrats than Bob Dole.

Shortly before the Illinois primary, one of the more unusual incidents of the campaign occurred. At Meigs Field, a small downtown airport in Chicago, I received word that Dr. Armand Hammer, Chairman of the Board of Occidental Petroleum, wanted to talk to me. A man in his eighties, he has done as much as any single American to improve U.S.-Soviet relations. He has known all of the Soviet leaders since Lenin. A hugely successful American industrialist, he has used his considerable talents to do much more than make money. He has helped Soviet citizens emigrate, has enriched the art world through his impressive collections, and is a man of uncommon vision, whether the issue is energy or world politics. We have met and visited from time to time, though I do not know him well. I did know that he was close to the Gore family. Al Gore Sr., the former senator, serves on the board of Occidental Petroleum. I took the call, and Hammer told me that if I called a press conference and endorsed Gore for president, I could have any cabinet spot I wanted. He said the news would be dramatic and tip the presidential scales in Al's direction. The proposal came perilously close to a technical violation of the law, though I knew Hammer well enough to know that his intent was good, and he would not knowingly violate the law. I thanked him but I did not call him back, nor did I ever discuss it with Al, who probably did not know of the call.

My winning in Illinois confused the presidential race further and, for a time, most observers felt we were headed to a brokered convention. "Democrats Approach Gridlock," read the subhead of the *Baltimore Sun*.[7] "The [Illinois] result left the overall Democratic campaign even more confused," observed Thomas Oliphant in the *Boston Globe*.[8] Paul Taylor of the *Washington Post* wrote that the decision of Illinois voters "to give most of the state's delegates to Paul Simon only increased the prospect that no candidate will be able to win a majority of delegates by the close of this year's primary season."[9]

My aim now was to survive until New York, where we had a base of considerable support and a good campaign. The way to get there seemed clear: Bypass Michigan and do well in Wisconsin.

I had made two fund-raising appearances in Michigan, appeared on a few campuses, and spoke at a major Democratic fund- raiser in Detroit where, among other things, I said:

Some of you will be old enough to remember when an east coast governor ran for President. His name began with the letter "D."

This east coast governor had more money than anyone else. He had a better organization than anyone else. And he said that he ran his state efficiently.

And all the media said he had the inside track to victory.

But he ran against a plainspoken man from the heartland of America, who spoke from the heart, who frequently wore a bow tie. He wasn't as glamorous. He didn't have the finest organization. He didn't have the most media endorsements. But he had heart. He stood up courageously against special interests for the working men and women of America and for the less fortunate.

And Harry Truman defeated Thomas E. Dewey.

From the viewpoint of my candidacy the ideal answer would have been for Gephardt to take Michigan, slowing the Dukakis candidacy. But the press and the public perceived that Gephardt would make a weakened last stand with depleted resources, notwithstanding some United Auto Workers support. The Michigan selection process is a strange hybrid—not really a caucus, not really a primary. Most people chose not to vote, and the hybrid evoked intensity politics. Jackson had it; Dukakis did not; and Gephardt had it only in a few blue-collar suburbs. Jackson scored a big victory, fueled by enormous margins in the black community, a good showing in some college towns and considerable interest in Michigan's Arab population, the largest of any state in the nation. Jackson pulled one of the few genuine upsets during the entire preconvention period.

After Michigan, Gephardt withdrew as a candidate, narrowing the field to Dukakis, Jackson, Gore, and me. Dick withdrew rather than simply suspending his campaign to hold onto the delegates and exercise what influence he could have through them. Under Missouri law it seemed doubtful that he could simply suspend a campaign and be a candidate for the U.S. House. He did not dare risk clouding the legal status of his House candidacy.

Wisconsin seemed natural turf for me. It has a progressive tradition, and my grandparents were dairy farmers in Wisconsin. I still have relatives there—many more than I knew I had when I announced my campaign. I had to do well in Wisconsin to survive. I knew it and I said it.

But Michigan changed the dynamics of the entire race. What had been a multicandidate field, with Dukakis out front, suddenly changed into a race where it looked like Jesse Jackson might emerge as the candidate, a result feared by some for legitimate political reasons and by others for bigotry.

Michigan changed Wisconsin from a who-can-win question to a stop-Jackson effort on the part of many. The question posed by the national and local media: Can Dukakis stop Jackson in Wisconsin? As a result most voters viewed the race that way. The few dollars I mustered for television had little impact. Dukakis won. That turned into the key post-Iowa decision of the preconvention campaign, though it was not that clear at the time. Dukakis led the field by a wide margin with 47 percent, Jackson trailed with 27 percent, and the rest of us divided the remainder. I trailed Gore, who came in third.

After Wisconsin I suspended my campaign. I suspended rather than withdraw because I did not know yet what would happen, and I wanted to use whatever influence I had through my delegates at the convention. A deadlocked convention still seemed possible, though I recognized a deadlocked convention would not move in my direction. Former President Jimmy Carter said there was a 50–50 chance for a brokered convention. Some key people in other camps favored me as the fall-back candidate if Dukakis did not emerge, but a more likely scenario would be for the convention to turn to someone then not in the race, such as Governor Mario Cuomo of New York, Senator Bill Bradley of New Jersey, or Senator Dale Bumpers of Arkansas.

I had spent a year of my life attempting to influence the policy of my country through my presidential candidacy, and I was not about to simply throw that influence to the winds. Some in both the Dukakis and Jackson camps criticized my suspending and not withdrawing. But I am sure, had the situation been reversed, each of them would have done the same thing.

On April 7, I told the press:

> I am today suspending my campaign for the presidency.
> I am grateful to all who have campaigned with me and for me,

and I leave the field of active campaigning with no regrets for having made the race. . . .

Where I have had the opportunity to reach people, I have seen them respond with a selflessness that must be tapped. Americans instinctively know that we are one nation, one family, and when anyone in that family hurts, all of us eventually hurt. There really is a yearning across this good land for leadership that appeals to the noble in us, rather than the greed in us.

I wish I had been able to tap that yearning more effectively, but to the extent my supporters and I have been able to reach out and talk about programs and a vision of a better nation, to that extent we have helped to make possible the building of a better nation. . . .

The Polish writer, Kazimierz Brandys, tells the story of two who were approached during a period of ferment in Poland and asked to protest the illegal arrest and imprisonment of a leading intellectual. One refused to sign and said, "I can't. I have a son." The other immediately took out his pen and said, "I have to sign because I have a son." Both acts are understandable, but the legacy of honor that one leaves is vastly different than the other.

I entered this race because I have a daughter and a son.

I entered this race because I have had the good fortune to understand that vast difference in the lives of millions of people action by government can make. . . . I entered this race because I want this generation to give the coming generations a sound economy, not an uncontrollable debt. I entered this race because I see a nation indifferent to the wasted lives of far too many— children in schools where fear dominates rather than learning; older citizens and their families financially devastated by long-term care needs; hardworking farmers devastated by short-sighted government policies; people eager to work who cannot find a job, who lose pride in themselves and their families and their nation; and communities gripped by the terror of crime. I entered this race because I know that the President of the United States can lead our nation and other nations away from the arms race. The blight of the arms race and unemployment and crime and inadequate health care and educational shortcomings are not the result of acts of God, but the result of insensitive leadership, chosen by a people who sometimes are not as caring nor as careful as they might be.

I know we can do better. You know we can do better. I want leadership that will provide that.

I said that I would remain technically in the race, though not an active candidate, at least until after the last primaries. The New York primary virtually sealed the nomination for Dukakis; and the final primaries in California, New Jersey, Montana, and New Mexico on June 7 did lock it up. The next day I announced I would vote for Dukakis at the convention. In my statement I paid tribute to Jesse Jackson for his campaign efforts and for calling our attention to the needs of the less fortunate. While there is a time to fight, I felt that now the time had arrived for healing. Some Dukakis leaders put substantial pressure on my delegates to announce for him prior to June 7, and I received several calls urging me to do the same. I felt that as long as there still was a real contest, in fairness to my delegates and to Jackson, I should not declare. I saw no point in continuing any contest after the last primaries. For the same reason I declined the advice of friends who wanted me to go through the business of being nominated and pick up my approximately 180 delegates on the first ballot. Some of my delegates, particularly six from Minnesota, wanted to vote for me as a gesture even if no one nominated me, I dissuaded them. The contest was over.

A few in the black community, including Jesse Jackson, were unhappy with my endorsement of Dukakis, since Jesse and I are both from Illinois. Perhaps I should have handled it more tactfully, but I felt the fight was over and the sooner the party pulled together, the greater the possibility of victory.

Some speculation emerged about my becoming a vice presidential candidate shortly after I got out of the race. A few around the nation wanted to organize a campaign quietly to increase that possibility. I asked them not to do it. First, I felt that Dukakis would move to his right to select a vice presidential candidate. Second, life is too short to be doing something you might not enjoy. The vice presidency by its nature is largely ceremonial, attending state funerals, cutting ribbons on grand occasions, representing the president at an inauguration, doing a host of things that are important but not my "cup of tea." My interest is policy making. I should stick to what I know and enjoy and I am good at. I conveyed to the Dukakis people my noninterest, though I don't believe they would have come my way anyway.

A few days after the last primary Dukakis called me, and I gave him my evaluation of various vice presidential possibilities. I recall that the four we talked most about were Senators Bill Bradley, John Glenn, Dale Bumpers, and Lloyd Bentsen. Several other names were discussed briefly, and I told him that if geography were not a factor, Senator George Mitchell of Maine should be considered, but two candidates from New England was just too much politically. He agreed, expressing a high opinion of Mitchell. I also mentioned that had things gone my way, one of the names I would have considered was one that he probably could not, Bill Moyers. Well-respected by the media and with Texas roots, he has background enough in the presidency through his White House work to understand the role there and, so far as I know, is sound on the basic issues. But I added that in Mike's situation, he almost had to get someone with congressional experience.

On two other occasions I discussed the vice presidential situation with Dukakis, once with Bill Bradley, and once with Dukakis's campaign chair, Paul Brountas, who had made a uniformly favorable impression upon those on Capitol Hill with whom he talked. Mike had a high opinion of Bradley but said he would not run. I talked to Bradley—for whom I have a high regard—about the possibility, but he remained rigid, clearly unwilling to consider it.

As of Sunday night, July 10, I thought it would be John Glenn, though neither Dukakis nor Brountas told me that in so many words. Tuesday morning I had breakfast with Tom Dine, executive director of the American-Israeli Public Action Committee, and in the midst of breakfast I received a phone call from Dukakis telling me he had chosen Lloyd Bentsen. I told him Bentsen was a great choice and that I would do everything I could to help.

I had studied the electoral college votes enough during the course of the campaign to know how vital Texas would be. Lloyd Bentsen would help there and also in Oklahoma and Louisiana because of their sensitivity to energy problems. More than that, during my years in the Senate I had come to respect Bentsen a great deal. He does not fit conveniently into any philosophical pocket, but he has humanitarian instincts, sound judgment, and he wears well. He also fits well with Dukakis. He is anything but brash, not typical of what some think of Texans. While there were critics of the choice, John F. Kennedy received far more criticism of the Lyndon Johnson selection—in part because of Johnson's style, in part because of Johnson's record. Both Johnson and Bentsen were effective but with totally different styles. Johnson could be noisy, crude, a man who grew up in poverty and felt he had to prove himself. But aside from foreign policy, where his record was not an illustrious one, he effectively moved the nation toward major achievements on the domestic front. Bentsen is low-key, polished, and has a great sense of self-confidence. A reporter described Bentsen to me as "a nice beige, not primary colors."

The New Republic called Bentsen "a lousy choice," but even that editorial did not receive prominence in the magazine.[10] Criticisms were few and mostly muted. The reaction in the Senate that morning to the Bentsen selection was overwhelmingly positive among both Democrats and Republicans. The Kennedy-Johnson ticket carried in 1960, with 303 electoral votes, but those same states today produce only 285 electoral votes, only 15 more than is needed to win.

☆ 4 ☆

THE CANDIDATES

After interviewing all the candidates but one—George Bush, who declined the hour-long interview—Marvin Kalb wrote: "I developed a grudging admiration for almost all of them. The people who ran for President of the United States in 1988 are serious men and sturdy patriots. They are well-educated and well-informed."[1]

I had known all of the Democratic and Republican presidential candidates, with the exception of Bruce Babbitt, before entering the race. But insights into your fellow candidates grow.

Bruce, known to me only as a vague figure in his service as governor of Arizona, came to be more central in the campaign than his vote count ultimately indicated.

He formally announced his candidacy on March 10, 1987, but he had been making moves prior to that. Two years earlier, Bruce had arranged for young people to help candidates and the party organizations in both Iowa and New Hampshire, working it so that the cost would not be attributable to his ceiling on expenditures for these two states imposed by the Federal Election Commission. He, Dick Gephardt, Joe Biden, Jesse Jackson, and Gary Hart were the first to start their campaign efforts and planning. Mike Dukakis followed. Mike had early planning but less public and less obvious campaign activities than the others. Al Gore and I trailed badly in the advance efforts.

Bruce had pockets of strength in both Iowa and New Hampshire.

Nonideological and blessed with a good mind, he often brought a fresh approach to issues. He had reflected more than most non-federal officials on foreign policy and had a good comprehension of the general sweep of historical forces. He did more than master details on issues. He had a weakness, however, often shared by candidates without federal government experience, in not having a feel and an understanding of what is achievable and what is not. A president has to lead with initiatives for the nation, but he must also understand which initiatives Congress might pass and which would have no chance whatsoever. Lack of background leads to simple mistakes. Babbitt criticized a proposal I made to eliminate two totally unneeded new nuclear aircraft carrier flotillas that are now on the way to construction at a cost of $36 billion. His inaccurate criticism simply reflected his lack of knowledge of the federal budget process.

Babbitt's proposals to increase taxes resulted in his becoming the media's favorite candidate. Anyone who is willing to commit political suicide in public, and do it on a rational basis, has a ready market with political commentators. One editorial writer edged close to what others thought: "The question many have about Bruce Babbitt: Does he want to raise taxes because he is single-digit in the polls or is he single-digit in the polls because he wants to raise taxes?"[2]

The only significant unfavorable publicity that Bruce received came after Al Gore's disclosure that Gore had smoked marijuana as a student. The issue arose when a Supreme Court nominee, Alan Ginsburg, admitted that he had smoked marijuana. A reporter asked the same questions of Gore. Then the rest of the candidates were asked the same question. Bruce said he had also smoked marijuana. As the oldest of the candidates at age fifty-nine, I said that not only had I never smoked marijuana, but I had never even been invited to smoke marijuana. To some, that may have indicated that I have a much too limited social circle. I told reporters that I did not know of anyone who smoked marijuana or used drugs when I went to high school and college. In high school if we really wanted to do something beyond the pale of authority, we would get a six-pack or case of beer and go off into the woods somewhere with a few friends and drink it. I indicated that I felt that a youthful indiscretion should not disqualify either Babbitt or Gore, and I believe most people feel that way, though a former United States Attorney berated me for my stand. "I've had to stand up to pressure to put people into prison for selling marijuana," the prosecutor told me, "and now you tell me that someone who buys the stuff, who is a partner in that crime, should be considered for the presidency."

The marijuana matter lasted only a few days and then all but disappeared.

But Babbitt for a brief period received more favorable publicity than any candidate. That, plus a sizable investment in early Iowa television, somehow did not significantly raise him in the polls. As his failure to rise in the polls became apparent, Bruce became a little desperate. He became the candidate of gimmicks in debates, and became a little too "I'm virtuous and you're not" toward other candidates for anyone's comfort. The few sour notes—and we all had them—did not detract from someone who emerged from near oblivion to become a known quantity on the national scene, someone who would make a good Secretary of the Interior, or fit into a foreign policy post. Gary Hart presented himself as the champion of "new ideas," but if there was one candidate among us who offered more new ideas—some of them impractical—Bruce Babbitt deserves the credit.

Bruce had one other major problem: He and television did not mesh well.

Joe Biden came closer to putting it together than most political analysts realize. He emerged as the tragic figure in the campaign, his significant effort derailed by a mistake in political oratory. Next to Jesse Jackson, Joe had the best oratorical skills of any candidate. But those oratorical skills helped sink his candidacy. In an Iowa debate Biden did not mention that the eloquent words he used were from another speaker. Soon his mistake became front-page news and perhaps even more devastating, every political cartoonist in the country had the American people chuckling. Joe made the only realistic decision he could; he stepped aside.

Biden had a well-financed campaign. He had been building his war chest for a long time. He had the best campaign staff of any candidate in Iowa. And more than most of us, he had built a small core of supporters in all areas of the country, particularly in the Jewish community.

The Delaware senator's oratory caused him problems in another way. His first speech in any locality really lifted people. There emerged the expectation that that lofty level of inspiration could be maintained, and no candidate or speaker can do that. One reporter described him to me as "very personable, and a good hand-shaker when he felt like it, but too often he didn't seem to enjoy that personal end of the campaign." He also came across to some as less than thoughtful and a little abrasive, but his candidacy did not last long enough to discover whether those criticisms would have been meaningful.

The polls did not show him to be a major factor in the race when he withdrew, but those polls were deceptive. At this point the only polls that really had importance were in Iowa and New Hampshire. He did not look like the winner-to-be when he quit the race, according to the national polls, but when you factor in his superior staff—a crucial factor in a caucus state like Iowa—and his oratorical skills, and the fact that he handled himself well in debate, Joe Biden might have ended on top of the heap in Iowa and been launched toward the nomination.

Governor Michael Dukakis emerged as well financed, well programmed, and somewhat cautious. I wish I could have been the first of those three. But the primary reason he came out on top is not because of those three attributes. If money alone could do it, John Connally would have been nominated for the presidency.

Michael Dukakis's great virtue turned out to be a simple one: He didn't try to fashion himself along the lines of anyone else. He did what he felt comfortable doing and ultimately that turned out to be a great strength in getting the nomination. Robert Farmer, his indispensable financial wizard, related to me: "The day before the Iowa caucuses, we made the rounds of airports in that state for press conferences and appearances. No one knew what might happen, but we felt that we had a real chance to be first. Then the votes started coming in, and it became clear we would end up in third place. That night some of our key people started talking about dramatic changes, particularly changes in Michael's approach; that he had to become much more aggressive, become much more negative. After listening for a while, he turned to us and said, 'No.' That was it."

Mike learned about the nation in the process of the campaign, as we all did, but I sense that he learned more, that he had a longer road to travel. He understood parts of Boston and New York but not Iowa and South Dakota. The campaign developed a more rounded Michael Dukakis.

He enjoys campaigning less than some candidates do. The smile is sometimes forced. In the multicandidate setting of the Polk County (Des Moines) Democratic Steak-Fry, when some of the other candidates shook hands wherever a hand could be reached, Mike shook hands for a period but then sat down and ate. Sensible, some would say; not good politics, others would comment. I perceived that this grew less out of a need for food than from a sense that it offered an opportunity to get away from the handshaking routine.

But his great weakness as a candidate—and perhaps would have been as a president—is that he does not convey passion. What does he believe in *strongly?* On the problems of poverty and poor-quality urban education, would he work at the edges of these issues, or would he really lead and march on the problems? I don't know the answer. A college classmate has described Dukakis as "bright but somewhat remote."[3] That is the impression he gave to many Americans.

The Massachusetts governor has said, "People say I'm not a passionate guy. . . . My wife thinks I'm passionate and so does *Playgirl Magazine*."[4] But obviously a different kind of passion is needed to form and guide and lead policy through the rugged course that real presidential leadership requires. *U.S. News & World Report* observed about Bush and Dukakis, "They are tinkerers who will only be forced into the bold stroke by circumstance."[5] Born within five miles of each other, the two candidates share much, though there are substantial policy differences between them. How much visceral commitment there is to those policy differences, I cannot judge.

A small incident in his New York campaign illustrates both Mike's strength and weakness. Addressing about five hundred people gathered on the street in a Jewish area of New York City, he gave them his standard speech about the economy and the need for new leadership. He said nothing about Israel, nothing about his wife being Jewish. Someone in the crowd shouted at him, "Say something significant!" Dukakis ignored the comment. To his credit he did not pander, he did not demagogue. But neither did he stir an audience that wanted to be stirred.

After I suspended my presidential campaign, I met on a legislative matter with a nationally prominent leader of the Jewish community, and we started talking about the turmoil in the Middle East. I said that I felt that significant steps toward peace between Israel and her neighbors could be achieved despite hardening positions on both sides, but that it "would take a president with a real gut commitment to achieving peace in that area. The road will be rocky." He agreed and added, "I know both Bush and Dukakis and have met with them several times. I know some of those close to each man as well. I regret to say that gut commitment is lacking in both of them."

He may be wrong. I have heard people say that Michael Dukakis lacks the toughness to be a good leader. I know the answer to that. He has it. Lack of visible toughness is not always a sign of a lack of real toughness, and lack of visible passion is not always a sign of a lack of inner passion.

People close to Dukakis say he should broaden himself a little. Someone has described him as "poetic as a slide rule."[6] That is not fair, but there probably should be a little more poetry in his life, a little less prose.

I like his analytical mind, his lack of pretention. He is cautious yet hard-driving. There would not have been great surprises in a Dukakis administration. But I hope he would have detached himself enough to climb figuratively to a mountaintop to see the big picture and then inspire us, as well as manage us. A little more of that in the campaign would have helped.

The Massachusetts governor surrounds himself with capable people; however, he needed to develop further public evidence of a strong sense of direction and purpose. But this nation would have been much more likely to act on our difficulties and our potential with Michael Dukakis at the helm than we are with George Bush there.

Congressman Dick Gephardt started as a total unknown on the national scene and through hard work emerged as a significant factor in the campaign. He started early, working Iowa and New Hampshire before some of us were seriously thinking about the race.

Initially Dick seemed unlikely to have an impact. Both his personal campaign style and speaking ability were criticized. He worked hard and improved the latter immensely, emerging as one of the better stump speakers among the candidates. Whatever stiffness and routineness he had in shaking hands with people were more than offset by the warmth of his wife's abilities in that category.

His basic message of fighting "the establishment," of standing up for working men and women against entrenched interests, may not have been totally consistent with his legislative record, but it ignited a spark in Iowa. He delivered his message well, both through television and in person. For his media handlers, he was almost the ideal candidate because he could change to a different jacket or a different speaking style or a different position with apparent ease.

My sense is that the Missouri congressman is more cut out to be a legislative leader than to lead in the executive branch. There is a difference. On two occasions I've had my legislative colleagues come and ask me to pursue a noncommittee legislative leadership post, and on both occasions I have declined because I am not cut out for that. A minority or majority leader constantly has to be concerned with the opinion of his colleagues on any given subject. If I want to be the only Democrat to take a stand on a certain issue, I want to maintain the freedom to do that. I don't want to be worrying constantly about offending my colleagues and losing my leadership post. To be an effective president, on the other hand, you need a strong sense of conviction and direction; you have to *believe* in your causes. The criticism leveled at Dick Gephardt of shifting substantially on significant issues is justified for someone seeking the presidency, but what is a weakness in the presidency can be a strength for a legislative leader. My guess is that he could emerge eventually as Speaker of the House or a Senator from Missouri and make a significant contribution to the nation.

Albert Gore, Jr., shared one of my campaign's problems: getting into the race late without advance planning. His father, a former Tennessee senator, once had presidential ambitions and came close to becoming the vice presidential candidate with Adlai Stevenson in 1956. The family had inhaled the presidential air and Al caught the germ. Albert, Sr., passed it along to Albert, Jr., not as a genetic flaw but more like influenza: proximity to the disease.

The youngest of the candidates at thirty-nine when he announced, his youth occasionally showed in a brashness of style that time usually tempers in successful politicians. But the in-depth knowledge that he has on certain aspects of defense and arms control offset the youth factor. Few took his candidacy lightly.

Several times journalists described him as "an older man's version of what a young man ought to be." His candidacy did not take off on campuses—where some expected him to do well— nor in Iowa and New Hampshire, and he had invested substantial time in both states. In a conversation with me, one reporter noted Gore's "inability to really relax." Even in debates, he told me, he sounds "like he got tips from his speech teacher five minutes ago" and is trying too strenuously to put the lessons into practice, concentrating more on that than his message. He came across to some viewers as the deliverer of a "canned" message, rather than someone with genuine beliefs. One reporter described him to me as "nice-looking but a long way from being ready for the presidency." Many shared that feeling. That is not age alone, though in my opinion he is infinitely closer to being ready for the presidency than is the slightly older Dan Quayle, Bush's vice presidential choice.

Al's substantial abilities were clouded somewhat by charges of pandering and his shift in emphasis after Senator Sam Nunn made clear he would not become a candidate, a real watershed moment in the Gore campaign. Gore's strategy helped him in the South but not elsewhere. He ended doing better than most experts predicted and has emerged as a national figure.

My sense is that Al is still sorting out who he is and what life means to him. His passion is to have an impact on the arms race. Here his motivation is the best, even though he has accepted too readily the notion that by piling up weapons you can force arms control agreements.

He will be a presidential candidate again and probably a better one the next time he runs.

Gary Hart played the role of a loner in the U.S. Senate and played a similar role in the campaign. Saying that by itself does not give him his due. Gary's much-publicized initial departure as a candidate obscured a role he had in the Senate, as a candidate, and as a thoughtful observer. A little on the dull side as a public speaker, he looked better outside the political ring than inside it. Even when he led the political polls in the first leg of his candidacy, there were relatively few Democratic leaders who endorsed him. He neither gave enthusiasm and warmth nor received them. After the Donna Rice matter became public and he stepped aside, he continued to run strong in the polls. That strength surged temporarily following his reannounced candidacy. But despite the high poll numbers, on the scene in Iowa and New Hampshire support appeared to be thin.

My daughter Sheila and her husband Perry Knop spoke to two high school classes in Iowa after Hart's reemergence as a candidate. When the subject of his candidacy came up, Sheila asked the class how many of them would vote for Hart. Not a hand went up, but the class giggled. In a second class one student raised his hand, and the rest of the class laughed at him. "Sorry," that embarrassed student immediately responded and hastily pulled down his hand. The significance of those two classes is that they are much like a caucus, where you have to stand up before your friends and neighbors and say whom you support. Not many wanted to be laughed at by their neighbors, and Hart's support diminished rapidly.

Hart fashioned himself as the candidate of new ideas. There were not many. Most of us who come up with what appear to be new ideas acquire them from others, and frequently what are presented as new ideas are rephrased old ideas. One new idea Gary had that should have received more attention: joint U.S.-Soviet research on arms verification. For a great many reasons that makes sense; and until Gary Hart proposed it, I had not heard the idea.

In some ways Gary was more the philosopher than the candidate, more the observer than the participant. He seemed somewhat remote from reality, an easy position into which a candidate can place himself or herself. More than the other candidates, he is self-focused, introspective, and reflective.

Three days after his few flickering hopes disappeared on Super Tuesday, Hart gracefully exited. "I got a fair hearing. And the people have decided. Now I clearly should not go forward."[7]

He is too bright and too thoughtful not to contribute to public service in the future, whether through writing, or with a foundation, or in some other form. Gary Hart will reappear but probably not as a candidate. Sometimes defeated candidates are consumed by cynicism and bitterness. If Gary Hart can avoid those two pitfalls, he can contribute much to the nation in the decades ahead.

In many ways the most fascinating personality in the cast of characters of the campaign is Jesse Jackson. Both very open and an enigma at the same time, among the contributions he made to the party and the nation was seeing to it that those less fortunate were not forgotten.

Both feared and loved, he became the celebrity of the campaign. His instinct for the right phrase, the quick response that makes national television, and the crowd-pleasing dramatic gesture, marked him as the real professional before an audience while the rest of us were amateurs.

Never did Jesse Jackson grip an audience more than when he talked about his own background. In a New Orleans debate at Tulane University, cohost Hodding Carter asked us about the nation's poor. Jackson's response came from the heart; we all felt it:

> Hodding, of the people on the stage I was the poorest the longest and the most recently. I was born to a teenage mother who was born to a teenage mother. Now, how do you break out of that cycle? A combination of things: spiritual, personal, and governmental. A mother who cared and who did not surrender was a factor. Love is a factor in making people come alive and dream of their predicament. Secondly, the option to get an education. A public school system that worked for us, and when teachers gave homework, mother made me be home to do that work. It was a partnership between school and home, of teacher and parent. That was a factor in getting out. Secondly, a public housing system, Fieldcrest Village, gave us for the first time a concrete floor and heat and a refrigerator. That was a factor in getting out. My father came home from the military service and got those extra ten points and became a janitor at the post office and mama was able to go back to school when I was about twelve to become a beautician.
>
> It was a combination of private initiative and government support to break that cycle.[8]

Jesse Jackson's audience-gripping speech to the Atlanta convention reached its emotional height when he talked about his childhood, his background. Then we sensed the *real* person, opening his heart, not simply an eloquent preacher.

Sometimes Jesse seemed more exuberant than thoughtful, but at other times he penetrated to the heart of issues in an uncanny way.

Essential details in his proposals often were missing, and also absent from time to time was any sense of what could and could not be accomplished.

At first the press wrote him off as a serious possibility, as did the rest of the candidates. Neither the press nor the candidates said that in so many words, but it remained the unspoken assumption. That resulted in his sometimes receiving less than serious questions in the first part of the campaign; and then when his candidacy took on a more serious cast, those questions seemed inappropriate, rude.

Observers expected Jackson to be a disruptive force in debates and in the campaign as he was in 1984. Instead, during the primaries he became a reconciler and healer more than any candidate, though that role shifted a bit prior to the convention and after it.

Along with his many more traditional supporters, Jackson had what one observer described as "the weird element" supporting him. The reporter meant those who dress unconventionally and appear to think in less than traditional ways. Jesse became almost a cult figure to some. That he could turn them on and bring them into the process is a tribute to him, as well as to our system.

The slowness of our society to fully integrate all of our people resulted in an awkwardness that his campaign presented, the same awkwardness that the Patricia Schroeder candidacy would have presented had she become a candidate. If you are part of a stop-Dukakis effort, or a stop-Gephardt move, it is only that. If it is a stop-Jackson effort, for many it takes on the tone of racism. John Kennedy's Catholicism presented political leaders with a similar dilemma in 1960. How do you honestly differ and yet dissociate yourself from those who differ because of bigotry?

I have known Jesse about a quarter of a century. When I first knew him, he wore a dashiki and had an Afro hair-style. His speeches startled people. Today he wears a three-piece suit, and from his haircut to his shoes he exudes success. But he does not feel success; his spirit is restless. And he still startles many with his speeches.

In my 1984 race for the Senate against incumbent Senator Charles Percy, Jackson had some mixed feelings. He did not like Percy's embrace of Reagan and Reaganism and felt much closer to me on domestic issues, but Percy had befriended him and his organization Operation PUSH. He felt closer to Percy's stands on the Middle East than to mine. He ended up endorsing neither of us.

After the election Jesse and I had breakfast, and he asked why I had not pushed him for an endorsement. I explained that I understood the dilemma he faced, but since he had been a Democratic candidate for the presidential nomination, I should not have to ask for his support. I also told him that I felt I was in reasonably good shape in the black community, with my strong civil rights record and Chicago Mayor Harold Washington's vigorous support. I added, "And Jesse, you're not the most popular guy in the Polish wards in Chicago." He laughed.

"But one other thing is more than political," I recall telling him. "You're a Baptist minister, and I'm the son of a Lutheran minister. We were both involved in the civil rights struggle. The portion of the white community that supported us most strongly in those days was the Jewish community. I am concerned that you are sending the wrong message to people in the Jewish community and to others.

"When I get on a radio call-in program with a predominantly black listening audience, occasionally I get anti-semitic phone calls from people who assume that the name Simon is Jewish. I do not suggest that there are not some Jews who have prejudices against blacks. But you should use your immense talents to be a force for reconciliation."

Our conversation became vigorous at that point. He asked me to read a speech by Congressman William Clay of Missouri commenting on black/Jewish relations, to understand more fully the black perspective, which I did.

Jesse and I did not see each other for several months, and then I met him at a reception. "I've been working on that sermon you preached to me," he said. No one around us knew what he meant, but Jackson and I knew.

David Broder writes about an encounter this famous Baptist minister had with a former Klan member who wanted his picture taken with Jesse because, as the man explained, "I don't want to be on the wrong side of history again."

Then, talking to Broder, Jackson added this significant commentary, "They've come so far, these people, and this country's come so far. . . . Racism is not irredeemable. It's not genetic. It's the product of the environment, and the environment is changing."[9]

Jesse could have been talking about himself.

He is repelled by discrimination against Arab-Americans, as he should be. He sympathizes with the plight of the Palestinians. We all should. He has grown since his 1984 reference to New York City as "Hymietown," but I don't know that he fully understands why Jews react as they do to this and to his failure to move more decisively away from the Nation of Islam leader Louis Farrakhan, who has made some vicious anti-Semitic statements. And while he has greater understanding of the plight of Israel, he does not comprehend completely how impractical it is to talk about things like "internationalizing Jerusalem" and how that sends all the wrong signals.

Jackson has grown over the last four years, as I hope we all have. When relations between blacks and Jews became tense in Chicago and Los Angeles, he visited the Israeli ambassador in Washington. I do not know what happened at the meeting which took place shortly after the Atlanta convention, but the fact that a meeting took place was good for those cities, good for the Middle East, good for the United States, and good for Jesse.

At one point in the campaign, shortly after Gary Hart initially withdrew, Jackson told me that he was seriously thinking of withdrawing. We sat together on a plane and talked for more than an hour, our longest single one-on-one visit of the campaign. His nature is sometimes to be either very up or very down in mood, and on this day he felt down. A combination of things caused his down mood, including several death threats and reporters talking to friends of many years ago, prying into his personal life.

We talked about the contribution he might ultimately make to the nation if a Democrat were elected president, assuming Jesse would withdraw. While we talked about a variety of possibilities, I sensed that ultimately he would like to maintain a position of independence, yet in some way help significantly in assisting third-world nations.

The slight tension that built before the convention between Jackson and Dukakis was not really over the phone call that Jesse did not receive on the choice of Bentsen for the vice presidential nomination. Much more it is the difference between two dissimilar personalities. Jesse is open. What he thinks and believes, how he feels, is worn on his sleeve. We all see it. He is sometimes moody. He is an improviser. Mike is reserved, much less open, has a shell that few penetrate, and has a very stable personality that is not volatile. He is a manager not an improviser. And the clash between a winner and a loser adds some inevitable bruised feelings. This clash between two differing personalities likely would have continued on a modified basis with a Dukakis administration. Jackson wants to be inside the tent enough to influence the decisions but not so totally inside that he cannot challenge. He wants to be free to create controversies, but he also wants to be called upon to resolve controversies. Dukakis senses that and understands that, though the personality chasm between them is profound.

There are prominent national black leaders who privately are critical of Jackson and his role. "When he stands up and speaks and receives national attention, I feel a sense of pride," one major civil rights figure told me. "But then I ask myself: Could he get elected governor of any state? I conclude that he could not. Could [Congressman] Bill Gray? Maybe. [Los Angeles Mayor] Tom Bradley? Almost. [Atlanta Mayor] Andrew Young? Maybe. Congressman Allen Wheat? Maybe. Illinois Comptroller Roland Burris? Maybe. [Attorneys] Vernon Jordan or Bill Coleman? Maybe. But Jesse Jackson? No chance. He frightens too many whites. If he can't get elected as governor, he certainly cannot get elected president. When he talked about empowering blacks through his candidacy, he is in fact doing precisely the opposite. His candidacy has deprived blacks of taking part in the real choice. The real choice ultimately was between Dukakis and Gore and Gephardt and you. Many black leaders would have supported you. But because of Jesse's candidacy, we ended up as nonparticipants in the real choice."

The difficulty with the latter part of that argument is that if it is followed logically, no black will ever run. And that clearly is not in anyone's best interest. I recall some Roman Catholics using the same argument against John F. Kennedy becoming a candidate. Catholics would vote for him, denying themselves a role in the real selection, went the argument.

Jesse understood well before the 1988 election that he was not likely to be chosen president this year. But he pioneered. For the first time in two-hundred years, a black candidate for president attracted significant numbers of whites to his cause. The day will come when we will have a black president. It may not be Jesse. But like John the Baptist he preaches about, he has helped prepare the way.

Equally important, he prodded our conscience about the ignored and forgotten among us.

There were non-candidates who had brushes with the presidential possibility: Governor Mario Cuomo of New York, Senator Dale Bumpers of Arkansas, Senator Sam Nunn of Georgia, Senator Bill Bradley of New Jersey, Representative Patricia Schroeder of Colorado, Governor William Clinton of Arkansas, Senator Charles Robb of Virginia, and a few others.

The most publicized and talked-about of these, Mario Cuomo, never came close to an actual candidacy. He would have been a formidable candidate for the nomination and the election and a strong president. Pat Schroeder came closer to announcing but opted against it. Her possible candidacy generated genuine interest around the nation. Her experience should in no way deter consideration of her for high public office in the future.

In addition to these serious possibilities, there were perhaps a hundred people who would emerge from time to time in the campaign and hand you a card saying they were a candidate for president. Two of these unknowns offered me the chance to run for vice president on their tickets. One man from Florida, who referred to himself as Poet Ray Rollinson, offered to run for vice president with me. In his letter he supported "new capitalism, the higher plateau, phasing out all federal personal income taxes in three years," and a variety of other proposals, including raising the salary of the president to $12,888,000 a year. Precisely where that figure came from, I could not ascertain. At the bottom of his letter, below his name, he wrote: "American soldier 3 years, moving man 8 years, salesman 20 years, union waiter 12 years, presidential candidate 12 years." He gave me four weeks to announce the "Simon-Rollinson victory ticket." He added these words of encouragement: "How else could you get ten million dollars worth of free press and media coverage short of immolating [yourself]?"[10] Some candidates were laughable and laughed at, but a few had serious ideas. In a free society, who knows what may happen. The Republicans nominated Wendell Wilkie in 1940, not a total unknown but almost.

The Republican candidates, whom I saw less than the Democratic candidates, were:

Vice President George Bush. He was loaded with the advantage of money, staff, and eight years of campaigning, and had the disadvantage of lacking strong convictions, and of being so perceived.

Senator Bob Dole was the strongest Republican in the general election and the Republican who would have made the strongest president, but his appeal to Democrats and independents made him suspect to many of the right-wing within his party.

Former Secretary of State Al Haig was an amateur in elective politics who showed that over and over.

Congressman Jack Kemp was a hero to many conservatives who had worked hard for years to build support. He had some ideas to appeal to conservatives, like returning to the gold standard. But Jack also was one of the few Republican candidates not frightened by a new idea.

Former House member and Governor Pierre DuPont was a person of ability from a small state who tried to achieve attention with the brashness of his ideas. The high point of his campaign came with the endorsement of the *Manchester Union-Leader* of New Hampshire.

"Pat" Robertson was a well financed newcomer to politics and had an army of religious followers, but he could not expand his base much beyond that. He turned out to be much more of a factor than pundits originally predicted.

One line all candidates had and probably sincerely believed: "I am the most electable candidate." I could point to Illinois as a micro-cosm of the nation, which it is, and that my last general election vote totaled more than all the other Democratic candidates' votes com-bined in their last general election—a tougher test in a more signifi-cant state—and I could also cite the large number of Republicans who crossed over to vote for me in the Reagan landslide year of 1984, when I ran against incumbent Republican Senator Charles Percy.

Each candidate had impressive credentials in electability and could show why his candidacy would strengthen the party most in a general election.

"———— is a fine person, but he can't be elected in the fall," each of our enthusiastic supporters said about the other candidates. This happened in both political parties.

Polls between potential general election candidates were almost meaningless at this point, and those experienced in political ways had to make the judgment call. The candidates were more difficult to measure on this standard than on the issues. What we said on the question of electability tended to confuse the voters rather than clarify anything, though the tendency to confuse is not confined to the electability issue.

While candidates have their down moments, there were also moments we shared or shared with others that we will never forget: the presentation of a quilt by the Indians from the Pine Ridge Reservation in South Dakota, or the excitement in the air on campuses when you see students "turned on" for the first time by political involvement. One of my favorites is described in an article in the magazine *Mother Jones*.

> One of the bills Simon is proudest of sponsoring mandates equal education opportunity for the disabled. And so his staff has arranged for him to speak at the Iowa School for the Deaf. Some 60 deaf students and their teachers turn out to see him. He wins their hearts immediately by saying "Hello, I'm happy to see you" in sign language.
>
> Then, speaking slowly so that students can read his lips and a school official can sign all he says, Simon takes a hearing aid out of his own ear to show them; he talks about how lucky they are to know sign language, which is universal, unlike English or Russian; he tells them about his barber in Springfield, Illinois, who is deaf; he says that Abraham Lincoln, as an Illinois legislator, supported creating a school for the deaf.
>
> The students, however, ask remarkably sophisticated questions about all sorts of other things: Judge Bork (Simon voted no), abortion ("that question has to be answered by a woman and her physician"), the death penalty (he's against it: "punishment we reserve for poor people"), and aid to the contras ("I don't think we should be trying to overthrow governments we don't like. That's two-thirds of the governments on the face of the earth. We'll have our hands full").
>
> Simon is impressed: "Your questions are much better than the questions I've been getting from these reporters." At that, the deaf children applaud enthusiastically—not by clapping, since that presupposes an ability to hear. Instead, a forest of small hands waves in the air.[11]

One other thing all presidential candidates had in common: exhaustion.

There are candidates who manage to campaign at a leisurely pace, Ronald Reagan and the late Henry Cabot Lodge among them. But few can campaign at that pace and be successful either in a national race or in statewide contests.

It is not simply that you are "on the go" all but the six or so hours a day when you sleep, it is also the time zone changes that affect you. Flying from Washington, D.C., to Los Angeles to attend a dinner that lasts until 11:00 P.M. may not seem significant, but eleven at night in Los Angeles is two in the morning in Washington, and I'm tired at two in the morning.

Occasionally critical decisions have to be made at the only time your staff can reach you—late at night. Sometimes weariness then dictates a decision more than reason.

Two weeks after I suspended my campaign I had a chance to relax with my family for a week in Puerto Rico. From there I called Jesse Jackson at his hotel in Philadelphia. I wanted to straighten out a misunderstanding that had arisen in Illinois. It was the day after the New York primary. After a brief conversation I said to him, "Jesse, you really sound weary." "Paul," he responded in a voice husky from overuse, "only you can understand how exhausted I am."

The race for the presidency is not only a test of ideas and political skills, it is also a physical endurance contest. Anyone who survives is likely to be in reasonably good physical condition for four years of the presidency, which is more demanding than a campaign in what is required in judgment calls but less demanding in its physical requirements.

Some would add another requirement to physical ability to handle a campaign. They suggest that you have to have an obsession that you have to become president, and everything you say and do must fall into a pattern that helps promote that end. That probably helps to get you elected, but I believe it is not essential. Nor is it desirable from the viewpoint of the public.

More important than any other test is the test of character, of judgment. Whose judgment do you trust for the fate of your children? Years ago, Horace Greeley—an unsuccessful presidential candidate—wrote, "Fame is a vapour, popularity an accident, riches take wind, and those who cheer you today will curse you tomorrow. Only one thing endures: character."[12] Obviously issues are important, ideology is important, and competence is. But there is a basic need for character, for judgment, that no one can measure precisely, yet each of us must seek as we choose our leaders.

☆ **5** ☆

DEALING WITH THE ISSUES

Between the time he withdrew and then reannounced his candidacy, Gary Hart and I met late one evening at the Denver home of a mutual friend, Mark Hogan, former lieutenant governor of Colorado and former state chair of the Democratic party in that state. Mark called him early in the evening, and Gary stopped by after events each of us had attended. Contrary to the image people have of all politicians, Gary is somewhat shy and reserved. No one would describe him as a backslapper.

My guess is that before he stopped by, Gary had a beer or two, or a drink of whatever he happens to like. Not enough to dull his senses in any way but enough to make him more talkative than usual. Out of the conversation came his suggestion about what I should do: Ignore the political meetings; ignore the fund-raising and political calls your staff wants you to make. Instead, for six months go to a mountain retreat and reflect on what the nation needs, and then come down and give that message to the nation.

It is true that a candidate ought to plan to take some time off during the campaign to get a better perspective. Surrounded by reporters and the Secret Service, rushed from one speech to another, from one television appearance to another, it becomes easy to do all the little things well but to lose sight of the bigger picture. Mike Dukakis took each Sunday off. I should have done the same. I spent too much time working, not enough time reflecting. The Easter weekend, for example, is not a good weekend to get much done. I

61

remember having political meetings in Iowa on Sunday afternoon of Mother's Day. It should have surprised no one that our audiences were almost nonexistent. We should have prepared a schedule that included time off periodically.

After I had been in the race two months, Mitchell Locin of the *Chicago Tribune* wrote: "Knowing that he has to act quickly to build and retain his poll standing, Simon has been on the road almost constantly or else on the telephone road. In the car between stops, he dictated thank-you letters to people he had just met and receives quick briefings on his next appearance."[1] The article was not meant critically. What he described accurately portrays too much of my campaign. Pam Huey, who worked on press, wrote: "I remember sitting through one scheduling meeting during the summer of 1987 when they were mapping out the next three months. I noted to Kathleen Crowell, Paul's scheduler, that there was not one day off planned. We were both appalled but our objections were vetoed."[2] I would have been wise to take more time off, to reflect a little more on what I was doing wisely and where I could improve my candidacy. And also simply to ponder a little more on the course of the nation and of the world. Candidates are programmed to speak a great deal and think very little.

What Hart suggested is in many ways more logical than what we did. It can be argued that since the party did not nominate me anyway, his strategy could not have been worse than mine. Perhaps. It certainly would have been less expensive! My guess is that if I had done what he suggested, I would not have come close to winning Iowa, and it would have been even faster and further downhill from then on.

The reality is that personality, rather than issues, tends to dominate our presidential nomination and election process. If the gimmickry of going to the mountaintop had set me apart from the rest of the crowded field, then it might have worked. It is doubtful that anything I might have said on the issues would have given me the nomination. I might have received some favorable editorials for the 5 percent or so of the population who read editorials, but to believe that the public is eager to devour a full course of detailed issues is, I regret to say, unrealistic.

But I could and should have done better than I did.

In the rush to become a candidate, as we put the staff together, those who structured my campaign effort recognized that I had greater issues knowledge than most of the candidates. So basic decisions on personnel to deal with the issues were handled with the view that "down the road" we would pick up that key person who combined knowledge of the issues with good political instincts. We had a solid person handling issues temporarily, Paul Furiga, and later another talented person, Mike Calabrese, but neither had depth on the political side. Issues cannot be judged in the abstract. They must be framed in ways that attract votes rather than repel them, and they must be approached on the basis of what is achievable politically in Congress, not on the basis of an abstract theory.

The defect was more than simply a lack of the right combination of skills and experience. I also lacked some central theme around which to develop the issues. Failure to take time off to develop that meant frenetic campaign activity that had less of a point than it should have had. We needed at least one evening "bull session" to go over ideas for a theme. For a brief time some of our commercials ended with the words, "Isn't it time to believe again?" Exactly where that came from I'm not sure, but it did not strike me as strong and obviously didn't strike the voters that way either. It emerged without careful thought. Theme development is the type of decision in which a candidate should be involved, and that decision should be made early.

I asked a friend to inquire of six people he knew who followed politics (but not too closely) what people thought of when the names of specific candidates were mentioned to them. Six people is hardly a scientific sample, but it is of interest to see the response:

Babbitt—taxes
Dukakis—efficiency, Greek, Central America
Gephardt—trade
Gore—defense, pro-Israel, conservative
Hart—women, new ideas
Jackson—black, pro-Arab, helps "the little guy," extreme
Simon—bow tie, traditional Democrat, education, honest
Biden—foreign affairs, speech stealing

The only two of the candidates who came through clearly were Babbitt and Gephardt. Babbitt was tied to taxes, not the message he wanted to deliver; he tried to come across as the candidate of candor. Gephardt was associated with trade, a message he did want to deliver.

The rest of us came across less decisively. That can turn out all right, as Dukakis proved in the primaries, but it is also true that the right theme could have been used effectively by any of us. Themes are not necessarily issues, though ideally they should mesh. Themes can be simply campaign gimmicks.

When issues fail to dominate a campaign—and that is generally true for U.S. elections, unlike European elections—the danger is that the quirks of personality will and that the nation will select a less than superior leader.

It would be an error to suggest that issues do not play a role in the campaign; they do. But they are not as dominant as they should be. There are people who quiz candidates carefully on issues of special concern to them, particularly in Iowa and New Hampshire. There were enough inquiries to cause my staff to put together a book of four hundred pages plus on issues including remarks I had made, interviews I've given, and stands I had taken, listed alphabetically, ranging from acid rain to World War III. Those statements and issue papers did have some influence. But limited. Very limited.

The result of failure to pay more attention to the significant issues is that even when issues emerge, they are often trivial relative to the responsibilities that a president faces. In the weeks after it became clear that Dukakis would be the Democratic nominee, George Bush took out after Dukakis primarily on one issue, judging by news media coverage. Was that the question of arms control? Was that a question of how the nation can meet the ignored problem of the underclass? Was that a question of long-term policy, such as how we can find an inexpensive way to convert salt water to fresh water? Was it a discussion of the vital issue of improved education? Was it the problem of how we make the United States more competitive again?

The answer is no. The question was on the furloughing of prisoners in the state penal system in Massachusetts for occasional weekends, a practice followed by thirty-eight states and the federal government. One prisoner on furlough, Willie Horton, committed a brutal murder. In a not-so-subtle appeal to racism, Willie Horton's picture went on the campaign literature, a black man who did the killing. When Bush attacks, Dukakis has to respond. I traveled with

Dukakis to five speeches and press conferences four weeks after the last primary and three weeks before the convention. At all but one, the question of prison furloughs arose. I felt like standing up and saying to the questioners, "He's running for President of the United States, not warden of the local prison."

I thought the campaign had reached a low with that issue, but it sank even deeper. Suddenly the Pledge of Allegiance to the flag became a national issue. (It probably would have shocked a few who clasped this issue so firmly to learn that the author of the pledge is believed to be Reverend Francis Bellemy who was a strong Socialist.) George Bush traveled the nation loudly proclaiming that Dukakis had vetoed a bill to require saying the Pledge of Allegiance in Massachusetts. The unspoken implication: Dukakis is not as patriotic as the rest of us.

The Bush use of the Pledge of Allegiance issue said more about Bush than it did about Dukakis.

It was wrong in substance. Jehovah's Witnesses brought this issue to the U.S. Supreme Court before either Bush or Dukakis was involved in politics. The Witnesses, as they call themselves, believe pledging of allegiance is an idolatrous act; it violates their religious tenets. The Supreme Court ruled that no one can be forced to say the pledge. That's part of free speech, they said.

When the Massachusetts legislature passed a measure requiring that the pledge be recited, Dukakis did what a governor cannot do in most states: He sent the measure to the Massachusetts Supreme Court and asked for an advisory opinion as to its constitutionality. They told Dukakis that it violated the U.S. Supreme Court decision and was unconstitutional. He vetoed it, as he should have.

The pledge issue is wrong for other reasons. One is that it hauls out the flag to shield the nondiscussion of the real issues upon which a campaign should focus. It is also a shabby use of the flag. Real patriotism welcomes a discussion of the genuine issues, knowing that through such a discussion, the nation becomes better informed and ultimately better governed.

Columnist Steve Daley summed it up: "Empirical evidence tells us that in 1988 the political high road is closed for repairs. The cynical advisers are on to something. Demagoguery works."[3] Even where there was a discussion of issues, both before the convention by many candidates and after the convention by two, those of us seeking the presidency broke little new ground. We tended to speak in comfortable phrases and clichés about yesterday's needs, rather than tomorrow's. A former president of NBC News wrote during the campaign, "No one has yet begun to come to grips with the momentous changes that we know we shall have to confront in the decade ahead."[4]

Six days before New Yorkers voted in the primary, the *New York Times* editorialized on the primary there: "It's mainly snapping and snarling, lacking substantive bite. . . . What's remarkable so far . . . is how little content there is in it. . . . The primary campaign remains largely sterile, for one big reason. So far, most people, in New York and elsewhere, want it that way."[5]

That's part of the answer. It is also true, however, that the *New York Times* asked all of us who were candidates for detailed medical records but did not ask us where we stood on the problems of the impoverished in that city. I was the only candidate to offer a specific program to deal with the needs of the underclass, and it received praise from the few who looked at it seriously, including Senator Daniel P. Moynihan. But interest in specific programs to help lift those most desperate in our society has been minimal on editorial pages and with the public.

It is incorrect to place all responsibility on the doorstep of the nation's journalists. As a people we have to do better. The situation is summarized by the heading on a Robert Wagman column: "Voters Bored with Emphasis on Issues." Wagman writes, "Polling here [in New Hampshire] seems to show that voters are actually being turned off by the current emphasis on issues."[6]

Political observer William Schneider advises candidates: "Stay away from big ideas; they will only get you into trouble."[7] Pat Robertson told Marvin Kalb, "Any candidate who gets too specific about budget cuts will remain perpetually a candidate."[8] He could have broadened his conclusion far beyond budget cuts. Elizabeth Drew writes that there is "a political consensus that the Democratic Party can't talk very much about the needs of the poor and win the election."[9] Obviously the Republicans do not talk about these needs, so the problem is virtually ignored. But is William Greider perhaps correct when he writes, "There are millions of citizens who stopped voting when Democrats began to sound more and more like Republicans?"[10]

Newsweek called the Democratic and Republican presidential nominees "the two blandest and most cautious in the field."[11] Cheers rang out in the convention hall when Dukakis said in his acceptance speech, "This election is not about ideology. It's about competence."[12] One journal noted that the two nominees "are offering muzzy messages to the voters, being highly unexplicit about what they plan to do if elected."[13] The *New York Times* commented in June: "It is noteworthy that Mr. Dukakis and Mr. Bush not only raised more money than their rivals but also kept their messages much more bland."[14] Two scholars who studied the 1984 New Hampshire primary reached this conclusion for candidates: "Do not try to create a clear-cut image. . . . Remain vague and elusive."[15]

The question: Can you win if you are reasonably explicit on the issues? The answer: It is more difficult, but it has been done, and it can be done, and a candidate who does it makes a contribution to the public dialogue that is essential in a free country. But the public must demand it.

Groups with specific agendas help on issues. The AFL-CIO, for example, circulated a five-minute video-taped statement each candidate made that forced the candidates to reflect at least a little on labor-related issues. Kenneth Blaylock, then president of the American Federation of Government Employees, and Vincent R. Sombrotto, president of the Letter Carriers, did their own tape for governmental unions with good, specific, pointed questions that related to their interests—the way they should be. Questions should be posed so that it is difficult for a candidate to avoid answering. The National Education Association did a tape with questions in the general field of education. Their first attempt at this, it gave their people at least some glimpse into what the candidates believed.

Another first-time entrant into the field, the American Association of Retired Persons (AARP), did a video and also sponsored a debate in Des Moines. However, the debate permitted the candidates to escape too easily. When the question of long-term care arose, for example, Dick Gephardt and I were both cosponsors of at-home long-term care, but I was the only candidate willing to commit to the necessary taxes to meet the ignored and growing problem of long-term care for those who require nursing home assistance. I suggested paying for it in one of three ways: a half-percent increase in Social

Security taxes, taking the cap off Social Security (we now pay Social Security only on the first $45,000 of income), or a series of "sin taxes," taxes on cigarettes and alcohol. The AARP is still new to the political arena, and their failure to pin down candidates more explicitly weakened the impact of their endeavors. I had far more volunteers through the Council of Senior Citizens, a much smaller group, than I did from the AARP, even though I had the strongest stand on the key issue of long-term care of any of the candidates. A two-page spread in the AARP publication with three paragraphs on each candidate in both parties made all of us sound good. The reader had to be a political sophisticate to understand that there were significant differences among us. The AARP and other groups must understand there is a tendency for candidates to be fuzzy on the issues when it serves their purpose; the organizations should not add to the fuzziness. My guess is that in 1992, the AARP will be more effective. The political power of senior citizens has yet to be tapped as fully as it should, and a key to doing that is pinpointing candidates on where they stand on the issues of concern to older Americans, not that seniors should or will vote only on that basis.

There were local issues, like the Seabrook nuclear energy issue in New Hampshire or relations with Cuba in Florida, both with national implications; but most groups taking stands and confronting issues had national agendas. Arms control groups tended to endorse Jesse Jackson and me. Environmental groups tended toward Al Gore, Mike Dukakis, and me. Organizations made an important contribution in moving candidates away from gray, palid statements that sounded good but said nothing. At one point, the *St. Louis Post-Dispatch* editorialized, "With the possible exceptions of Sen. Paul Simon and the Rev. Jesse Jackson, all the contenders are saying pretty much the same uninspiring things."[16]

Our campaign put out an eight-page flier on my educational stands and circulated it to teachers in the early states. The polls showed I had a substantial lead among teachers. This turned out to be one of my success stories: We got out a good folder, told the story on issues in concrete terms, and it got me votes and supporters. But financial limitations prevented my doing that for more than three or four key groups. Where we did have the money to target effectively, the polling evidence is that I carried.

A good illustration of the limitations imposed by money—and

how an issue can help—is the Puerto Rican situation. More delegates were elected in Puerto Rico than in twenty-five states. The party situation there is different from any of the fifty states, and leaders tend to work with U.S. officials of both political parties, a lesson they have had to learn to survive.

Puerto Ricans are American citizens but undeservedly second-class citizens. Puerto Rico had a higher percentage of troops—and casualties—in the Korean conflict and in the Vietnam disaster than all but three of the fifty states. But because they are voiceless in the United States Senate and have only one nonvoting delegate in the House, it is easy for political leaders in both parties to ignore Puerto Rican needs. Eventually there must come an end to second-class citizenship, an end to a more pleasant-sounding name that we use: commonwealth status. That's colonialism pure and simple. Eventually Puerto Rico has to have independence or statehood, but the decision must be first made by the people there. Then Congress can act.

I have been one of the few members of Congress who has taken an interest in Puerto Rico's problems and potential. That Puerto Rico would have been one of the naturals for me in a presidential race is illustrated by a column written for the *San Juan Star* by Roland Perusse, professor of political science at Inter American University: "The Democratic party now has at least seven declared or undeclared candidates in the race. Some writers refer to them as the Seven Dwarfs. I take exception. Keeping in mind the New Progressive Party platform on statehood, I see at least one Snow White among the Seven Dwarfs. He is Paul Simon of Illinois. . . . Paul Simon wrote and spoke on Puerto Rican statehood for ten years as a U.S. Representative from a congressional district deep in southern Illinois without a single Puerto Rican, long before he became a U.S. Senator."[17]

The head of the New Progressive Party, San Juan Mayor Baltasar Corrada, favored my candidacy, as did his chief rival for leadership within the party, former Governor Carlos Romero. But getting to Puerto Rico is costly in dollars and time. At one point I had a trip scheduled, but for reasons I don't recall it was canceled. A combination of a few more dollars, two trips to Puerto Rico, and a win in Iowa would have given me the chance for a substantial Puerto Rico victory.

As it turned out, I came in third in the popular vote behind Jesse Jackson and Michael Dukakis.

But Puerto Rico is an exception to the "issues are not that important" syndrome. The issue there is the status of the island: statehood, commonwealth, or independence.

On one issue I did not do well, and I should have. The basic question: "How can you be for balancing the budget and, at the same time, advocate various social programs? Isn't that inconsistent?"

Because there appeared to be an inconsistency early in the campaign, I should have prepared a solid, documented outline on how you can construct such a program, that it is not only possible, but essential for the nation's future.

An article appeared in the *Washington Post* suggesting an inconsistency in my position, and a usually good reporter for *U.S. News & World Report,* Michael Kramer, wrote a story accusing me of "sloppy thinking" on fiscal matters, in an article unfortunately loaded with sloppy reporting.[18] But it furthered questioning on the same problem.

A few days later, NBC had its debate among the candidates. I had moved into first place in the polls in Iowa, so I could expect to be a target, and these articles illustrated a perception problem that could grow. It would become the most widely seen debate in the entire series, with twenty to twenty-five million viewers. Instead of resting and preparing well for it, I rested not at all and had only brief preparation, lulled into that in part by the fact that I had already participated in a series of debates. Instead of preparing a good, concise answer on the fiscal question, I accepted the suggestion that in the one minute permitted you cannot give an adequate explanation so provide a generality, and say that you will provide the detailed response shortly. My answer flopped, as it should have.

I merited the editorial criticism I received for the debate. The *Peoria Journal-Star* commented, "Particularly disappointing was Sen. Paul Simon, who did a poor job in the debate defending his policies. . . . He must be listening to his pollster now that he has risen to the rank of front runner in Iowa."[19] Another newspaper editorialized, "Illinois Sen. Paul Simon . . . probably came off the worst of the Democrats. Most observers commenting afterward felt he did little to defend his positions."[20] A respected and influential reporter from the *Des Moines Register*, David Yepsen, wrote that "Richard Gephardt and Paul Simon lost ground [in the debate]. . . . Simon was rated poorly for his explanation of how he can balance the budget while supporting a massive public works program."[21]

All of the criticisms unfortunately were valid.

On the other hand, there is also validity to the proposition that in one minute you can't offer a sensible answer on how you balance the budget and move vigorously on the nation's problems at the same time.

Marvin Kalb described the situation accurately: "The process distorts the way the candidates feel compelled to present themselves. Understandably, they wish to give as little offense as conscience allows, while at the same time looking and sounding 'presidential'— no easy task. They are crammed with set responses to nearly every conceivable question, little mental tape loops twenty seconds in length or forty seconds or even as long as a minute." Then Kalb added, "To go on much longer, to give a subject the nuance and detail it deserves, is to risk getting what vaudevillians used to call the hook. Paul Simon took four and a half minutes to answer my opening question about how he was planning to balance the budget in three years. Click, click, click went televisions sets all over the country, as benumbed viewers sought relief in football. Maybe that was one reason why Simon, after Iowa and New Hampshire, suddenly found himself out of money—and opportunity."[22]

I later outlined my fiscal program in a fourteen-page white paper. I had the disadvantage of serving on the Senate Budget Committee, knowing enough about the subject to understand that simplistic answers do not work. The reaction to my white paper was almost predictable. My opponents were unimpressed and critical. Among most journalists and economists who actually read it, there was a favorable response. Those who reacted to news accounts of it, or to reporters' descriptions of it, reacted negatively. The *Philadelphia Inquirer* editorialized, "The blueprint in his white paper more than meets the 1988 norm for fiscal specifics."[23] Stuart Eizenstat, who served as chief domestic adviser for President Jimmy Carter, called my outlined goals "ambitious but not impossible targets. . . . [Simon's tax options] are relatively painless and reasonable."[24] A leading economist who criticized my proposal in the media, called me after I sent him a copy and told me that when he read it, rather than having it described to him by a reporter, it made sense.

What I suggested in detail were three spending priorities:

First, that education must receive a higher share of the federal budget. At the present time, education (excluding the school lunch program, which is primarily nutritional in aim) takes 2 percent of the federal budget. We have to do much better with intensive pre-school education programs in disadvantaged areas, with adult illiteracy, and curriculum enrichment. These are not peripheral luxuries that would be nice to have; they are essential if tomorrow is to be better for our children, and if this nation is to remain competitive with the rest of the world. After Hubert Humphrey's death, Norman Cousins described him as someone "who had no difficulty in regarding the next generation as a constituency no less deserving of attention than people who would go to the polls next week."[25] How we need that attitude today! The president has to speak to the nation about the importance of education and be a real leader in this field so that at the state and local level there will be responses, including raising pay and standards for new teachers. By shifting federal priorities, growth in education spending can be accomplished without increasing the total budget. Ninety-eight percent of the budget can be squeezed a little so that education receives more than 2 percent. It is not done simply or easily, but as as member of the Budget Committee in the Senate (I also served on the Budget Committee in the House), I know it can be done.

Second, we must face up to the problem of the underclass in our society. We have largely pretended there is no underclass, or that having it is somehow inevitable, like the rise of the sun each morning. Those who have taken the time to look seriously at the problem have come to the conclusion that a jobs program with an educational enrichment component is essential. Before I entered the race, I wrote a book calling for such a program, *Let's Put America Back to Work*[26] and introduced legislation to do it, cosponsored by Senators Daniel P. Moynihan of New York and Harry Reid of Nevada. Since we will not let people starve if people cannot find work, we face a choice of paying them for doing something or paying them for doing nothing. Permitting them to be productive is, by far, the wiser course for a host of societal reasons. Under my proposal, people out of work five weeks or more would be given a public service job and paid the minimum wage for thirty-two hours a week—which comes to $464 a month—or 10 percent above welfare or 10 percent above unemployment compensation, whichever is highest, so that everyone earns more for being productive, rather than being nonproductive. This would be a tremendous economic lift to the least fortunate. The average payment for a *family* on welfare in Illinois is $315 a month, better than many states pay. The average *family* on welfare in Alabama receives $113.70 a month! Paying $464 a month to an *individual* under this plan is not much, but it is more than all but three states pay to a *family* on welfare. A local committee of thirteen would select the projects on which applicants work.

People would be screened as they come into the program. If they cannot read and write, they would be placed in a class or given a tutor (who might also be unemployed, doing this as his or her project). If they have no marketable skills, they would be given the opportunity for training. The program calls for working four days so that the fifth day can be used to seek a private sector job. If they do get one, even at the minimum wage, that would increase their income 25 percent. The incentive should be toward private sector employment. The minimum wage public sector jobs should be the launching pad for most people, not the landing field. The cost of the program would be five billion dollars the first year and up to eight billion dollars the third year, a sizable amount of money, but *less than 1 percent of the federal budget.* In a very short time, the program would reap a huge economic harvest for the nation, as well as a decline in the ills that accompany unemployment: crime, drug dependency, and teenage pregnancy. Five to eight billion dollars can be found with adjustments in the present budget by shifting priorities slightly. Long-term savings in welfare expenditures, unemployment compensation outlays, and improved productivity in the nation would be enormous.

Does this nation have the will to give people the chance to become productive? Of course we do—if we have the leadership to direct the way and to challenge us to do what is economically wise and what is humanitarian.

More than a month after I suspended my presidential race, CBS's Dan Rather commented: "It was Paul Simon—once a candidate for president, now a distant memory—who proposed the kind of massive public works project that may be the only way to solve the problem of our country's crumbling infrastructure. Simon was immediately attacked by both Republican and Democratic opponents. He was called a big spender. . . . But worst of all, he was labeled a traditional liberal Democrat for his troubles. It's too bad that Senator Simon didn't think to remind people that the largest public works project in our nation's history was launched by one of the most conservative presidents in our nation's history—the Interstate Highway System, under Dwight D. Eisenhower."[27]

Praised by sociologists like William Julius Wilson and economists like Lester Thurow, my jobs proposal was criticized by at least three of the Democratic presidential candidates and a variety of columnists, none of whom—I would guess—had taken the trouble to look seriously at my proposal or at the problem. If I had simply talked vaguely about providing opportunities for people, I would have received applause and no criticism. The lesson for candidates is clear: Be vague. Sound knowledgeable but don't become too specific.

My third major spending priority: long-term care for those who need it, primarily senior citizens. There is no way budget priorities can be shifted to accommodate this. There has to be a self-financing mechanism. A look at the demographic factors of the nation suggests this need is going to explode on us. By financing long-term care through a series of modest tax options (described earlier in this chapter), there actually would be a reduction in the federal deficit because of savings in Medicaid and Medicare expenditures.

There are other spending priorities the nation should have, such as more research in the environmental field and on AIDS and other diseases, but these are relatively small ticket items in a federal budget. Housing must once again become a federal priority, but there are ways to stimulate that without large federal expenditures, primarily through guarantees to foundations and nonprofit organizations that can use some of their resources in this field.

Those three big ticket items constitute the "massive spending" program—as it was frequently described—that I advocated. Compare those numbers with the increase in gross interest expenditures under the Reagan administration, from $83 billion to $234 billion and climbing. That is an *increase* of $151 billion for interest, for which the nation gets nothing other than higher interest rates. Compare that $151 billion increase, resulting in nothing, with the most criticized of my programs, the jobs program that costs $8 billion even in the later fiscal years. My jobs program would cost less than 6 percent of the annual *increase* in interest fostered by this administration, and would enrich the life and economy of the nation enormously.

The second part of my economic program was to eliminate the deficit in three fiscal years, by Fiscal Year 1992. I provided a specific timetable for two reasons. First, as a writer I frequently have people come to me and say, "Some day I'm going to write a book." I mentally note that that person is never going to write a book. "Some day" never comes. If someone tells me that he or she has started a book or is taking off next summer to write one or has a specific timetable, then a book may get written. The same is true for candidates. When candidates tell you that "some day" they will balance the budget, you can write it down in your little black book that "some day" will never come.

Second, by providing a specific timetable the financial markets are reassured *if* the person making the pledge follows through immediately after the election with a program to accomplish the deficit reduction. If the follow-through takes place, then there probably would be a slight reduction in interest rates almost immediately.

How do you reduce the budget deficit to the point of zero in three fiscal years?

The present projected deficit (as this book is written) for Fiscal Year 1992, is $50 to $100 billion, depending on whose projection is used. I pledged to do it with these steps:

(1) A reduction in defense expenditures of $20 billion, or slightly less than 7 percent from the present projections. That can be done by management reforms, something I talked about long before the Pentagon scandals broke—and something many others also talked about. The Packard Commission, appointed by President Reagan, made recommendations that would save about $38 billion a year. In addition, money could be saved by eliminating redundant and unnecessary weapons, and by gradually and carefully reducing some of our overseas commitments, asking our allies to bear a fairer share of the burden. A $20 billion saving per year through this combination would in no way impair the defense of the nation.

(2) By moving to coordinate trade and lower the trade deficit, by doing more to stimulate private sector employment, in three years

the unemployment rate can be reduced by at least 1-1/2 percent. For each 1 percent reduction in unemployment there is a savings of $30 billion a year. One and one-half percent would reduce the deficit $45 billion. All of these are conservative estimates, and I outlined in my paper in detail how I would act on the trade problem and the private sector employment stimulus.

(3) As you move on the first two of these, what will follow will be a reduction in interest rates. With a $2.5 trillion national debt, each time you reduce the interest rate 1 percent, there is a saving of $25 billion. Because there are long-term bonds, that is not all saved in one year. But the first year the savings will be approximately $15 billion, and they will be higher each year after that. Each reduction of $50 billion in the deficit probably will reduce the interest rates approximately 1 percent. By my third fiscal year there would be a reduction of 1-1/2 percent in interest rates, perhaps more, and a savings of at least $37 billion a year and more in succeeding years.

Those three items together total $102 billion by my third fiscal year, more than enough to balance the budget. Add to that $9 to $18 billion from an oil import tax, and the budget would be balanced, barring major shifts in the economy.

I made clear my deep commitment to balancing the budget and pledged that if a disciplined, tough administration was not able to put this package together, as a last resort I would ask for modest tax increases, and I outlined the revenue I would request.

My fourteen-page white paper provided much greater detail on an overall program that was—and is—sound and politically achievable.

But the negatives in the press prior to my white paper prompted Senator Edward Kennedy, a supporter of Dukakis, to say in a Harvard speech: "Candidates are raised up, only to be torn down, and . . . the whole field is falsely characterized as unimpressive and insubstantial. It is now happening to Paul Simon. I know him well, and he is a man of principle—and not simply because he refuses to give up his bow tie. . . . Now that his season has seemingly dawned, we have seen a rash of stories revealing in reproachful terms that he doesn't have a plan to pay for every proposal he has ever made. That is hardly news about him—or virtually any presidential candidate in this field or in my memory. When was the last time a platform was enacted whole into law?"[28]

I also favor buttressing this economic program with something many of my friends oppose: a constitutional amendment requiring that the budget be balanced, unless there is a 60 percent vote of the House and Senate authorizing a deficit. In 1796, Thomas Jefferson wrote that if he could add just one amendment to the constitution, it would be to require that the budget be balanced. But he favored a rigid requirement, something I do not favor, because there are times when a deficit is desirable.

We have made something that is occasionally desirable into a habit, and that habit is causing major long-run problems for the nation.

The irony of the situation is that those who should be speaking for such an amendment, those who favor programs for the less fortunate, are among those opposing the idea. This is an outgrowth of history. When Franklin Roosevelt faced a depression, he called for modest deficits, and the F.D.R. haters screamed about the budget not being balanced. People of progressive bent got into the habit of defending deficits, and what they could once say is logical no longer can be defended.

We are borrowing from our children and grandchildren to run the country. But we are doing more than that. Because the fastest growing item in the budget is interest, it is squeezing out our ability to create programs that could build a better future. The gross interest expenditure by the federal government for Fiscal Year 1989 is $234 billion. Our spending for education—all federal education programs combined—is $19.5 billion, less than 10 percent of what we spend on interest. Our ability to act on education, health care, and other needs is limited by the burgeoning interest spending.

We also add to the inequity of the distribution problem. Who pays the tax money that goes for interest? Most is paid by people of limited means. Who ultimately receives the tax money that goes for interest? Generally those who are the most fortunate economically, and increasingly that is now the most fortunate economically beyond our borders.

In 1986 the Senate came within one vote of passing a soundly drafted constitutional amendment to require a balanced budget. If we were to approve such an amendment, it would be a strong signal to the financial markets and interest rates would decrease. As this manuscript is being typed the prime rate of interest in the United States is 10 percent, and Germany recently raised her prime rate—to 3 percent. In Japan it is 3-1/2 percent. We can do better.

In the middle of a December 1987 story on a *New York Times/ CBS* poll, this paragraph appeared: "Senator Paul Simon of Illinois has been viewed skeptically by policy experts because he supports both a constitutional amendment to balance the budget and a new federal jobs program. But it turns out, that is exactly where the American people are: They overwhelmingly support both the balanced budget amendment and a federal responsibility for providing jobs."[29]

Let me add that while I favor a constitutional amendment, I strongly oppose a constitutional convention to achieve it. States can petition Congress for a constitutional convention, something this nation has not had since the present constitution came into being. No one knows what a constitutional convention might do. The basic framework of this nation is sound. We should not tinker with experiments like a constitutional convention.

In one form or another, the question of taxes kept surfacing in debates and question periods. With the exception of Bruce Babbitt, the candidates did not bring up the topic. Increasing taxes receives low marks in all polls, unless the idea is very carefully phrased. Candidates know that headline writers are not known for careful phrasing. Besides, if the deficit can be resolved without substantial increases in taxes, and I believed prior to the savings and loan problems that was possible, why commit political suicide by calling for across-the-board, general tax increases? Bruce Babbitt received praise for his stand calling for tax increases, praise that followed him all the way to his political demise. If he had become the nominee and had lost, many of the same journalists who praised his courage would have turned on him like vultures attacking a small rabbit, questioning why he had ever called for a tax increase.

When Mondale made his famous acceptance speech calling for a tax increase, Senator Wendell Ford of Kentucky was on the stage but appreciably below the elevated platform from which Mondale spoke. After Mondale's remarks on taxes, the camera gave a large view of the front of the convention, and Senator Ford could be seen dialing a number on a telephone. Asked about it later, he said, "I was trying to reach dial-a-prayer."[30]

I supported an oil import fee. A ten-dollar-per-barrel fee would bring in $18 billion in revenue. Hart and Gephardt also supported that. It is a politically achievable tax. Babbitt tended to favor taxes that sound good in the deserts of Arizona but would die and wither quickly in the much hotter air of Capitol Hill.

People will support a tax that goes for a specific purpose. I favored a pay-as-you-go program for long-term care, outlining three possible ways to pay for it. I received almost no criticism and much support. I also pointed out that every other day a bridge in this nation either is closed or collapses, that we have major transportation needs to meet, and that I favor a six-cent gasoline tax; one-third for state and interstate highways and bridges; one-third to local roads and bridges; and one-third for mass transit. I pointed out that the tax would meet a national need and put about 200,000 more Americans to work. The people to whom I explained it supported it.

Understanding of the inequity of our present tax structure emerged occasionally. I invariably received applause when I told audiences that I voted against both the Reagan tax bill of 1981 and the tax bill of 1986, that I was one of three in the Senate to vote against that misguided 1986 act. I explained that during the seven-year period of the Reagan administration, taxes on the wealthiest of Americans were reduced from 70 percent to 28 percent while one-third of middle-income Americans got tax increases. I used that in one television commercial but I never sensed the inequities of the tax structure caught on in a major way. If the key primaries had come after April 15, I would have had an issue for garnering votes.

Religion as an issue reared its head from time to time, though less than I expected. We had two ordained Baptist ministers in the race and both, on the basis of their faith, arrived at opposite political poles, one on the left, one on the right.

Both did better than most observers expected. Robertson stunned Bush and the nation by coming in second to Dole in Iowa, Bush trailing in third place. Robertson came in first in Hawaii, Alaska and Washington, and second in Iowa, Minnesota, Colorado, South Dakota, Louisiana, Texas, West Virginia, and Idaho. Jackson came in first in eleven states, plus the Virgin Islands and Puerto Rico, and came in second in thirty-one states.

Of the two, Jackson had been through a presidential campaign before and had learned the hard way to be somewhat more careful in what he said. Though Pat Robertson's father had served in the U.S. Senate, Pat became more of a loose cannon in the campaign, in large part because he had never gone through the rigors of a race. He is bright, a Phi Beta Kappa, cum laude graduate of Washington and Lee, and a Yale Law School graduate. The other candidates and I always found him genial.

His interest in politics did not come suddenly. In 1981 he had talked about the federal government being run by "Spirit-filled Christians," and he reflected on what the nation would be like if "every member of the Cabinet was Spirit-filled, the President was Spirit-filled, and the Senate and the House of Representatives were Spirit-filled."[31] While he moved away from any comments like that in the campaign, he did move from one slip of the tongue, or crisis, to another. Pat accused George Bush of being behind the disclosures of the sexual escapades of fellow-evangelist Jimmy Swaggart to indirectly harm Robertson, but he offered no proof for the charges. Pat said he once knew where the captives were in Lebanon and that the United States could have rescued them if we had moved swiftly. No evidence ever came forward to prove the remark. He said he would not have hesitated to kill Muammar el-Qaddafi, the Libyan leader, had he been president and called for escalating the cold war. "I would step up the propaganda war," he told Marvin Kalb, and said he would aid revolutionary movements trying to overthrow unfavorable governments.[32] He announced that Soviet missiles are again in Cuba, but the administration quickly batted that down. He told a New Hampshire congregation why he became a candidate: "I heard the Lord saying, 'I have something else for you to do. I want you to run for President of the United States.' " He added, "I assure you that I am going to be the next President of the United States."[33] Kemp, trying to deal with the Robertson support, much of which came from Kemp, at one point had more than one hundred "Iowa evangelical pastors" endorse him. Their statement noted Kemp's anti-abortion stance and added: "He can and will be elected . . . not for one man, not for one party, but for one nation, under God."[34] On

Robertson's campaign literature the words religious or evangelist or Christian did not appear. At one point Robertson, who made a major issue of abortion, said, "I wouldn't want any morality legislated. I don't think that's the appropriate role of government."[35] Robertson found himself ill at ease making the transition from evangelist to presidential candidate.

Jesse Jackson never made similar claims as the basis for his candidacy, nor in 1988 did he make the mistakes in speeches and interviews that Robertson made. By 1988 Jesse had become a political pro, while Pat was still an amateur. Jesse had learned through experience. He did use the black churches as a political base, but frank political talk at worship services has been accepted by the majority of black churches for well over a century. The churches provided the only independent base for black social and political action for decades, and many of the present black churches reflect that heritage.

Organized religious groups seemed to focus more on abortion than any other issue but with widely differing conclusions on what the moral answer is. Abortion did not become a major issue in the preconvention period, but after the first Bush-Dukakis debate, it became one of the five or six most talked about issues.

Each of us who were candidates tried in different ways to walk the narrow line between acknowledging the importance of religious groups while not abusing or misusing their sincere efforts. Jack Kemp hired Tim LaHaye, described in news accounts as "a Christian activist," to help Jack deal with the religious right; but when some anti-Semitic remarks LaHaye had alledgedly made became public, Jack quickly dropped him. Bush later had a series of resignations from advisers and personnel who allegedly were involved in anti-Semitic activities or statement.

The Greek Orthodox and Lutherans have never had a president, so journals representing each featured either Mike Dukakis or me. My wife is Roman Catholic and when we were together on a Sunday—which did not happen often during the campaign—we sometimes attended both a Lutheran and a Catholic service.

In an article in the magazine *The Lutheran,* I described myself with some accuracy, I felt, as "an inadequate Christian."[36] I received a few comments from people who found that description less than theologically sound.

An unusual offer of assistance came to me from a Baptist minister, Reverend Robert Thompson of Evanston, Illinois, who has a history of leadership on social concerns. He called and stated he would like to organize some clergy of all persuasions who knew me from Illinois, to contact their friends in Iowa and New Hampshire. He said, "The religious right is organized and active. Those of us who have differing views shouldn't sit idly by and do nothing." He made clear it would be a low-key sales job, with no claims that I had some divine mandate to be the candidate. They did a good job and had in their group a variety of Protestant, Catholic, and Jewish leaders.

But organized religion generally played less of a role than it did in 1984, when Geraldine Ferraro's stand on abortion caused a major furor, and less than it did in other recent presidential races going back to 1960, when John F. Kennedy's Catholicism emerged as the major issue in much of the nation.

We had reached the point of maturity as a nation so that an Associated Press photo from the New Orleans Republican convention caused only smiles, not outrage. A demonstrator carried a sign: "Bush Will Win Because God Is A Republican."[37]

The lessening of religious tensions in a campaign is good. When the dogmas of religion get confused with the flexibility that government policy requires, both religion and government suffer. George Will touched on that indirectly when he described Dukakis as "a man frequently faulted for lack of passion, but at least he lacks the passion of moral pride . . . the especially insulting vanity of the virtucrat."[38]

In the midst of Oliver North's testimony before the joint committee of Congress, the mail and phone calls in my Senate office ran approximately fifty-to-one in support of North. Other offices experienced the same. It discouraged me, and I knew I had to say something. On July 14, I spoke to the National Association of Counties convention in Indianapolis one hour before President Reagan addressed the same group. The president had earlier called Colonel North a hero. Without checking with my staff, because I knew there would be objections, I prepared my remarks that included these words:

> The current television coverage of the Iran-Contra problems and the public reaction to the hearings cause me to divert attention for two minutes from my message about the future of county government. . . .
>
> I do not question the sincerity of Lt. Col. Oliver North, but he is not an American hero. No one deserves the hero rank who admits that he lied, he cheated, he shredded evidence, and he violated the laws of our nation he swore to uphold.
>
> Our heroes should be those who live within the law and serve the public . . . .

Then I quoted from a speech that Abraham Lincoln made in 1838 at age twenty-eight, after a mob had killed a newspaper editor: "Let every American, every lover of liberty, every well-wisher to his [or her] posterity, swear by the blood of the [American] revolution never to violate in the least particular the laws of this country; and never to tolerate their violation by others. . . . Let every man remember that to violate the law is to trample upon the blood of his father and to tear the charter of his own and his children's liberty."[39]

I knew what the immediate reaction of that audience would be. The Associated Press summed up what many saw on television: "County officials from around the nation . . . booed the Illinois senator when he said Oliver North was not a hero."[40] But the immediate negative reaction of the crowd turned into complete silence when I read Lincoln's words.

In retrospect, I have two serious concerns as I view the issues of the campaign.

First, I am struck by how rarely fundamental questions were asked that lack general public appeal. Third world debt is an example. I referred to it in a few speeches but because there was no widespread interest, I brought it up infrequently. I had question and answer periods at almost all meetings, but I doubt that anyone asked about third world debt four times during the process of a year's campaigning. Part of that responsibility is mine. I should have used the opportunities to raise the issue more. But there is a political maturity that is yet to be developed among our people, when a candidate gets several questions every day about the Contras and the Sandinistas and Nicaragua, with its three million people, and there is indifference and almost total lack of knowledge about the debt problems that threaten the future of 70 million people in Mexico, 138 million in Brazil, and 31 million in Argentina, to pick three graphic examples. Some of the poorest nations have even greater burdens relative to their economic base. If those debt problems are not resolved satisfactorily, the long-term impact on the United States and on the fragile democracies in these countries will be infinitely greater than the impact from whatever happens in Nicaragua.

A second concern I have is the lack of focus on the nation's less fortunate. With a few exceptions, such as former Senator Lowell Weicker's and former Senator Robert Stafford's concern for the disabled, Senator Bob Dole's work for the disabled and the poorly fed, and Senator Pete Domenici's help to the homeless and the mentally ill, I find little interest among Republicans in programs that would lift the less fortunate. I expect that. But I do not expect that in my party. I hope the shift taking place in the Democratic party can be arrested. The political difficulty is that the poor are concentrated more and more in isolated geographical areas: the inner cities, Indian reservations, and scattered rural counties. They are no longer on our doorsteps, no longer visible where most Americans live. So the immediacy of the problem disappears. Since the poor vote in smaller numbers, the political necessity for paying attention to them also diminishes.

Talking of my jobs program, Gary Hart said, "You can't spend your way out of difficulty simply with more programs."[41] And I agree with that. But I fail to see Gary and too many others dealing in a meaningful way with the problem of the underclass in our society. Saying that you can't solve the problem by throwing money at it is true, but bromides like that do nothing to solve it.

Someone who has worked closely with Dukakis told me that he learns best by experience. But it becomes difficult for a governor or a president to really experience and understand the increasing desperation many Americans feel. The income of the top twenty percent of our population is growing, while the income of the bottom twenty percent is shrinking. If that course continues, it will lead to greater and greater economic stagnation and ultimately to political explosions. Both George Bush and Michael Dukakis have been somewhat insulated from understanding life as many see it. Elizabeth Drew, in commenting about Dukakis, wrote, "He hasn't seen much of life."[42] In some ways, Bush has seen even less. When Hodding Carter asked

Mike in one debate, "Is there a hardcore, unemployed . . . living in a culture which is outside the standard American culture?" Dukakis responded: "I don't believe there is."[43] In another debate I referred to America's underclass, and Mike said there is no underclass in the nation. I do not doubt his sincerity or nobleness of purpose. But there is a lack of understanding that concerns me, and it is a lack of understanding that is shared by the American public. It requires leadership to change that.

One of the substitutes for issues is labels. Someone is a "liberal" or a "conservative" or a "neo-liberal" or "right wing" or any one of a dozen or more labels. Labels are a shorthand convenience to reporters or candidates but often devoid of much meaning. I avoid describing myself by label, other than saying I'm a traditional Democrat, because those descriptions can convey totally erroneous impressions. I am usually called a liberal but in the minds of many people that means you favor wasting money, which I clearly do not. I favor a balanced budget unless there is a recession or emergency. Does that make me liberal or conservative? If by liberal you mean fighting for working men and women and not for the economically elite, trying to create opportunity for those less fortunate in our society, helping those in this country and abroad who are in desperate need of assistance, preserving our environment and civilization itself, you bet I'm a liberal. I favor not wasting the minds of children in our innercities with poor-quality schools. Does that make me liberal or conservative?

Fortunately, the American people are not that much enamored of labels. They want practical answers to real problems, and if a candidate provides those or has that certain chemistry of personality they are looking for in a leader, they will support the candidate.

I had to overcome this minor hurdle constantly: "A traditional Democrat who really espouses programs that help working men and women and the less fortunate cannot win in the fall. Look at Walter Mondale. He lost, forty-nine states to one."

It is an interesting argument because it assumes that the American people vote on a philosophical basis. It reverses precisely the same argument that many Republicans used in 1980 for not nominating Ronald Reagan. "He can't win. Someone who is too obviously conservative will lose. Look at Barry Goldwater in 1964." Despite those predictions Reagan won, and the media assumed there had been a huge philosophical shift by the public, rather than the more accurate assessment that the public, for the most part, does not vote on the basis of political philosophy.

When confronted with this question by someone in a large group, I would respond by asking, "Let's rerun the 1984 election. Let's assume that Reagan ran on the Mondale platform, and Mondale ran on the Reagan platform. Who would have won?" I asked the audience to raise their hands in reply. The results were always seven-to-one to twenty-to-one that Reagan would have won. Walter Mondale somehow did not communicate to people the compassion and vision for the nation that I know he has.

Let's try the same question another way: If Walter Cronkite had been a candidate for the nomination in either political party, would he have been nominated? I think he would have. He has the highest credibility rating of any well-known public figure. Where does he stand on the issues? It is a deeply held secret. But people instinctively like him and trust him.

For the most part, in 1984 people did not make their decision on the basis of the issues, and that held true in 1988 also. In my race, I did not come across as well as I needed to win. Exit polls in Iowa indicated that among college graduates and among those with a strong interest in the issues, I had a significant lead. The *New York Times*/CBS exit poll of Iowa caucus voters showed that among those with "some college and more," I received 29 percent, Dukakis 21 percent, and Gephardt 17 percent.[44] But among those with high school or less education, Gephardt led me decisively and won. Obviously I did not communicate effectively enough to the non-college portion of the population which is more heavily reliant on television. Somehow a combination of my appearance, my presentation, and my paid media did not click as effectively as I would have liked. The ABC exit poll in New Hampshire among college graduates showed Dukakis at 29 percent, I had 25 percent, and Gephardt had 12 percent, but Gephardt nosed me out for second place in New Hampshire on the votes of those less well educated.[45]

The fault rests with me and my presentation, not the issues. Media attention to the nonissues aggravates the problem of candidates who attempt to focus on issues. The American people are ready to follow someone who *really* leads on the problems of urban education, jobs for those who now feel totally left out by our society, a safer environment, long-term care for those who need it, arms control, and similar issues. The public is ready and eager for such leadership, but the fog of personality and media trivia and campaign commercials prevents them from getting a clear picture.

☆ 6 ☆

THE DEBATES

An unprecedented number of debates occurred during the 1987–88 preconvention period, almost all of them on the Democratic side. By the time I suspended my candidacy, I had participated in more than thirty debates, missing three where there were serious schedule conflicts and in one case because it was scheduled in a Super Tuesday state after I had abandoned serious Super Tuesday contention.

The Republicans had far fewer debates, primarily because George Bush tried to avoid them and because the number two candidate, Bob Dole, did not want them if Bush did not show. Dole could only lose ground to his other rivals and not gain on Bush. Only Bush, of all the Republican and Democratic candidates, declined to be on the one-hour series of shows Marvin Kalb had on Public Broadcasting. His representative told Kalb, "An hour of substantive talk with Marvin Kalb and the Harvard community will not advance his [Bush's] candidacy."[1] Kalb later reflected that Bush's declining to participate "revealed a propensity in Bush and his operation for overcalculation, overcaution, and overconfidence—qualities that could create problems for him as . . . his country's president."[2] When Ted Koppel asked both Dukakis and Bush to appear on a one and one-half hour "Nightline" (ABC) special, Dukakis accepted but Bush declined. Bush appeared on the David Frost show, the only lengthy interview format he accepted during the entire campaign. The Republicans had only three real encounters with all Republican candidates present, though there were a few minor skirmishes in which only two or three of the candidates participated.

The Bush strategy, traditional for a front-runner, paid off. As the front-runner, he would have had everyone pouncing on him and might lose that front-runner status. Dole, in his role as one of the two Senate leaders, received good press to reinforce his status.

Dole probably decided against many debates in part because he has a biting wit and if provoked, a short fuse. Those who work with him in the Senate see it and understand it. He is sometimes caustic in his treatment of others, but he is also willing to take it and willing to laugh at himself. He is a substantial legislator, sometimes hampered by a sharp tongue. The public does not see the full person. The sharp tongue might have helped him or caused him problems in debates. On the day of the New Hampshire primary, candidates traditionally make the rounds of the polling places in New Hampshire to shake hands and encourage supporters. Under New Hampshire law and tradition, political activity is tolerated much closer to the place of voting than is the case in Illinois and most states. Those going to vote sometimes enter through an "honor guard" of volunteers on both sides of the sidewalk urging the voters-to-be to cast their ballots for various candidates. Signs and placards are in abundance, both to influence the voters and to catch whatever television coverage may come to that precinct, and in Manchester precincts that is substantial. I came to one precinct right after Dole. One of my supporters related that as Dole headed toward his car after talking with his supporters and reporters, a DuPont volunteer carrying a placard thrust a sign in Dole's face and asked, "Why did you support the 1982 tax increase?" Without a smile and without a moment's hesitation—but with no reporters immediately present — Dole, who had already received unpleasant news from the early exit polls, turned on his heckler and quietly said, "Go back to your cave."

Dole is superb at those jabs, but they don't gain a candidate votes in a presidential campaign.

Despite that weakness, Dole would have been the strongest candidate the Republicans could have put up and would have made the best president among them. He would have appealed to groups that traditionally have not voted Republican—minorities and the disabled particularly—and he would have had a broader appeal because he has one thing that is essential for a strong leader: a sense of direction and purpose. Bush does not have it. Bush tries too hard to please. As one of his defenders noted in the middle of an interview with the *New York Times,* "He's not a deep person. He doesn't have the courage of his convictions."[3] President Reagan's former press secretary, Larry Speakes, noted the same in different words: "Seldom did I hear [Bush] speak up, either in Cabinet meetings or in private sessions. . . . I never heard him say, 'Mr. President, my advice to you would be, this is the wrong thing to do.' Or, for that matter, 'This is the right thing to do.' . . . He was the perfect yes man. . . . With Bush the popular image may be accurate: that he does not have a strong philosophical base, that he is not decisive, that he is not willing to take stands on the big issues. He agonizes endlessly . . . and is a bit wishy-washy when he takes a stand."[4]

My own impression is that Bush has inclinations rather than convictions. Dole is tough enough to make the difficult economic and foreign policy decisions a president must make. His foreign policy background is not as great as Bush's, but my guess is that he would have chosen wisely and carefully in that field, as he put his key players together. Choosing wisely is not a substitute for experience, but Dole's more limited experience, plus the right advisers, probably would have kept him away from major foreign policy blunders. Those who differ with that conclusion point to his southern African foreign policy record. My impression is that his none-too-illustrious African record is largely a combination of inattention and a desire to do a few things to satisfy the far-right among his GOP Senate colleagues. There is reason to believe that as president he would have had more enlightened policies than the Reagan administration.

On the Democratic side, no one had the kind of lead Bush had until early April. Hart held a significant lead until his initial, hasty departure, but even that lead had little depth. Unlike Bush, no Democratic candidate could risk avoiding the debates.

But "debate" is really the wrong word. They were as different in style and substance from the Lincoln-Douglas debates of 1858 as a musical radio commercial is from a Beethoven symphony. The pattern for most of these discussions was a one-minute open and/or close, and then a series of questions by a panel. The candidates' responses were limited to one minute in most instances, forty-five seconds in one debate, and thirty seconds on one occasion.

The result: little new in the way of questions and even less new in the way of answers. They became contests in sloganeering rather than a test of thoughtfulness and substance. The way to win: Get a good one-liner that makes the evening television news.

A few debates had a short period for candidate-to-candidate questions, and that improved the dialogue a little. But in most instances the candidates and the reporters who followed us could predict with not-so-amazing precision what the answers would be.

Certain lines were part of every debate.

We knew that Mike Dukakis would refer to his Greek immigrant parents; that Joe Biden would invoke the generational theme; that Jesse Jackson would ask the audience how many own VCRs, all made in Japan, and then ask us how many own nuclear warheads made in the U.S., then tell us we're making things that don't sell, and Japan is making things that do sell; that Al Gore would win the old joke award, usually the chicken and ham joke, with the pig noting that the ham and egg breakfast required only a donation from the chicken, but a real sacrifice from the pig; that Gary Hart would pull out the "budget" that he put together and display it; that Bruce Babbitt would not very modestly note his courage and candor and usually offer a surprise line or gimmick, the lines usually pretty good, the gimmicks less so; that Dick Gephardt would display carefully trained passion at some point and assert, "It's your fight too," a public relations line that never caught on. I had Hubert Humphrey stories and other lines that I repeated over and over and over again. I was as tired of hearing my own lines as my fellow candidates were. Why didn't we change our lines more often? You learn what works with the public, and you have a limited time to acquire anything really new, so you go with the tried and effective. For most of the audiences our lines were new.

With the time constraints, new lines or new thoughts were an ill-afforded luxury.

In fairness to the sponsors of the debates, they had a time problem in the number of candidates: eight at one point, later seven, and then six. It's difficult to construct a meaningful dialogue among seven talkative candidates in a limited time span.

In a few debates we asked questions of our colleagues that either pressed our opponents or got in some points about where we stood. Dukakis became the exception, almost always asking softball questions that did not score but did not antagonize. It's difficult to knock a home run with a softball question.

Jackson used more audience participation than any of us and had great skill at occasionally evading questions. "Should we modernize our weapons as we approach arms control?" Gephardt asked Jackson in the Iowa STARPAC (Stop the Arms Race Political Action Committee) debate. Jesse responded, "We ought to modernize our thinking." And then he was off answering the question he wanted to answer.

The two candidates with strong gestures in debate were Dick Gephardt and Jesse Jackson.

Al Gore strenuously tried to shift his image to the right after Senator Sam Nunn of Georgia declined to get into the race, and he succeeded at least partially. Gore consistently showed a good mind, though his liability in debates according to reporters who watched him on television was his wooden appearance.

Winner of the rapid speech award: Mike Dukakis.

Better than the debates were the one-on-one interviews conducted by David Frost and Marvin Kalb. In the case of Frost, he interviewed the candidates and the candidates' wives in our homes, talked with us for about two hours, and condensed that into a one-hour show. In the case of Marvin Kalb, he had a one-hour program before a live audience at Harvard. He asked questions for approximately thirty minutes and then let faculty and students ask questions.

My guess, however, is that the ratings for the Kalb show and the Frost show—if they had been taken—would be even lower than for the joint appearances. The NBC debate of all the candidates, hosted by Tom Brokaw, ranked fifty-eighth out of seventy programs rated by Nielsen for that week. Joint appearance had at least the hope of a little theater, a little fireworks, and the brevity of the answers had some appeal. Americans appear to like their politics in the form of appetizers rather than entrées. Two recent studies of network news found that the average length "sound bite" of candidates speaking in 1984 ran fourteen seconds, and in 1988 nine seconds.

In three of the better debates in which I participated, only two of the seven candidates appeared. In one debate at Rivier College in

New Hampshire, sponsored by the organization Beyond War, Dukakis and I discussed foreign policy. It gave the immediate audience and the television viewers much more of an insight than the more traditional discussions with six or seven candidates. Two-person debates permitted lengthier answers and greater depth on the questions. At a debate in Birmingham, Alabama, only Gore and I showed. Again, because of the paucity of candidates, the immediate audience and the statewide television audience—whatever there may have been of it—got a better look at two candidates than they would have at seven. In Atlanta, a debate sponsored by the two daily newspapers in which all candidates participated was followed immediately by a debate sponsored by environmental groups, but only Al Gore and I appeared. The two of us have strong environmental records, and there probably would have been more fireworks if some of the other candidates had been present. A debate of limited focus— such as on the environment—can provide greater insight into a candidate's understanding and attitude than can the more general debate that covers the universe of issues, particularly one with seven candidates.

I participated in one debate at Fordham University with Jesse Jackson and Al Gore, and during the New York primary there were three debates in which Gore, Jackson, and Dukakis participated. After New York, Dukakis and Jackson were the only participants. The more limited numbers did not always produce better debates, but better debates were possible and sometimes happened.

An "almost candidate" did not appear in the debates. Representative Patricia Schroeder of Colorado came close to announcing and, in the words of William Buckley, cohost for the first debate, she "applied to be included in the program, but unhappily, too late to be included in the mechanical arrangements."[5] I urged the hosts to include her. She would have brought an added dimension on defense issues and on issues where women have shown a greater sensitivity. In two later debates, she declined to participate and then, on September 28, announced that she would not be a candidate, a decision signaled by her nonparticipation in debates.

There were several joint appearances by our wives, one formally structured. I did not get to see this, though I'm told that Jeanne did exceptionally well.

And there were debates featuring surrogates everywhere, sometimes members of our family, but frequently some volunteer or staff member who took on the task. Those exchanges often were more feisty than the debates by the principals. Our daughter Sheila and her husband Perry Knop were at one where the Bush and Dole representatives almost came to blows. The restraints of friendship and the desire not to appear too negative kept the debates of the candidates fairly tame—much tamer than many had predicted or wanted.

The three most significant debates prior to the suspension of my candidacy were the initial Houston debate broadcast on public television; the NBC debate; and the *Des Moines Register* debate, each important for different reasons.

The Houston debate, broadcast nationally on PBS had as its hosts William Buckley, columnist and Republican stalwart, and Robert Strauss, the former Democratic national chair and a respected political negotiator. As the first encounter it received national media buildup. No clear winner emerged, but Bruce Babbitt became the clear loser. We felt it there on the stage, and the television audience sensed it even more. Widely watched as the first debate, it did serious, if temporary, harm to Babbitt's campaign. Bruce's body movements bothered television audiences. What a way to pick a president! But these things become important. Bruce sensed immediately that he did not do well, hired a television coach, and spent hours preparing and improving his style; and it did improve. A viewer of the North Carolina debate some weeks later would not have guessed that Bruce ever had any difficulty.

In the Houston debate, Bruce did what some advised me to do at various times during the campaign. He announced who some of his cabinet appointees would be. It received hardly any attention, and it pleased me that it did not. A presidential candidate should avoid those public commitments during a campaign so that if elected, he or she can select the best possible people. A president can almost literally get anyone to accept a cabinet position. The freedom to pick the finest people available should be reserved for a president-to-be until the last possible moment, so that if better choices occur just prior to the appointment time, the president is free to select them. It also avoids the preelection danger of picking big names—who may not be that good—and pandering to various interest groups with the selections.

One of the better lines in the Houston debate was mine, and I wish I had written it. The candidates were told well in advance that the opening question would be, "Which president's picture would you hang on the wall of the cabinet room?" My answer, "The cabinet room is a working room, and instead of a tribute to our heritage, I would like to see a steelworker from Pennsylvania and a coal miner. I would like to see a farm family there, a working mother, a teacher, some inner-city school children. I want to see America on that wall. I want to remind those cabinet members [that] they work for those people. . . . It is a great honor to serve in the cabinet, but they are there to serve and help the people of this nation."[6] Those lines came from Arnold Bennett, one of our early volunteers. Like most good lines in all the debates, they were not original with the candidate.

William Batoff, a Democratic fund-raiser and business/civic leader from the Philadelphia area, employed Wheeler and Associates, a Seattle polling firm, to have Iowa citizens sit in front of "electronic response systems" to evaluate the performance of candidates in the Houston debate and in the later NBC debate. Eighty-five Iowa citizens watched on a large screen and recorded their responses as the Houston debate proceeded.

The eighty-five were asked to evaluate the candidates, both before the debate and after it. The results:

Post-Debate (Describes Candidate Very Well)		Net Change In "Very Well"
Has the experience and qualifications a President needs		
42	Simon	+17
37	Dukakis	0
27	Gephardt	+5
26	Biden	+1
15	Gore	+7
14	Jackson	0
4	Babbitt	−7
Is a strong leader		
56	Dukakis	+5
32	Simon	+16

28	Gephardt	+8
27	Jackson	−13
25	Biden	+4
19	Gore	+4
4	Babbitt	−6

Is intelligent

55	Simon	+22
54	Dukakis	+16
41	Jackson	0
36	Biden	+4
33	Gephardt	+5
27	Gore	+5
18	Babbitt	−6

Has good ideas

48	Dukakis	+10
42	Simon	+21
32	Jackson	+5
31	Biden	+3
27	Gephardt	+7
20	Gore	+6
11	Babbitt	−2

Is persuasive

45	Dukakis	+5
40	Jackson	0
33	Biden	+2
28	Gephardt	+13
26	Simon	+10
22	Gore	+10
5	Babbitt	−14

Is close to you on the issues

36	Simon	+17
31	Dukakis	+5
24	Gephardt	+3
24	Biden	−5
22	Jackson	0
18	Gore	+6
5	Babbitt	+1

Understands the problems Iowa faces

34	Simon	+12
29	Jackson	+4
29	Gephardt	+3
21	Dukakis	−4
14	Biden	+1
11	Gore	0
4	Babbitt	−2

When asked to evaluate who won the debate, these percentages were recorded:

Mike Dukakis	23
Dick Gephardt	21
Paul Simon	18
Al Gore	13
Joe Biden	11
Jesse Jackson	2
Bruce Babbitt	2
Don't know	10

To some extent those figures reflect support at that point in Iowa. I had gained the most in the process, and Bruce Babbitt had lost the most. Jesse Jackson's figures were not high because the expectation level for him exceeded his performance.

NBC had the only encounter in which all the Republican and Democratic candidates appeared. The two parties alternated each half hour with Brokaw moderating. The NBC debate had added significance because it was the only debate carried in full by any of the three major commercial networks.

Tom Brokaw—unlike most debate moderators—really took charge and was strict on time. In most debates the candidates too easily outtalked the moderators, and time rules often disintegrated. The greatest abuser of the time limitation rule, by far, was Al Gore, with Jesse Jackson running second. But as each of us saw the moderator of any particular debate not strictly following the clock, all of us went over our time limit.

Moderators and questioners also made another mistake—not following through if candidates failed to answer the question asked.

In the North Carolina debate Judy Woodruff of PBS became one of the rare exceptions to that rule. The oldest gimmick in these settings is to avoid the question and answer the one you want to answer. In two debates, much too lengthy introductions of the subjects and the candidates got the discussion off to a slow start.

NBC gave us one minute to respond to a Brokaw question. That time limitation turned into an important factor in the results of that debate.

Because I had been dissatisfied with debate preparation for the previous debates, I asked Joel Hyatt of Cleveland, a trial lawyer who also understands politics, to join in our debate preparation this time. We had less than two hours of preparation time and compounded that error by a staff decision that I approved, allowing Lesley Stahl of CBS to tape much of our debate preparation—a factor that inhibited our discussion. After the limited late-afternoon debate preparation, Hyatt went to the office of his father-in-law, Senator Howard Metzenbaum, and told him, "Paul is tired, and he has had poor preparation for the debate." Joel was right on both counts. The results showed it.

When you are bone-tired—which you are sometimes—you recognize that you are not as sharp in interviews. I remember struggling to stay awake during one radio interview. I was on "automatic pilot" answering questions, and I could have really created problems for myself. I tried to sleep late at least one morning a week, and I also tried to get at least six hours sleep each night. When I missed those six hours two or more days in a row, I could feel that I did not do well. It shows. After some of the televised debates, friends or my staff would tell me, "You looked tired." They were right.

Dukakis had three three-hour preparation sessions before major debates, plenty of sleep, and separate time for relaxation between the preparation and the debate. I would have been wise to follow the same procedure.

Prior to the NBC debate, articles had appeared suggesting that my call for spending on jobs and education and long-term care, and my simultaneous call for a balanced budget, were inconsistent. The charge had enough superficial appearance of validity to make it sound believable. (The issue is discussed in greater detail in Chapter 5.) We felt that Brokaw would ask a question on this, and as we discussed how to respond, we agreed that in one minute you simply cannot provide an answer for that complex a matter. I decided to say that I would provide the background material and that it could be done. It was a major error on my part. I should have worked hard on devising a one-minute summary and then get cut off, if necessary. I appeared to be ducking.

Brokaw pointed out that I favor both a balanced budget and increased spending in certain areas and then asked, "Aren't you in danger of being tagged with voodoo economics in 1988?"[7]

After responding that we have to move on education and a jobs program, I said, "We have to do it on a pay-as-you-go basis. And we can do it. I've served on the Budget Committee in the House and Senate. I understand the figures. We can do it, and we're going to do it. No question about it."

Hardly a satisfactory answer.

Dick Gephardt, who had voted for the Reagan tax bills of 1981 and 1986, both of which I had opposed, called my plans "Reaganomics with a bow tie." I responded that he should be an expert on it since he had voted for the 1981 tax bill, the centerpiece of Reaganomics that had caused the huge budget and trade deficits.

The polls in Iowa the next day—the only state that really counted at this point—showed a negative reaction to Dick's attack on me and showed me coming in second to Dukakis in "winning" among Iowa viewers. But this debate affected my candidacy negatively. Again, Bill Batoff of Philadelphia teamed with the Wheeler and Associates firm to measure the Iowa response. Their analysis of the response is of interest:

On Babbitt: "They are slow to accept his sometimes unusual framing of and solutions to problems. . . . He was neither helped nor hurt by his debate performance."

On Dukakis: "The debate forum . . . requiring concise and powerful answers appears tailor-made for Governor Dukakis. His performance . . . was very consistent with his previous [Houston] strong showing among an Iowa voter audience. . . . He does not directly attack individuals. The benefits of this critical, yet depersonalized, approach are seen in the positive marks Republican respondents gave his hard-hitting criticisms of Reagan foreign policy."

On Gephardt: " . . . the evening's disaster story. From relatively high, positive pre-debate assessments of his qualifications, Gephardt plummeted in every candidate attribute category along with the perception of his ability to deal with specific issues."

On Jackson: " . . . has an oratorical style which is subject to highs and lows. . . . The Iowa voter audience rewarded his performance with relatively high marks in many areas."

On Simon: " . . . vaguer and less forceful [than in the Houston debate]. . . . He lost significant ground. . . . lack of dynamism and apparent tentativeness in addressing the issues."

Republicans polled thought that among the Democrats, I had won the debate, and Democrats thought that among the Republicans, Bob Dole had won—significant numbers for a general election, but we did not face a general election, rather a crucial Iowa party caucus.

Among Democrats the estimate on who won: Dukakis 23 percent, Jackson and Simon 13 percent, Gore 10 percent, Babbitt 7 percent, Gephardt 2 percent, and "no clear winner" 33 percent.

But long-term I got hurt. My exchange with Brokaw reinforced genuine concerns with my budget and spending proposals. The real loser in the NBC debate, the most widely watched of any of the debates: Paul Simon. Not by a wide margin but the loser nevertheless.

A mid-October memorandum from my pollster, Paul Maslin, to key campaign staff and to me noted: "Despite several good performances, Paul is still an inconsistent debate performer. . . . Mock debates and intensive rehearsing are the only mechanisms to guarantee a consistently strong performance level. There is no substitute."[8] Unfortunately we paid no attention to that memo six weeks later for the NBC debate. Its advice was sound.

The *Des Moines Register* sponsored the third really key debate, critical because of that newspaper's sponsorship and because of Hart's reentrance into the race. The newspaper has a role of preeminence like that of no other newspaper in any other state, and a respected role. The debate also had wide viewership in Iowa.

Thirty-one days before the *Des Moines Register* debate, Gary Hart reentered the race. That overwhelmed the news for days. At one point Gary gave as a reason for coming back that the candidates were not discussing the issues. He could have said that we were not discussing them adequately or almost anything else, but the reality is that we were discussing the issues, though not always well, and receiving little attention for doing it—and appreciably less after Hart reentered the race. For three weeks after Gary's announcement, almost all the media questions focused on Hart.

The combination of the great attention to his reentrance and his suggestion that the rest of us already in the race were not doing an adequate job raised expectations for his performance. Perhaps because he had not participated in as many debates as the rest of us, Gary never looked comfortable in these settings. And the almost universal reaction after his first debate performance was that he "bombed." Congressman David Nagle, former Iowa Democratic chair, told the newspapers, "I think six guys won and one guy lost. You'd think the guy who's got all the new ideas would have shared one of them with us tonight."⁹ The headings in the newspapers the next day told the story: "Hart Makes Six Opponents Look Good in First Debate Appearance with Rivals" *(Wall Street Journal)*; "Hart Fails to Impress at Debate in Iowa" *(Boston Globe)*; "No Winner, but Hart Loses" *(Ft. Dodge Messenger)*. The expectation that he would be decidedly different from the rest of us was heightened visually at the debate when he appeared wearing a sport jacket and cowboy boots. Actually he did as well as the rest of us—no better and no worse—but the expectations were so high that he became the loser. His performance did nothing to slow a continued downhill slide of his candidacy. After Mike Dukakis had clinched the nomination, Dukakis told me that he thought the *Des Moines Register* debate turned into the decisive moment of the preconvention campaign because it plummeted Gary Hart in the polls, and it virtually ended all the talk about "the seven dwarfs."

To the critics who charged that no conflict arose in the debates, they either did not listen to, or view, many of the debates or were seeking a brand of violent encounter that would not be good for the party.

For example, here is one exchange from the NBC debate:

MR. BROKAW: It's that portion of tonight's presidential debate format in which they ask each other some questions. We begin with Senator Gore who has a question for Congressman Gephardt of Missouri.

SENATOR GORE: Dick, you tried to answer this question earlier and you didn't get a chance. We've all agreed that the principal problem with domestic policy and our economic policy is Reaganomics. And the centerpiece was the unfair and inequitable tax bill of 1981. [All] of the others of us who had a chance to vote on it, voted against it. You're the only one who supported it, and I want to give you a chance to explain why you voted for Reaganomics.

REPRESENTATIVE GEPHARDT: Well, Al, you know as well as I do that I led the fight in the Ways and Means Committee and on the floor for the Democratic alternative, and we came within a few votes of passing it. But let me ask you a question. Are you—

SENATOR GORE: I'd prefer that you answer the question that I asked you and that Paul Simon asked you because we haven't heard the answer yet.

REPRESENTATIVE GEPHARDT: Well, let me ask you a question: Are you for repealing the Reagan tax cut and raising taxes on middle-income Americans by $260 billion?

SENATOR GORE: I voted against that tax cut because I thought it was unfair and inequitable.

REPRESENTATIVE GEPHARDT: Just let me—are you for repealing it? Are you for repealing it today?

SENATOR GORE: Did you vote for it because you thought it was a good idea?

REPRESENTATIVE GEPHARDT: I thought we were about to have a recession. I thought we were about to have a recession, and I thought we needed a tax cut. I fought as hard as I could. And I led—you were a back bencher—I was leading—to pass the Democratic bill.

SENATOR GORE: We came at the same time, Dick. We came at the same time.

REPRESENTATIVE GEPHARDT: I understand. But I was leading to pass the Democratic alternative.

SENATOR GORE: So you thought it was a good—you thought the Reagan tax cut was a good idea?

REPRESENTATIVE GEPHARDT: I thought we needed a tax cut, Al.

SENATOR GORE: Even if—

REPRESENTATIVE GEPHARDT: I wish we had gotten the Democratic tax cut. We couldn't pass it. We came nine votes or ten votes short. But my question to you, are you for repealing it? Do you want to raise revenue by repealing the '81 tax cut?

SENATOR GORE: I voted against it. And I voted to repeal major portions of it.

REPRESENTATIVE GEPHARDT: Do you want to raise taxes on middle-income Americans?

MR. BROKAW: How's the hearing in Tennessee and Missouri, gentlemen? The chime man [who controls debate time] was going cross-eyed during the course of that. Thank you both very much.[10]

There were light moments in the debates. At one encounter on agriculture Jesse Jackson held up one of those tiny cereal boxes, about three by four inches and one inch deep, and said that the box of Wheaties he held cost $1.25 at a grocery store. I told him he had better get someone to advise him before he went grocery shopping again.

Sometimes the light moments backfired. Al Gore gave up on Iowa and disappeared from that state when, despite a sizable expenditure of time and money, the polls showed him going nowhere. Suddenly he showed up at the *Des Moines Register* debate. Bruce Babbitt welcomed him back, commenting, "I thought we would see you show up on one of these milk cartons," meaning the cartons that display missing children. But one of the first missing children displayed on a milk carton came from Iowa, a boy carrying newspapers who went out on his route one day and never returned. The Babbitt remark, not intended to offend anyone, caused a small stir and he apologized.

One other insight into the debates: As I prepared for this manuscript, I played the tapes on our home VCR, going through them late at night in our bedroom. Jeanne frequently fell asleep. Sometimes I did too.

The debates resulted in a reasonably good feeling among the candidates. That did not include Al Gore initially. Al made some sweeping charges, such as that the rest of us were advocating policies of "retreat, complacency, and doubt," a charge that suddenly emerged after Senator Sam Nunn announced his decision not to run. It is one thing to accuse me (or any of us) of being wrong in opposing the MX missile or on any other specific position. Specific charges we can respond to, adequately or inadequately. But broadside attacks are difficult to deal with and were resented by all the other candidates. This Gore approach came under discussion in the debate sponsored by the Democratic National Committee in Washington. It included these exchanges:

> SIMON: Al, I'm pleased to detect a little different tone in your comments here today, I think all of us are. . . . I don't think it helps you or any of us to be knifing each other.

> GORE: Well, now, wait just a minute here. Wait just a minute here. If you want to—if we want to have another spirited debate about defense and foreign policy, then we'll have some sharp disagreements about these issues.

> SIMON: Okay, let me finish and I'll be happy to let you respond. One of the things that we have to keep in mind is that one of us is going to emerge after Atlanta as a candidate, and we should be conducting ourselves in such a way that there is meaning to these debates, not just sound, and that we are pulling our Party together, not tearing it apart. That is absolutely essential.

> CHAIRMAN PAUL KIRK: Senator Gore has asked for the right to respond. I would like to believe, as a preface, he feels the same way.

> GORE: I do in fact feel the same way, but to pretend that there are no differences in our Party is completely unrealistic. We have disagreements within our Party. . . .

> JACKSON: I must say categorically that we must assert our differences and our distinctions in ways that do not lend to division because when it's all said and done, it's not the particulars of our single vision, it's the building of this network that will give us enough people for victory in 1988. And that's the spirit of Paul Simon's position, and I support that basic spirit.

> SIMON: Al, in a foreign policy speech on October 4 you criticized those in the Democratic Party who advocate, and I quote, "the politics of retreat, complacency, and doubt." Now, as one who favors a stronger conventional force, who has voted for Midgetman, who has voted for the Stealth and the Cruise missile, I don't

think I fall in that category; I don't think Mike Dukakis does; I don't think Dick Gephardt does; I don't think Bruce Babbitt does; I don't think Jesse Jackson does. It would be healthy, if you didn't mean any of us, to say so right now. If you do, we ought to be named.

GORE: All right. We've had some sharp disagreements in debates over the last ten days or so on issues relating to defense and foreign policy. A couple of issues on which I find myself in disagreement from my competitors here include two that have been mentioned, the Persian Gulf and the proposal for a flight test ban. . . .

GEPHARDT: Al, we ought to debate differences, but let's not bring up phony differences, and let's not talk about each other the way Jeane Kirkpatrick or Ronald Reagan talks about Democrats.[11]

Most political observers did not sense the friction that existed. But one columnist noted, "The party did seem divided last week. Gore was on one side, all the other candidates were on the other."[12]

Al soon sensed in debates that his approach was both ineffective and resented. With the change in style came greater acceptance of him by the other candidates.

Shortly after the Democratic National Committee debate just referred to, Gore appeared on the Marvin Kalb show, and Kalb followed through:

KALB: You've been very tough in criticizing the people who are running for the Democratic nomination. You have said that you are in the race with people who are advocates of retreat, complacency and doubt. Now that's pretty tough stuff. . . . Who are you talking about among your colleagues who's advocating retreat, complacency, and doubt? Are you talking about Dukakis?

GORE: What I said specifically was that the politics of retreat, complacency, and doubt may appeal to some, but they don't appeal to me.

KALB: Who are you talking about?[13]

Gore, once again, was not specific in naming anyone.

Adequate preparation for debates is essential, but going from preparation to showmanship was a role I did not relish. It is a difficulty the staff had with me. I recognize that it is a political defect. I believe that if you do something with which you do not feel comfortable, you will not do it well—so don't do it. I declined to put on an Indian headdress in front of cameras in Des Moines, declined to pose with innumerable hats various communities and organizations and companies gave me, declined to milk a cow in Wisconsin, and declined to do the gimmicky things in debates that my staff wanted me to do. For example, in New Hampshire where I ran a television ad comparing my record and Dick Gephardt's, Dick said at a press conference that I should get rid of my bow tie if I was going to run ads like that. My staff wanted me to pull out a long tie in the debate the next day and say to him, "If you can show me one inaccuracy in that ad, I'll wear this tie." I came close to saying it, even taking the tie up on the stage in my pocket, but when it got to that point in the debate, I simply did not feel comfortable doing it. It somehow did not seem to fit me or the dignity of the office I sought. My staff had said—accurately—that if I did it, it would make all the national television news shows. I recalled John F. Kennedy watching Richard Nixon raising both arms skyward on national television. Kennedy commented, "If I have to do that to become president, I won't become president." There is nothing immoral about raising your hands or wearing hats or flashing ties in a debate, but these actions fit some people and do not fit others. In addition, gimmicks sometimes detract from what should be a serious look at the issues and who should lead the free world.

My staff wanted me to do some shouting in order to show toughness during the debates. I recognize that there are those who equate toughness with shouting, but it is not my kind of toughness. I've taken on everything from organized crime as a young newspaper publisher to the problems of corruption as a state legislator, and I got action by a more low-key, solid but tough approach. I've been able to get a great deal done in the House and Senate through the years, but none of it by shouting and screaming. Showmanship should not be a substitute for quiet strength in a presidential debate or in the presidency. But in terms of presidential politics, my staff may have been right, and I may have been wrong.

There were the inevitable little struggles in the debates. The candidates liked to debate with tables in front of them. You could put notes in front of yourself and make notes about the comments of others more easily. And you didn't need to be bothered about the problems of crossing or not crossing your legs, which always evoked advice from staff and viewers. For reasons that were never completely clear to me, the television people involved in the debates did not want tables, and too often they won. Television producers who viewed all the debates found that the North Carolina debate had the best set for television, and there the sponsors used tables. Boston radio-television personality Jerry Williams had one of the best structural setups in the debate he hosted. He had us around a relatively small table. Crowded, yes, but the exchange somehow became more spontaneous, less contrived.

Who won the debates?

If you were to pick one winner, overall, my award would go to Jesse Jackson by a slight margin, with Mike Dukakis second. That's a subjective call, but Jesse is superb with the phrases and with the short response that makes a good sound bite for television. Mike did not shine as Jesse sometimes did, but he came across as unflappable and competent. In most of the debates it was close, with no clear winners or losers.

The *National Journal* asked four college debate coaches to analyze the debates, scoring us on analysis, reasoning, evidence, organization, refutation, and delivery. I did poorly in delivery, where Jackson emerged on top, and I came out on top in analysis and reasoning. Overall, in total points, Jackson came in first, I came in second, Dukakis third, Babbitt fourth, Gephardt fifth, and Gore sixth.[14] But are college debate coaches good judges of what impresses the public? I don't know.

The encounters did bring about a comradeship among the candidates that transcended our differences. When Bruce Babbitt's father died, the exchange among the candidates prior to a debate that Bruce had to miss showed a genuine feeling for Bruce and his family and what they were going through. Before each debate, we gathered behind a stage or in a side room and exchanged banter. I had as my campaign symbol a small bow tie pin with no name on it. It's a pin that people actually wear, while almost no one wears campaign buttons except at rallies. In two debates, Jesse Jackson put on my bow tie pin. A few sharp-eyed television viewers spotted it and wrote, asking me if there was any special significance to it. There was not, just a little "horse play" among the candidates.

Bruce Babbitt recently related something I had forgotten. At the end of the NBC debate in which Bruce literally stood up for a tax increase, I turned to him and said, "You're going to be in the first paragraph of tomorrow's stories. Good performance."[15] We commended or criticized or jested with each other in private. After the Democratic National Committee debate, in which I admonished Al Gore to tone down his rhetoric a little, each of the other candidates came over to me afterward to thank me.

Republican debates had more bloodletting, though the GOP decision came early enough to heal the wounds. On our side, the wounds were less deep, but fresher, as the general election approached.

The sense of belonging to—and sharing in—an extremely small fraternity of Democratic candidates for president made it unlikely that the Democrats would approach the general election deeply divided.

The debates helped to create that sense of fraternity.

The first debate in the general election between Bush and Dukakis gave Mike a boost. In part that lift came because Dukakis outscored him on any point-for-point analysis. In part it helped the Democrat because of expectations. Bush had been talking about his superior experience, and as vice president people anticipated that he could provide a better performance. The expectations game, always important in politics, helped Dukakis. Bush softened what would have been a devastating blow to him by coming across as the less polished of the two but the more likable. Several journals referred to the Dukakis performance as "icy." But despite a lack of projected warmth, Dukakis got a campaign boost.

The second debate between the two had fewer viewers, but Bush received the boost. The expectations game no longer helped Dukakis. Mike had already shown that could do well. Both candidates came across the television screen as more relaxed than in the first debate. In debate points it came close to a draw, but again Bush portrayed a warmth of personality that Mike did not, though Dukakis's was an improved performance in this regard. *Time* magazine summed up the second debate with the heading, "Bush Scores a Warm Win."[16]

The Lloyd Bentsen/Dan Quayle debate generated much conversation in the days that followed, and for pure entertainment purposes, it topped the three debates. The climax to the Bentsen-Quayle debate came when Quayle compared his experience to John Kennedy's, and Bentsen coolly replied, "You're no Jack Kennedy." Prior to the debate, Democrats worried that because expectations were high for Bentsen and low for Quayle, a well-programmed Quayle could come out of the debate doing well. His handlers did program Quayle thoroughly, too thoroughly. He did well until an unexpected question arose—the most basic question—about what he would do if he had to suddenly take over the presidency. Then he faltered. The debate made Lloyd Bentsen a political star. He even looked presidential.

Neither Dukakis nor Bush scored a similar knockout punch in their debates. Those of us pulling for Dukakis hoped for a repeat of the 1960 John F. Kennedy victory over Richard Nixon. Instead, like most debates, neither side scored a decisive victory.

☆ 7 ☆

SHOULD IOWA AND NEW HAMPSHIRE BE SO DOMINANT?

A Herblock cartoon shows a teacher speaking to a civics class filled with wide-eyed children, saying, "And any native-American has a chance to become President if the voters of Iowa and New Hampshire approve."[1] The cartoon echoes the criticism I hear from people in forty-eight states. "Why should we in New York [any other state's name can be inserted] be squeezed out of the big choice by a few thousand people in Iowa and New Hampshire?"

Raymond R. Coffey writes in the *Chicago Sun-Times*: "Why should anyone in Chicago—or New York, Boston, Philadelphia, Pittsburgh . . . or any other genuine citadel of our political enlightenment—care what they care for in Iowa or New Hampshire in the way of a president?"[2] The move in Congress to shift to several regional primaries in the nation reflects that criticism.

Should Iowa and New Hampshire continue to have a role far beyond their relative populations in the process? The arguments against it are:

Iowa and New Hampshire are not representative of the nation in population composition.

This is the most valid of the criticisms. In terms of black population and Hispanic population, these two states are not representative of the nation. Iowa is 1.4 percent black, compared to 12.2 percent for the nation, and 0.9 percent Hispanic compared to 10.9 percent

110

for the nation. In New Hampshire, the figures are 0.4 percent black and 0.6 percent Hispanic.

Iowa is more liberal than the rest of the nation.

In 1976 Iowa voted for Jimmy Carter, arguably the most conservative of the Democratic candidates. In 1980 the race was between Carter and Senator Ted Kennedy, and the more conservative candidate, Carter, won. In 1984 Hart, Cranston, and McGovern would be considered more liberal than Mondale, but Mondale carried the state decisively. In 1988 Dick Gephardt was one of the two most conservative candidates and he carried the state. The reality is not like the image.

New Hampshire is too conservative, not representative of the party.

In a general election New Hampshire is overwhelmingly conservative and Republican. But that is not true of the Democrats who vote in the primary. I have seen no specific statistics but my impression is that New Hampshire is fairly representative for Democrats philosophically, with a good percentage of blue-collar workers in Manchester and Berlin but also a healthy infusion of suburban people who work in Boston and are interested in arms-control issues, environmental matters, and other things ordinarily identified more with the liberal community.

It is true, for reasons that I only partially understand, that Iowa and New Hampshire are less parochial than is the nation as a whole. They are more "international-minded," as some of the critics say, but I applaud them for that.

We need a national primary or a series of regional primaries to avoid undue influence by two small states.

There is legislation pending in Congress to do precisely this. There is some immediate appeal in this argument. But let me present the other side—and I do so as one who did not win either state and might be among those who would be expected to jump ship on the present arrangement.

Let me use my own situation as an illustration.

I believe I have a good record in behalf of the public, but I have offended just about every special interest group that exists, particularly those with the big financial contributions: the defense industry, big oil, the American Medical Association, the insurance industry, and I could go on and on. If, instead of the first two tests being in Iowa and New Hampshire, I had faced a regional primary, frankly I would not have considered becoming a candidate. The costs of a regional primary would have been too great. My voting record would not have appealed to enough of those who have become accustomed to financing presidential campaigns. Someone with my type of record—favoring the public rather than the privileged—would be squeezed out.

Iowa and New Hampshire are not states that can be bought. Yes, having substantial sums of money helps, but a candidate of limited means has a chance. No one can carry either state simply by coming in with a slick media package, smothering a state with television, and then walking away with the prize. Money still plays more of a role in these two states than it should, but nowhere near the role a regional or national primary calls for.

If you shift the choosing of the president away from two states with early tests, you turn over the apparatus for choosing a president to powerful financial interests. The only exceptions to the big-money rule in a regional primary situation would be those candidates who are celebrities like Jesse Jackson. But could two people who would make excellent presidents—Senator George Mitchell of Maine and Senator Dale Bumpers of Arkansas—consider starting out in a regional primary? I doubt it. The nation will be the loser if even more really qualified people are forced to reject the possibility of seeking the presidency.

I am not wedded to the first states being Iowa and New Hampshire. They could be New Mexico and North Dakota, Arizona and Vermont, South Dakota and Arkansas, Oregon and Rhode Island. New Hampshire's early primary emerged by accident. In 1915 state legislators decided they could save some money by having the primary the same day as the Town Meeting Day, so they moved the date back two and one-half months, and since 1920 New Hampshire has had the first primary. Iowa now precedes it with the caucuses. Starting in two states where candidates are forced to go into people's living rooms and talk with real people about real problems is desirable. The regional primaries will call for TV commercial blitzes, huge rallies in large cities, airport press conferences, and media events. There will not be stops in Webster City, Iowa, and

Hollis, New Hampshire. The artificial will become even more dominant.

A reporter covering the Super Tuesday regional primary wrote the day after that event: "Super Tuesday was at best a parody of American democracy. At worst, it was . . . generally dangerous to the political health of the United States. . . . For the last three weeks, it has been virtually impossible to find a candidate in either party or a political reporter more than ten miles from the nearest airport. . . . The candidates realized they couldn't cover all the ground so they flew over, dropping cassettes of their television commercials, attacking any and all opponents in generally vicious overstatement."[3]

One other point that every candidate would recognize who has been through the process: The people of Iowa and New Hampshire take the presidential selection process seriously. They make their commitments with considerably more caution and care than do most citizens in other states. They have been educated to the process. Sometimes they are too reluctant; sometimes they seem unable to make a decision. But their decisions are not casual. They understand the key role they are playing in selecting the next leader of this country and of the free world. That has been said so often it sounds trite, but it is true. And they do understand that.

The year 1988 changed the political map slightly. Ordinarily whoever carries Iowa and New Hampshire wins the Democratic and Republican nominations. This time confusion reigned and the two who came in third in Iowa but first in New Hampshire, Dukakis and Bush, ended up with their party nominations.

The day after the Iowa caucus the media carried the stories: Gephardt and Dole were the winners, Simon and Robertson placed second. If Gephardt and Dole had also won in New Hampshire, they probably would have been their parties' nominees. Only if contestants within one party are major, significant figures on the national scene will these two states not dominate. Mario Cuomo, for example, *might* have been able to win the nomination bypassing Iowa and New Hampshire. Some see Iowa's win for Gephardt and Dole and their failure to be nominated as a sign that these two states, where candidates spend a huge amount of time, have become less important. The reality is that their importance has not diminished.

The candidates who did not do well in either state fell by the wayside in both parties. Even with the confused results in Iowa and New Hampshire, these two states once again served as the screening process for the nation, reducing the choices in other states.

History is instructive. In 1976 Jimmy Carter got a grand total of 23,000 votes in New Hampshire, after doing well in the Iowa caucuses, and the next week he saw himself on the cover of *Time* and *Newsweek*. New Hampshire is the ninth smallest state in the nation, and Iowa is not one of the largest. But those two states dominate media coverage until their caucuses and primary are over. The primary and caucuses brought Carter, an outsider to the Democratic political establishment, to the nomination in 1976. Only eight years earlier, Hubert Humphrey had become the nominee without entering a single primary. Between 1968 and 1976 the caucuses and primaries took on increasing importance, and by 1988 they had become all-important.

In 1988 when Hart and Babbitt failed to make the top three in either Iowa or New Hampshire, they were through even though they had not announced it yet. Al Gore's southern strategy might have succeeded with a win in either Iowa or New Hampshire.

On my first venture into Iowa I had a well-attended press conference in Des Moines and then went to Webster City for a meeting in the home of Leo and Cleone Menage. Perhaps thirty people gathered to hear this little-known presidential candidate, but significantly among them were two reporters from *Time*, a reporter from *U.S. News & World Report*, and national columnist Jules Witcover. In a real sense that first stop represented Iowa: meeting in someone's living room, answering questions, and having national media with you.

Because we had no advance planning and at that point a staff in Iowa of only one person, Chuck Pennachio, attendance at most events was small indeed. We reached a low point in Anamosa where I had a meeting on the second floor of the Casual Cafe (properly named) with a grand total of two local people present plus John Carlson, a reporter from the *Des Moines Register* who duly noted the turnout for Paul Simon. The story reached its high point in the third paragraph: "Simon met with retirees Melvin Noll and Edward Flaherty and discussed his intentions to bring the Democratic Party back to the traditional issues that carried the party to victory during its glory years."[4] Later in the campaign that same second floor had people packed in for a campaign appearance. But in the early days those interested were few. Running for president almost seemed like reverting to my first days in politics, running for the state legislature, when I was pleased to have a half-dozen people listen.

Gradually as I became a known quantity in the state, things picked up, both in numbers of people at meetings and in the sense of momentum.

Volunteers were coming in; campuses were beginning to get turned on. Don Johnston, affiliated with the Operating Engineers Union, moved around the state organizing union leaders. My daughter and son-in-law were meeting with farmers and others. Enthusiasm was rising. The volunteers came from at least eighteen states, and approximately 1,500 people from Illinois volunteered to campaign in Iowa. How many of those volunteers actually came in I do not know, but a high percentage did, and it helped to overcome the time and money investment of other candidates. Our follow-through with volunteers was not as effective as it should have been—in some cases just plain bad—but they played a key role in moving me from a candidate viewed as someone without a chance to becoming a real contender.

All of this to influence 100,000 people who go to the caucuses in one state.

Because the numbers in each caucus do not necessarily equate with the vote strength of the caucus, tabulating votes on caucus night is not easy. It is weighted by the vote for governor in the previous election so that, in theory, if in one precinct five people show up and the votes for governor in that precinct totaled fifty, those five people count as fifty people. At the same time in another precinct fifty votes cast by fifty people also could count as fifty. Having said that, it is still true that in general there is a close correlation between the numbers showing up at the caucus—the popular vote—and the weighted vote. Because of the complexity of the weighted votes, the networks reported only the popular vote.

Early in the evening of the caucuses, CBS called it Gephardt first, Dukakis second, and Simon third. On the basis of returns we were getting, we were reasonably sure that was wrong, but our returns also showed Gephardt with a slight lead over me. ABC called

Gephardt the winner and put me in second place, but with vote totals tight. NBC never did declare a winner, and three months later, their Sunday night news anchor carried this:

> JOHN DANCY: It appears that Michael Dukakis is going to win Iowa. Wait a minute, you say, didn't they hold the Iowa caucuses a few months ago? Well, yes and no. The caucus process takes months. This weekend, Iowa Democrats are holding their district conventions. Dukakis delegates are ahead, even though Richard Gephardt appeared to win in February. If you're confused by all this, our political correspondent Tom Pettit says you have a right to be.

> TOM PETTIT: Even though the caucuses were in February, today, three months and seven days later, Iowa Democrats still are not sure who won—after all this time, and they're a little embarrassed about [it]. . . . Gephardt may not have won the unofficial popular vote. Looking back now at this small midwestern state, for Democratic presidential candidates, Iowa was a twilight zone. . . . Thirty percent [of the vote] never was counted—not that night, never. While Gephardt won more delegates, it is possible that Simon won more votes.

> HUGH WINEBRENNER: If all the votes were counted, it is possible.

> PETTIT: Hugh Winebrenner, political science professor, Drake University.

> WINEBRENNER: It's impossible to know who won. It's that simple.

> PETTIT: More than a hundred thousand Democrats went out to caucus in February to pick county delegates, not to record their initial preferences. State Democratic chair, Bonnie Campbell.

> CAMPBELL: It's certainly possible. It is certainly possible.[5]

One week prior to the NBC report, the *St. Louis Post-Dispatch* ran a story under a heading, "Simon May Have Won Popular Vote in Iowa," in which reporter Kathleen Best wrote: "Unfortunately for Simon, many of the precincts that went uncounted were in areas of the state where he was predicted to do well, such as Johnson County, home of the University of Iowa."[6]

Months later, an article titled, "Think You Know Who Really Won the Iowa Democratic Caucuses? Think Again," appeared in the magazine *American Politics*. Reporter William Saletan wrote: "It's possible that Paul Simon was ripped off. . . . Maybe Paul Simon did lose the Iowa straw vote after all. But . . . that devastating verdict, if it was to be reported at all, should have been based on more than a probability curve."[7]

The headlines the next morning and the television and radio news all reported a Gephardt win; 31 percent for him, 27 percent for me, and 22 percent for Dukakis.

The fact that only 70 percent of the vote was counted did not get reported by most of the media. Those of us on the inside knew enough about it to view the result as somewhat clouded, and a prominent trial lawyer from California, one of my strong supporters, Walter Weiss, wanted immediately to file a lawsuit challenging the results. I felt that we had little chance to win the lawsuit, and if we did it would be after the New Hampshire primary. In the meantime I would simply look like a sore loser. The probability is that Dick won both the popular and precinct delegate vote totals in Iowa, enough to jump him at least an additional 10 percent in the New Hampshire vote and come in second there, 3 percent ahead of me. The final delegate counts in Iowa, after delegates met seven weeks later, were Dukakis 29 percent, Gephardt 28 percent, and Simon 26 percent, but that shift to Dukakis took place because of the intervening primaries and caucuses.

We were much better organized in New Hampshire than the Gephardt forces, and it is probable that had I made the headlines and the TV news spots the next morning after Iowa, it would have been close in New Hampshire between Dukakis and me. There is an outside chance I would have won and then the whole nomination ball game probably would have been almost over. Running a strong second in Dukakis's neighboring state would not have clinched the nomination for me like an Iowa-New Hampshire dual-win would have, but it would have placed me in the lead as we moved to the next states. It is probable I would have then carried the next two states, and that would have set up a Gore-Simon-Jackson contest on Super Tuesday. Then as we moved on to Illinois, Wisconsin, New York, California, and the other states, I believe I would have won. The Dukakis people knew all this. After first ignoring my candidacy, *Newsweek* reported that "suddenly [pollster] Tubby Harrison was warning them that if Simon won in Iowa he could upset Dukakis in

New Hampshire."[8] The *Washington Post* reported: "Dukakis's strategists were relieved when it was Gephardt, not Simon, who finished first in Iowa."[9] They knew that I represented a real threat to them in New Hampshire.

But that is all theory that anyone can legitimately dispute.

What is not theory are two realities:

First, that the Iowa caucus counting system should be improved. I like the idea of caucuses, where neighbors can come together and discuss the merits and demerits of the various candidates. But then let them vote, all votes counting equally, and let these results be reported to the secretary of state of Iowa, as well as to the news media.

Second, unless and until the two political parties can find some rotating system of having two other small states first, let Iowa and New Hampshire continue to screen candidates for the nation. If a system can be devised where two other small states can come first, fine; but do not aggravate the already horrendous problem of money dominating our selection process by going to regional primaries. Regional primaries will produce candidates of the wealthy, by the wealthy, and for the wealthy.

☆ 8 ☆

THE MEDIA

A short sentence in the *Washington Post* during the middle of the campaign gives an insight into our culture: " 'Meet the Press' (NBC, WRC) will be preempted by the finals of the French Open tennis tournament."[1] That appeared the Sunday before the Democratic primaries in California, New Jersey, Montana, and New Mexico primaries where 466 Democratic delegates were selected.

As a journalist by background, I watched the unfolding of the campaign not only from the perspective of a candidate but also with special attention to what happens on the news side.

There is no question that the media played the decisive role in scuttling the campaigns of Gary Hart and Joe Biden.

In Biden's case, the comparison of his remarks and those of Neil Kinnock were provided to the media and then used by those so favored. Cable News Network, *Time*, the *New York Times*, and the succeeding air and print disclosures were prompted by information from the campaign manager of a rival candidate. Legitimate news, it was inappropriately handled by the Dukakis campaign manager, both in the manner of leaking and in timing. It hit Biden only a few days before he began the important hearings on the nomination of Judge Robert Bork to the U.S. Supreme Court. Biden started the hearings with a tornado swirling around him. After John Sasso left the campaign, an indirect victim of the episode turned out to be Patricia O'Brien, talented and respected press secretary of Dukakis. Her advice within the campaign: Tell the truth. It is always good

119

advice, but often unwelcome. Resentment within the campaign became strong enough to cause her to step aside as press secretary.

The Gary Hart story bubbled beneath the surface, with rumors appearing in print periodically. Gary told the *New York Times Magazine*, "Follow me around. I don't care. I'm serious. If anybody wants to put a tail on me, go ahead. They'd be very bored."[2] The *Miami Herald* did just that. The resulting charge that Hart had an overnight guest was followed by stories and a picture of a weekend trip to Bimini, on a boat with the unfortunate name of "Monkey Business."

Political cartoonists had a great time. Jokes multiplied like rabbits. Hart supporters were dismayed and, quietly and sometimes not so quietly, left the campaign. Gary took the only course that reality permitted. He quit the race.

The media's intense coverage of his social life had forced him out. Weeks later, Hart commented in a speech at Yale:

> A culture that treats politics like a sport—and lumps political figures with soap-opera characters—is producing more celebrities than statesmen. . . . Journalistic standards are eroding, as they did earlier in Great Britain, because of a blurring of the distinction between the serious and the sensational press. To keep or capture a worried or confused reader or viewer, sex is often more expedient than seriousness. . . .
>
> This year's buzz word is "character" and character is defined in a totally negative sense as everything a candidate lacks or every mistake a candidate has made. . . . But are we seeing a new departure—a departure disturbing, if not dangerous? How far are we prepared to go as a society to peek into areas hitherto precluded? . . .
>
> The issue isn't whether a candidate has something to hide. The issue is one of self-respect and the self-evident value of privacy. Take that away and we'll have not only bite-sized policies, we'll have pint-sized leaders.[3]

You don't have to agree with Gary Hart on everything or support his candidacy to feel at least some unease at where we have come. I recall when the wife of an Illinois governor, known as an alcoholic, on almost a weekly basis made some kind of embarrassing public display of herself. Yet it never appeared in print, nor on radio or television. Today it would. If it were the governor instead of his wife, it should be in the public domain. It obviously would affect his ability to govern. We should at least weigh these words of Hart in the same Yale speech: "In the occasionally exciting prying into a candidate's minutes and hours, are we not obscuring in the years of a lifetime the undramatic acts of courage, fortitude, and determination that reveal true character? That we are even asking such questions seems a far cry from the America of Jefferson and Madison, from John Winthrop's City on a Hill. More like what might occur in capitals such as Managua, Sofia, or Santiago."[4]

Tom Winship, editor of the *Boston Globe* for twenty years, called this period after the Hart and Biden disclosures "a particularly miserable time for both the press and the candidates."[5]

Did the media handle the Hart matter properly? And what should the press do about personal life? How probing should journalists be?

The answers are not entirely clear, but some general principles about campaign coverage and its shortcomings can be drawn:

The media should probe deeply enough to be able to answer the basic question: Can I trust the candidate?

Precisely where you draw the line is not easy to determine. The highly respected *New York Times* went too far in its letter to all the candidates:

> We are asking each of the candidates to provide us with access to the following:
> Birth certificate, marriage license(s), driver's license.
> High school, college and graduate school transcripts.
> Employment record—Dates and positions of all jobs held.
> Net worth statement, with specifics on stocks, bonds, real estate, etc.
> Federal and state income tax returns for [the] last five years and, if your spouse files separate returns, a copy of those as well.
> List of all civil and criminal court cases in which you have been a plaintiff or defendant.
> Waiver of privacy rights to enable us to obtain any investigative files that might have been prepared by the FBI and other law enforcement agencies, waiver of privacy claims in Freedom of Information requests, and records of House and/or Senate Ethics committee.

Military records, and permission to obtain those records from [the] Defense Dept.

Medical records indicating treatment for mental or physical disabilities, and permission to discuss medical history with your physicians.

List of closest friends in high school and college.

List of present friends, business associates, chief advisors and major fund-raisers.

We realize that this request places a burden on your staff. However, some of this material should be immediately available. We would appreciate receiving all this material as soon as possible.

Sincerely,

Craig R. Whitney

Washington Editor[6]

It is worth noting that I received no similar request from them to outline in detail my agenda for reviving urban America, no invitation to spell out my views on arms control in detail, no suggestion that I provide the *Times* with specifics on what we should do to provide more quality education in the nation. The *Times* request helped to set the wrong agenda for the election.

At first I decided not to provide all the information requested by their letter, but when I learned that two other candidates were going to give it, I decided to comply. I felt that I had no political option. In an accompanying letter I said I had great misgivings about how far they had gone: "Your query left me a bit nonplussed. It goes far beyond any previous relationship between a candidate and the press. On the other hand, my whole political life has been one of openness. I started reporting my personal finances thirty-two years ago, when I first became an elected official—long before there were financial disclosure laws and in much more detail than the current laws require. . . . I trust you and your staff to use the information responsibly. But I fear that we are setting a precedent that will be exploited and misused by those of lesser integrity."[7]

Bob Dole commented: "It was a letter that heralded the kind of coverage presidential candidates could expect in the coming months on the campaign trail: issueless and negative."[8]

What is wrong with this request? Let me give you a hypothetical example. A fifty-year-old distinguished United States Senator who would make a superb president had some wild days as a youth and had at age eighteen contracted syphillis. Is the public entitled to that information? Or what if ten years ago the candidate had a bad case of hemorrhoids? You can imagine what Johnny Carson could do with that! We should know the details of that senator's finances; we should know the details of his present physical condition. But there are sensible limits beyond which we should not go, both because it brings into play matters that should not be in the public domain, and because it discourages potential candidates from seeking office.

Requesting "any investigative files that might have been prepared by the FBI and other law enforcement agencies" sounds innocent. I served in the army in something that no longer exists called the Counter Intelligence Corps. While working in a specialized field, our work had strong similarities to much of the work done by the FBI. Any reports or rumors we received were filed and given a coded evaluation. Whoever thinks I murdered my grandmother or spied for the Soviets or robbed a bank can report that to the FBI, and it becomes part of the record. If not handled carefully, loose charges that people make could suddenly become public knowledge. The newspaper story then reads, "The *Daily News* has learned that FBI records [or local police records] show that authorities once checked out a report that Paul Simon robbed a bank." And knowing that such stories would appear undoubtedly would stimulate more unfounded charges. That should not become part of the election process.

Detailed financial information is part of what is necessary to discover whether you can trust a candidate. Financial statements sometimes reveal whether officials have used their years as officials to fill their pockets or really to serve the public. Requesting detailed financial data can help provide an insight into what you seek in a leader: openness, candor. A candidate who refuses to release detailed financial data ordinarily should not serve in high public office.

Personal questions that go to the root of the character of the candidate are both proper and necessary. What is asked will vary from candidate to candidate, but what is desirable is a careful examination, one that does not expect perfection but does reveal the basic strengths and weaknesses of the person who may lead the nation.

Whatever might cause doubts in the mind of a reporter or editorial writer about a candidate's ability to serve as president effectively should be probed. What is simply titillating should not receive emphasis.

More attention should be paid to the issues, less to the horse race. USA Today commissioned a study of television coverage of the presidential race for January through part of April 1988. The conclusion: approximately 80 percent of network coverage focused on the horse race (who is ahead in the polls), 20 percent on the issues. That becomes significant when you understand that for most of the public the primary source of information about political races is television. I say that with regret, perhaps in part because I am a veteran of the print media, but also because television coverage tends to be so superficial. Candidates underscore the impact of television on campaigns by the huge expenditures on television, compared to radio and newspaper advertising. A recent chronicler of campaigns over the past five decades wrote, "In the pretelevision campaign of 1944, newspapers and magazines wielded considerable influence in politics."[9] The implication is clear: They don't have considerable influence today. That conclusion is an exaggeration and ignores one important reality: Television gets much of its information from magazines and newspapers. But it is hard to argue with the lead sentence of a *New York Times* article one week before the election: "The next President will have been chosen in a campaign dominated as never before by television."[10] The print media still has persuasive ability, but the dominant influence is television. And when television focuses primarily on the horse race, the public gets appreciably less information on issues than it should.

Judging by questions asked candidates, the media paid much more attention to the horse race than did the public. Attend a meeting of citizens in Iowa or New Hampshire or any state and almost all of the questions are issue-related. Talk to reporters afterwards and there is a significant shift.

Senator Edward Kennedy commented in a speech at Harvard, late in 1987: "A presidential election is more than a game. . . . My experience in national campaigns . . . has left me with a very real sense of a widening gap between real issues and the reporting. . . . Our attention appears to be riveted on politics at the expense of issues. . . . Staff shake-ups, major and minor alike, command more attention than a major speech. . . . What issues-coverage there is now comes largely in the form of labels—and if the candidates won't supply them, then the press corps will. It is easier to deal in caricature than complexity."[11] The very phrase "presidential race" implies a contest, but it is not a game. The stakes are infinitely higher than in a face-off between the Chicago Cubs and St. Louis Cardinals.

I understand why there is intense focus on the relative positioning of the candidates in the race: It's easy to cover and the public is interested. But it shifts attention from what a campaign primarily should be about: issues. A presidential campaign should be significantly more than entertainment.

Greater focus on issues would change the dynamics of a campaign. A candidate who does well in the polls is going to do well in the media, and if you do well in the media, you will do well financially. If you do well financially, you are going to get more staff and more paid media, and you are generally going to do well in the polls. What is missing from this admittedly oversimplified circle? The issues.

I recently met an Associated Press veteran reporter who had spent most of his journalistic years in Europe. I asked him what constituted the big difference in covering European elections and U.S. elections. "In Europe, most of the stories you write are about issues," he replied. "In the United States, most of the election stories are *not* about issues."[12]

Gary Hart's conclusion: "We have put image over substance in our choice of government officers."[13] Too often that is the case.

Newsweek noted accurately, "Saying anything very definite only attracts opposing fire."[14] The magazine might have added that one of the reasons is that the media is not paying enough attention to the issues. It's easy for a reporter to write a lead sentence on a story about the latest poll, more difficult to write that lead sentence about a discussion of the issues. But the more difficult task serves the public better.

Less attention should be paid to the trivia.

During my service in the state legislature, U.S. Senator Paul Douglas called one day and asked me to introduce a resolution in the Illinois General Assembly urging the U.S. Congress to make the corn tassel the national flower. He would then introduce the measure in the Senate. Because of my great admiration for him, I immediately said yes. But as I reflected, I thought that I really did not want to do that, a nonsubstantial type of thing with which I felt uncomfortable. That night I called the senator and asked, "Are you sure you want me to introduce a resolution on the corn tassel? Are you sure you want to introduce a resolution in the Senate?" The professor-turned-senator laughed and responded with a lecture that taught me something about politics and journalism.

"Paul," he said, "if you want to stay in public office, you have to get media attention. The substantial things you do generally will not get attention unless they are involved in a major controversy. But the media loves trivia. You have to do a certain amount of that to stay alive politically. No one will get angry with you because you want to make the corn tassel the national flower. And don't worry; it will never pass."[15]

Paul Douglas turned out to be right. His comments were not about the presidential race, but they might have been.

Infinitely more people know that I wear a bow tie than what my positions are on arms control or education. And we took advantage of that attention. We had to.

Newspaper editorials from Dallas to Cape Cod, as well as CBS News and the Scripps-Howard newspapers, noted that political cartoonists favored my candidacy because with the bow tie, hornrimmed glasses and big ears, I would be a natural for them.

Predictably, comments on my appearance abounded. One writer called me "the ugliest man in the U.S. Senate—no mean achievement considering some of the competition."[16] Another noted, "I'd heard he lacked charisma, but I was not prepared for Simon in the flesh. He is to charisma what Donna Rice is to political endorsements."[17] Columnist Garry Wills wrote, "Over and over I hear the same thing said, 'I like him, and what he stands for; but he is not glamorous enough to interest most voters.' "[18] *The Economist* of London noted my "amazing earlobes."[19] (My colleague, Senator Alan Dixon, told me after the campaign, "I didn't notice you had big ears until you ran for President.") *Time* commented on my "floppy earlobes, horn-rimmed glasses, putty-like face and bow tie."[20] One reporter observed, "I looked up to watch the candidate respond and noticed he had a couple of gold fillings on one side of his upper plate."[21] A columnist quoted one man, "Every time I see him on TV, he looks a little hung over."[22]

But others thought that my appearance could help. "One look at that haircut, those glasses and that bow tie, and voters are sure to believe him when he says he is running on his ideas," columnist Jeff Greenfield wrote.[23] Mike Royko observed, "I've become so used to candidates having blow-dried hair, tailored suits and Kennedy-style speech patterns, that it's almost a shock to see someone with the wet look, owlish eyes, a bow tie and a shapeless suit saying, 'I'm running for president.' "[24] And one pollster suggested, "People figure a guy who looks like Simon must be telling the truth."[25]

The bow tie caused comment from columnists, apparel magazines, and evoked recommendations—pro and con—from public relations people and citizens everywhere. There are some things that excite people! Typical of many was a letter from a woman in Connecticut who enclosed a contribution, but added: "Could you bring yourself to exchange the bow tie for some well-mannered long ties and maybe wear the bow tie in your pocket for luck?"[26]

It is difficult to disagree with the conclusion of one writer: "The crisis of the presidency . . . is that we choose the leader of the free world on the basis of professionally packaged TV images rather than on any demonstrated knowledge, experience or wisdom."[27]

There is no dramatic solution to this problem. The answer for both the candidates and the media is the obvious and the undramatic: Pay more attention to issues, less to the trivia.

Nothing surprised me as much during the campaign as some of the questions I received from reporters: If you come back to life as an animal, which animal would it be? I declined to answer. What is your position on infant baptism? "I don't think it will develop into a major issue in the presidential race." Do you ever curse or swear? "Only when I read your column." When once a year you really want to eat your favorite dinner, what is it? "Dungeness crab, though generally my tastes are simple. I prefer a McDonald's hamburger to caviar." Why didn't you become a minister like your brother? "I'm not sure. I'm not that good at self-analysis but each of us is serving humanity." What kind of music do you like? "Classical and semi-classical, primarily." What is your favorite musical? *Hello Dolly*. Why do you wear wing-tip shoes? "I don't know; I just like them." Do you hunt? "No." Do you fish? "Yes." What do you do for exercise? "I try to swim most days, and I play tennis occasionally." Do you have a dog or a cat? "We've had both, but we have neither right now." Are there any foods you don't like? "I like most foods but nothing too spicy; I also don't like green or red peppers." Have you ever employed an Albanian-American? "Not that I'm aware, but I have worked with the Albanian community here on some of their concerns." Would you like to become a college or university president? "I've had a few inquiries over the years, but I would prefer the White House or the Senate." Do you play chess? "Rarely." And an infinite number of questions on my bow ties.

On and on and on. Many of these questions are good for personal profiles, adding color, but too many are questions without much relevance to anything.

One newspaper devoted considerable space to analyzing the handwriting of all the candidates. Readers of other journals learned such vital details as the fact that I like to drink Pepsi and that I sleep six hours a night.

Superficial coverage with too much attention to trivia also results in using the press to create perceptions beneficial to the campaigns. The new word in this campaign was "spin." Press secretaries met with reporters to give the right spin to a debate or an event. When the focus moves away from issues, the spin emerges more dominant than it should.

We all had to take advantage of the attention to the superficial. My campaign learned that if I would bowl a line at the local lanes, television cameras always showed up in force. I am not a good bowler and what bowling has to do with the presidency, I don't know; but a bowling shot makes television with much greater certainty than an attempt to say something profound on arms control or any other issue. When Graceland College in Iowa asked me to come and speak, the invitation brought cheers from my staff, not because it was another campus to visit and discuss the issues but it associated closely enough with Paul Simon, the singer, and his *Graceland* album that they knew we would receive publicity out of it. They were right. It got national attention.

Both the easiest and at the same time the most difficult questions from reporters are those that deal with motivation. The glib answer is rarely correct. A young reporter told me that R. W. Apple, Jr., chief Washington correspondent for the *New York Times*, had covered so many presidential races that he was now coasting on past laurels, not doing his homework. But I found his questions among the most penetrating. He moved beyond the superficial to questions of motivation. It is trite but sometimes true: You learn through experience.

The lengthy personality/issue profiles by a few newspapers and magazines provided that small percentage of readers who actually study such a piece with more background than previous campaigns had provided. And I found them generally well done.

But too much reporting searched for some "new angle," some bit of trivia that could be magnified into something significant when it was not. The problem is not new. Woodrow Wilson complained that the majority of reporters were interested "in the personal and trivial rather than in principles and policies."[28]

More solid, balanced reporting is needed.

The major national newspapers generally provide this, but there is a tendency to look for the colorful, for the sensational, for the confrontational when they may not be there. Reporters for the *Wall Street Journal*, to use one example, do not need to do this but television coverage is more tempted, as is too much of the print media.

Columnist Mark Shields, who combines humor with truth, wrote: "After Iowa, the Democrats, historically a joyful gang of rakes, rascals and rogues, were left with three straight-arrow leaders—Representative Richard Gephardt of Missouri, Senator Paul Simon of Illinois and Governor Michael Dukakis of Massachusetts—who among them appear to be without a single redeeming vice. To celebrate their collective survival, the three men might go out together and paint the town beige."[29]

The *New York Times* quoted an unnamed adviser as saying that I was not confrontational enough, and then got this comment from me: "They would like me to get into a fight every day. That's not my style. I have to be myself."[30]

Politically my adviser was right. Confrontation, color, the bizarre make the news.

But what is a little more dull may be what the nation needs, and responsible journalism should not cater constantly to the more sensational.

Editorial writers should be more probing.

An observer of the 1984 nomination process in the two political parties advised future newcomers to the presidential sweepstakes: "Do not try to create a clear-cut image [if you want to win]. . . . Remain vague and elusive."[31] Unfortunately, it is much too easy to do. Most newspaper editorial writers do nothing to discourage that practice. They nitpick at candidates who do offer specific programs, and when candidates offer near-silence on issues, these editorial writers join the chorus of silence. Who wants to listen to a chorus of silence?

Newspaper editorials ought to probe and cajole. Candidates who serve up nothing more than warm fuzziness to the public ought to be called for doing that.

Columnist Mary McGrory spelled out some direct questions to Vice President George Bush on the Iran-Contra mess. She should have been joined—and preceded—by a chorus of editorials. An editorial asking each candidate to spell out specifically what might be of interest to that newspaper, and then following through if candidates provided only pleasant nothingness, should be much more a part of the presidential race.

What do the candidates offer on the issues of urban education, long-term care, the arms race? The editorials ought to be precise in their questions. Do the candidates favor intensive preschool education for disadvantaged areas, and if they do, what are they willing to spend? When candidates answer, editorialize on the answers. If candidates fail to respond, editorialize on that. Editorial pages should be much more demanding, much tougher with candidates who are vague. Candidates win in part by being imprecise, and one of the reasons candidates emerge successfully with a vague agenda is that far too many editorials are even more imprecise and vague. A dull knife has a tough time cutting even hard butter. A dull editorial filled with generalities cannot cut through the soft soap the candidates too often try to sell. And do sell.

Ultimately the most important responsibility a president faces is in the area of foreign affairs. Editorial comment in this arena rarely appeared during the campaign, and when it did, it often evidenced the lack of background of the editorial writers, a few large newspapers being exceptions. If the United States is to be more effective in developing a stable and peaceful world, more publishers should be encouraging and demanding foreign policy background—or at least interest—by editorial writers. Where those writers do not have that background, a once-a-year trip abroad somewhere by at least one journalist on publications where there are three or more editorial writers ought to be the standard practice. If the newspaper editorial pages of the nation do not demand more knowledge of foreign relations in candidates, we inevitably will produce presidents who will stumble through at least the first part of their administrations in a world that can ill afford such stumbling.

Editorial endorsements in the primaries and caucuses are much more important than in the general election, yet they occur with much less frequency. That should change.

In a general election most citizens make up their own minds between George Bush and Michael Dukakis, or between Ronald Reagan and Walter Mondale. The combination of party affiliation, television advertisements, and television news coverage—and to a lesser extent, print and radio coverage—have all combined to give most people their decision-making material. What the newspaper says editorially in a general election will have only a slight impact, if any, on the vote.

But in a caucus or primary situation, people vote within a party, and there is much more confusion among several candidates who seem to be saying much the same thing. Voters seek guidance, and while not every newspaper has much influence, many do, and too many do not even attempt to use whatever influence they have. A newspaper that would be and should be embarrassed not to take a stand in a general election between two presidential candidates (though a surprising number did that this time) often blithely ignores the caucuses and primaries, sometimes contending this is an "internal matter" for a political party to determine. Who will serve as the next president is not an "internal matter."

"We let our readers make up their own minds," was the lame excuse I heard more than once from newspaper editors.

By far the most significant choice is made in the primaries and caucuses among an array of candidates, narrowing the field to two. The most important choice is picking among them. Newspapers should take no pride in ducking the important choice. And newspapers that editorialize, lamenting the poor choice between two general election candidates, when they have remained silent during the primaries and caucuses, should add a sentence to their editorials: "This newspaper is partially responsible for the results we decry."

One other minor criticism: Reporters and editorial writers should be careful that they do not pick up the loaded labels and phrases of candidates. Critics of my jobs program called it "a massive jobs program." It could more accurately be called "a jobs program to substitute, in large part, for a massive welfare program." But relative to the welfare system it would in large part replace, it is not massive. But my debate opponents who tried to portray it negatively talked about my "massive jobs program." Soon straight news accounts and editorials were using the same phrase. Fortunately, reporters did not pick up a less-than-accurate Babbitt description: "the biggest public works program since they built the Egyptian pyramids."[32]

A few random media observations:

• Some television commercials contained more substance on the issues than some of the television news coverage.

• Camera crews should occasionally be interviewed. They have observed a great deal, often reflected on it, and no one ever interviews them. I found some of them sharper than a few of the reporters who asked me the questions.

• "Pack journalism"—reporters reading what a few among their numbers write and then writing the same—is alive and kicking. It is understandable but not healthy.

• Journalists from at least twenty other nations interviewed me during the course of the campaign.

• *Presidential Campaign Hotline*, a daily bulletin published by the American Political Network, brought information to the media and gave each campaign a daily opportunity to express its views and put the right spin on happenings. Terry Michael, my creative campaign press secretary, tried humor occasionally in his reports. One began: "Today is January 20th. One year from today Special Trade Representative Dick Gephardt, IRS Commissioner Mike Dukakis, Ambassador to Southern America Al Gore, Secretary of the Department of Jestering Bruce Babbitt, Patent Office Director Gary Hart (new ideas. . . . get it?) and Poet Laureate Jesse Jackson take office with President Simon."[33]

Each of us who were candidates could cite examples of mistakes by the media, columns that reached conclusions before they reached the facts. One major newspaper, the *Boston Globe*, quoted me as claiming in an editorial meeting at that newspaper that I was a foreign correspondent. The heading on the story read: "Doubt Is Cast on Simon Role as Foreign Correspondent," and the lead emerged: "Sen. Paul Simon has often cited experience in which he got his 'hands dirty' as a foreign correspondent and met with world leaders as a major reason he would be more qualified to handle foreign policy than other Democratic presidential candidates. A look at his overseas work, however, shows a record far less wide-ranging than such assertions would imply. In fact, the one-time country editor was never based overseas for any publication, and his experience as a foreign correspondence was limited to seven trips twenty to thirty-six years ago."[34] Fortunately, we kept a tape of the editorial meeting, and it substantiated that I never made such a claim. I had said simply that in addition to my work on foreign affairs in the House and Senate, prior to that I had traveled overseas occasionally as a journalist, doing stories for my own newspaper and some free-lance writing, getting at least some foreign policy exposure before entering congress. I never claimed to be stationed overseas for a newspaper or having served as a foreign correspondent. The *Globe* twice printed a correction, though in space substantially smaller than the original article. They also printed a letter to the editor I wrote referring to this. Later in an article on coverage of candidates, the *Wall Street Journal* quoted the *Globe* reporter who wrote the inaccurate story, "I have a favorable view of him [Dukakis]. My outlook and ideology can't be divorced from my copy, but as a reporter, I try to be dispassionate." She added that she expected Dukakis to win. "I would love to come to Washington."[35] Otherwise the *Globe* treated me fairly, as did almost all the media. Mistakes made in the Democratic race were not out of malice, with the exception of a few of the far-right journals. Generally what few lumps I received from the media I merited.

Sometimes I got breaks I didn't deserve. A reporter for the *Christian Science Monitor* interviewed me for a background article, and when she asked about my youthful ambitions, I replied, "I hoped to become the Walter Lippmann of my generation." I either was not as clear as I should have been, or the reporter did not know who Lippmann was. The article appeared and noted that I wanted to be the Walt Whitman of my generation. Several people wrote and said they liked a candidate with literary interests and were for me.

Michael Dukakis received more attention than other candidates from the *New York Times* and the networks in the early months, but part of that came from a healthier treasury that could encourage more coverage, part because of regional interests, and part because the other candidates and I did not do as good a job as we should have in creating the news.

Special recognition should be given ABC for having the first full-time reporter-producer, Dianne Terrell, on my campaign trail, and reporters also with other candidates. A few weeks later, producer Susan Reed of CBS joined the regular followers. NBC never did have anyone full-time with the candidates. The *Los Angeles Times* had someone virtually all the time with me, usually Keith Love.

Boston media followed Mike Dukakis much more closely than local media followed any other candidate on the Democratic side, and that helped Dukakis in New Hampshire as well as neighboring states receiving the Boston media. The *Chicago Tribune* and Hugh Hill and his television crew from WLS (ABC) in Chicago were most frequent among the Illinois media covering me. The *St. Louis Post-Dispatch* assigned reporters to both Dick Gephardt and me with some degree of regularity.

The once all-white, all-male gaggle of reporters following the candidates broke down significantly in 1988, Dianne Terrell and Susan Reed being two examples. The *Atlanta Journal and Constitution* had Steve Harvey with me frequently, and *Time* often assigned Steve Holmes, both black reporters who clearly merited moving up to the national arena.

Every four years, the chief political reporter for the *Des Moines Register* becomes the most important reporter in the nation. It is a position that could cause vanity and abuse. To his credit, David Yepsen handled this position with sensitivity and balance. And he worked hard.

A few newspapers did an especially careful job of covering and evaluating candidates, the *Lawrence* (Massachusetts) *Eagle-Tribune* a prime example. It not only had its own editorial people interview candidates, but had a citizens committee of about eight people who interviewed all the candidates from both political parties and then made recommendations to the editors.

I appeared on the morning shows of each network, and all of the news interview programs like "Meet the Press," "Face the Nation," ABC's David Brinkley Sunday morning show, and the evening news. But I really discovered the impact of television after appearing on "Saturday Night Live" on NBC.

Shortly after Joe Biden withdrew from the race, I received a request from "Saturday Night Live" to appear in a skit that basically made fun of Gary Hart and Joe Biden. I felt that it would not be in good taste and I declined.

Two or three months later I received an invitation to appear with the singer Paul Simon. I accepted. At the beginning of the program, the announcer said, "And now our host for the evening, Paul Simon." Both of us walked on, carrying on a mock argument about which one of us he meant.

I had known the singer for a few years and we both enjoyed doing the program. I found it fascinating to go through the process. We practiced together one time, then had a dress rehearsal before a live audience, and then did it the final time live, also before an audience.

The recognition I received walking down the street anywhere escalated appreciably after my "Saturday Night Live" appearance. It had the great political advantage of reaching an audience that generally would not watch the Sunday morning news shows. It turned out to be excellent politics.

A positive side of television is that it has helped to make us one nation. A slight surprise in the campaign came with the discovery that the questions in Iowa and New Hampshire, Louisiana and Oregon, and everywhere else were virtually identical. Some matters are local, like Indian problems in South Dakota or Mexican border problems in Texas, but these local issues did not dominate the questions. We have become a national family much more than we were twenty or thirty years ago, and television has played the major role in that.

The question of how frequently I would hold news conferences as president emerged only two or three times during the entire year of campaigning. It is more than a self-serving question for reporters. It is the public's assurance of some type of direct access to the president and that a president will not become too isolated from reality.

Calvin Coolidge and Franklin D. Roosevelt held press conferences almost twice a week, by far the best records of any presidents. Harry Truman averaged almost once a week. But Ronald Reagan and Richard Nixon—the two with the most infrequent press conferences of recent presidents—held them less than once every two months.

I pledged to hold a press conference at least once a week, and once a month hold a town meeting somewhere in the nation so that not only reporters but auto mechanics and teachers and physicians and homemakers and people of every background could feel some access to the presidency.

The issue received almost no attention from either the reporters or candidates. How open a presidency will be is a question of importance.

Media includes not only free media, it is also media a candidate buys. Paid media is less a factor in a presidential campaign than it is in a senatorial campaign but in any close contest it can play a decisive role.

The paid media of all the candidates would have to be described as above average. I have reviewed most of the paid pre-convention commercials of all the Republican and Democratic candidates and on a scale of one to ten, ten being outstanding, my purely subjective evaluation:

Bruce Babbitt, 7. He was at his best talking directly into the camera. Biography less effective.

George Bush, 8.5. Well done technically.

Bob Dole, 8. Biographical material particularly effective.

Michael Dukakis, 8. Particularly effective was a commercial with children and the closing scene on some later ads. Dukakis would have merited a 9 rating, but the choice of subject in Illinois backfired. There the basic message was: Vote for me or you'll have a brokered convention. It didn't sell. But generally he had a superior product in the primaries. In the general election the Dukakis ads blurred the issues and confused viewers. Aside from the distortions, Bush won the paid media exchange, at least until the last few days. Pollster Louis Harris said on the evening of the vote, "The simple story of this election is that the Bush commercials have worked and the Dukakis commercials have not."[36]

Pierre Dupont, 7. Not bad, but not great. Something was missing.

Richard Gephardt, 9. The best use of various television techniques of any of the candidates. His Hyundai ad—comparing car costs as a result of trade barriers between the United States and South Korea— received press attention, but the effectivenes of his ads was much more than that. They made Dick Gephardt appear presidential. The cumulative impact helped him immensely.

Albert Gore, Jr., 7.5. Some excellent, some not so good.

Al Haig, 8. Commercials were better than the candidate.

Gary Hart, 7.5. Not bad for an extremely limited budget.

Jesse Jackson, 7. He had no commercials in the first part of the campaign. When they came they were not bad, not great. They needed a touch of the presidential look that the Gephardt ads had.

Jack Kemp, 8. Good.

Pat Robertson, 7.5. Good, but they did not significantly broaden his base.

On my ads, the biographical spots were exceedingly well done, deserving of a 9 rating. The issue ads were less effective. I would rank them 7. My biographical ads were good enough so that when they began running, the polls picked up measurably. They were technically well done, and the polls showed they had appeal.

The deficiency of the issue ads ultimately was my responsibility. Handling my media was David Axelrod and Associates, a Chicago-based firm that is still relatively new in the field. Dave served as campaign manager in my successful upset victory for the U.S. Senate in 1984. He has good political antennae and his company will develop into one of the best political media firms in the nation.

But on the issues in Iowa our material lacked some of the appeal and spark it needed, and some follow-through from the biographical spots that ran during the first part of the campaign. There have also been criticisms of the timing of our ads, suggesting that more of our fire should have been saved for the last days of the campaign, less early in our endeavor. We ran some of our television ads early to establish my credentials as a real contender. Precisely what the right mix should have been is a judgment call, but since we lost the critics can speak with a greater air of authority. Incredibly we made two major errors that I can only blame on myself: As the only real rural candidate in the race in rural Iowa, we did not stress my rural roots in our television spots; and as the candidate with the strongest program on long-term care for seniors in a state with the highest percentage of older Americans, we did not stress that. The exit polls showed that I lost both rural and older groups to Gephardt decisively. If I had broken even with Gephardt with either of these two groups, I would have easily carried Iowa.

A candidate is sometimes reluctant to impose his or her judgment on well-paid media and polling people, but often the candidate will know the political terrain of the contested area much better than either the media or polling people. I should have followed my instincts more and had substantially greater input on the issue television ads. There is always a fine line a candidate has to draw between being the candidate and managing the campaign; the latter you have to avoid.

My paid media people wanted me to go with "comparative" (a more refined and acceptable term than "negative" but meaning almost the same thing) television ads against Gephardt in Iowa. I declined, in part because I have always been a little uncomfortable with these unless they are really done well, in part because the inconsistencies in the Gephardt record I felt would be much more effectively covered by the media than they were until after after the Iowa caucuses, and in part because negative campaigning is always a two-edged sword, particularly in Iowa where there is a strong sense of what is decent and fair and what is not. I finally compromised and permitted some radio ads comparing our records. In retrospect, some television ads tastefully done, pointing out our differences, probably would have helped. My media people were right and I turned out to be wrong. After Iowa, free media criticisms of Dick's shift in positions were abundant, some of them unfair.

When you come as close as I did to winning Iowa and, with that, perhaps the nomination, many things could have made the difference. A better performance by me in debates could have done it. Better paid media could have done it. Running more and earlier comparative ads, as my media advisers wanted me to, might have made the difference. Timing our media buy better might have made a difference. Better planning could have done it. Better use of volunteers would have made a difference. A host of "what ifs" can arise. They do no good to reflect upon, other than to record for historical purposes so that candidates in the future can avoid similar mistakes.

☆ 9 ☆

THE PROCESS

Former Senator William Proxmire of Wisconsin stated that 1988 produced the best set of candidates he can remember. Both George Bush and Michael Dukakis are unquestionably people of ability. You may or may not agree with Proxmire's judgment call.

But even if you agree with that conclusion, it is difficult to disagree with another: The process of picking nominees can be improved substantially.

There are two major flaws with the present selection process plus some minor ones. The two big needs: Shorten the process and make money less dominant. Neither change is easily achieved.

Pick the names of any three people you believe should have considered running for the presidency in the last eight years but did not. Ask them why they have not run and almost always it comes down to two things: time and money. Other factors are also there— the risk of embarrassment if you do not do reasonably well, the physical stamina that will be required, the knowledge that the best of intentions will be distorted, what is demanded of your family, and the list goes on. But all of these combined do not weigh as heavily as the big two, time and money.

I made public my intention to run for president nineteen months before the general election and one of the things I heard from knowledgeable people over and over: You're too late. While we might have won with a few changes, there is no question that had I

139

worked at it as long as Dick Gephardt or Bruce Babbitt, Jack Kemp or George Bush, my odds of winning would have improved significantly. The two candidates who were nominated, Michael Dukakis and George Bush, planned well in advance and did so carefully. In a Dukakis biography, it is noted that after the 1984 Mondale loss, John Sasso, Dukakis's chief of staff, knew that "planning had to begin *immediately*. [Emphasis added.] For this, Sasso turned to a group of his close friends and advisors . . . meeting regularly on Tuesday nights over pizza or Chinese food."[1] After Adlai Stevenson's defeat of 1956, John F. Kennedy and his people *immediately* started to work on the 1960 race. In March, 1987—twenty months before the 1988 election—Democratic political consultant Greg Schneiders said, "Anyone who is not in right now will probaby be starting too late."[2] Jeanne and I had made a decision—and it is a longshot for any candidate—that we would gamble taking nineteen months out of our lives, that the good that might be accomplished so surpassed the difficulties that it would be worth it. But how many people are willing to risk nineteen months of their lives on a long shot? We needlessly put barriers in front of potential candidates. In most parliamentary systems the candidates for prime minister (usually the title) are selected in a matter of weeks. Our system tires the candidates, reporters, and the public.

An observer of several political campaigns told me that the length of the campaign requires a physical stamina level, not only for the candidate but also for the staff, that has caused staffing to be turned over more and more to young people who are "too focused on politics. They have never had a child, never planted a garden. They have not experienced life enough, but because of the length of our campaigns they often end up being key advisers to future presidents and that has diminished the product of the presidency."

Achieving a shorter time frame for our nomination process will not be easy. How can you, in a free country where freedom of speech is protected, prevent anyone from beginning to run for president at any time he or she wants?

We need some experimentation to move us toward shorter campaigns and that will have to involve meshing the first major problem, the length of the campaign, with the second major problem, money.

The political parties can compress the time for the primaries and caucuses slightly. It would help if the first Iowa caucuses were in the middle of March, rather than early in February, and if all states were required by their respective political parties to move their caucuses and primaries further into the year by at least one month.

Then if you were to make this additional change in funding, the campaign could be significantly shortened:

Federal matching funds should cover only contributions that come in after January 1 of the election year, and they should cover only expenses incurred after January 1. At the present time matching funds are available for the candidate in January of the election year, no matter when the contributions are received. If a candidate collected $250 from John or Jane Smith in January 1987, $250 in matching money was available in January 1988. These funds can be used to cover any and all expenses, no matter when they are incurred. If both contributions and expenditures were limited to the year of the election, it would shorten the campaign. The extra incentive would no longer be present for the early fund-raising and spending.

If that change were combined with some type of practical financial reward for a candidate who does not announce more than four months before the first primary or caucuses, the process would be shortened.

These changes in both federal and state laws would not be easily accomplished but the broad-based consensus that our campaigns are too long should make these changes possible to achieve. Public campaigns would be shortened from at least two years to eleven months, an appreciable improvement. Nothing would stop would-be candidates from meeting with friends to plan strategy. They could accept speaking invitations around the country and hint at their probable candidacy, but this procedure would make less attractive the full-blown two-year candidacies that now harm the process.

The second major problem is money. In some ways it is not as great a problem in the presidential race as it is in the Senate and House races where there is no public funding. There have been a few voices calling for public funding for the House and Senate races for years, like Stanley Sheinbaum, a California activist, but their numbers have been few indeed until recently, when Common Cause added its strong voice to the struggle. In the Senate, leadership has come from Senator David Boren, Senator Robert Byrd, and Senator Edward Kennedy. We are finally at the point where a majority of the senators are willing to pass a bill. But we do not have the sixty votes necessary to block a filibuster.[3]

I am grateful to all who support me financially. But the present system of paying for campaigns encourages pandering to powerful financial interests rather than paying attention to the real and long-term interests of the nation. What citizens do not realize is that we have indirect public financing of campaigns now. We pay through poorer schools, health care needs that are unattended, an inequitable tax structure, and in a host of other ways that people do not relate to the way campaigns are financed. We pay through our attention to the wishes of contributors and our inattention to the needs of society.

From the time of their official nomination at each convention, there is now the same amount of money available to both presidential candidates, paid by the one-dollar voluntary checkoff millions of us make when we pay our federal income taxes. This is a vast improvement over the days when candidates—particularly Democratic candidates—had to scramble for money the day after they achieved the nomination, though this once extremely significant reform is lessening in importance as both political parties find ways to evade the intent of the law. The federal law restricts what can be spent "directly" to elect a president, so the fund-raisers are gathering in contributions that are not covered by federal law—often called "soft money"—that can legally be donated by corporations, labor unions, and individuals to state political parties and others who then help "indirectly." The line between what is direct and indirect is sometimes so fine that it is not visible. This once substantial reform needs to be revisited, and massive loopholes closed.

Prior to the nomination, any candidate who receives at least $5,000 from each of twenty states in donations not exceeding $250 per contributor becomes eligible for matching funds up to $250 per contributor. The difficulty with this is that the inequity and imbalance in contributions is compounded by the matching provisions. If one candidate receives $15 million in contributions and another receives $5 million, assuming 50 percent of these contributions are matchable, the first candidate will receive an additional $7.5 million in matching funds, and the second candidate will receive $2.5 million, increasing the already large disparity in expenditures between the two candidates.

But that is not all of the problem. The most fundamental evil is that initial imbalance of funds.

As a sitting governor Mike Dukakis had a powerful resource for raising money. He also had a superb fund-raiser in Bob Farmer, almost a twenty-four-hour-a-day supersalesman. Dukakis had an understandably excited and generous Greek-American community supporting him.

By comparison, I have offended most of the major political funding resources. Jerry Soderberg of Minnesota, a Hubert Humphrey Democrat, operated under that handicap as chair of my national finance committee and did a fine job but could not do it full time. I did come from a major state, and I had around the country friends like Einar Dyhrkopp, Judd Malkin, John Schmidt, Ed Joyce, Mike Cherry, Bill Levine, John White, Marjorie Benton, Stan Glass, Harvey Wachsman, Bernard Weissbourd, Joe Sullivan, Seymour Zises, Dick Phelan, Jim Sale, Ping Tom, Stephen Swid, Alfred Moy, Emery Klein, Paul Park, Bernard Rapoport, David Shefrin and many others who helped in a major way.

Bruce Babbitt, from Arizona with its small population, by any gauge became a serious candidate, propounding substantial ideas and sometimes fresh ideas. But his base could not compare to Illinois. He deserved to have as much money as I had.

Al Gore made no secret of the fact that he became a candidate after some major contributors and fund-raisers pledged substantial sums for his candidacy. I mean no disrespect to Al when I say (and he would probably agree) that Bruce Babbitt deserved to have as much money as Gore had.

Jesse Jackson was the exception to the usual money rules because he is a celebrity. He had high name identification before he became a candidate. He could boast, "I was outspent on Super Tuesday 50–1, but I got the most popular votes."[4] Jesse Jackson could do that on limited dollars, but no one who is not already a celebrity could. Jesse deserved to have as much money as any of the rest of us.

The two candidates with the most money were nominated. I do not suggest that money alone can nominate a candidate, but having enough of it is a powerful assist. Pat Robertson had more money than any Republican candidate other than George Bush but ran third to Bob Dole in most states. While there are exceptions to any precise equation of money and votes, there is much more of a direct relationship than there should be. If I were to advise a candidate, it would be don't announce without either $2 million in the bank or solid pledges of at least $4 million, which will come in at about half the rate pledged. Nothing will frustrate you as a candidate more than seeing great opportunities missed because you do not have the money to seize them.

Adequate funding permits more of everything, from bumper stickers to polling to personnel, and permits not only more of everything, it also permits a qualitative improvement in what a candidate can do. Adequate funding permits a candidate to campaign instead of spending a major amount of time raising funds. "Money is the mother's milk of politics," California's state political leader, Jesse Unruh, used to repeat, with accuracy.

The first matching funds announcement at the beginning of 1988 illustrates the disparity of the present system. Here are the matching fund totals received by candidates on January 2:

Republican Candidates		Democratic Candidates	
Bush	$4,847,851	Dukakis	$2,402,296
Robertson	4,495,607	Gephardt	1,737,216
Dole	4,338,141	Gore	1,313,836
Kemp	3,012,949	Simon	748,180
DuPont	1,868,762	Babbitt	631,489
Haig	100,000	Hart	100,000

Jackson had not yet filed for his money.

Those who already have an edge financially have that edge increased under the present system. For example, if Babbitt had had the same funding as Dukakis, Bruce probably would not have won, but it would have been a much closer race.

Before the federal matching funds came in, here are the year-end totals of contributions received by all the candidates during 1987:

Republican Candidates

George Bush	$18.8 million
Pat Robertson	14.2 million
Bob Dole	14.0 million
Jack Kemp	7.1 million
Pete DuPont	3.7 million
Alexander Haig	1.2 million

Democratic Candidates

Michael Dukakis	$10.2 million
Richard Gephardt	4.3 million
Albert Gore	3.8 million
Paul Simon	3.8 million
Gary Hart	2.2 million
Jesse Jackson	1.9 million
Bruce Babbitt	1.7 million

Those figures illustrate the present problem.

As of June 30, 1988—after the final primary on June 7—the candidates showed these total receipts, including loans:

Republican Candidates

George Bush	$31.6 million
Pat Robertson	28.8 million
Bob Dole	26.1 million
Jack Kemp	16.0 million
Pete DuPont	8.0 million
Alexander Haig	1.9 million

Democratic Candidates

Michael Dukakis	$28.5 million
Jesse Jackson	17.2 million
Albert Gore	11.5 million
Richard Gephardt	9.6 million
Paul Simon	9.1 million
Gary Hart	4.4 million
Bruce Babbitt	3.3 million

One discouraging side note not listed above. Lyndon LaRouche, taken seriously by no political observers I know, received $3.4 million in contributions, almost $100,000 more than the substantial candidacy of Bruce Babbitt.

After looking at these figures, it is difficult to argue with the logic of former Senator Thomas Eagleton of Missouri: "Being the best and brightest at arm-twisting and fund-raising may be a qualification for running the United Way, but it should not be the criterion for the presidency."[5]

After the convention Al Gore's campaign manager, Fred Martin, wrote: "In a dangerous way we're going backward. Throughout American history, we have steadily expanded the pool of people whose consent is required for government to exist—from the elimination of the last property qualifications in the 1850s, to women's suffrage in 1920, to the Voting Rights Act of 1965. . . . The modern nominating system entitles people to vote for only those candidates who have passed a daunting financial challenge. This is extraordinary and not unlike the situation of the early 19th century—only now the financial qualification is imposed on the candidates, not the voters. But voters are disenfranchised just the same, for power continues to lie in other than their hands alone."[6]

That financial qualification for the candidates gives power to those who contribute. And while fortunately there are many who contribute from the best of motivation, too many give because they expect something in return—and get it. The title of a Common Cause study is an insight into today's politics: "If at First You Don't Succeed, Give, Give, Again."

How can a better balance in funding be achieved?

If a candidate were required to raise at least $500,000 in sums not to exceed $250, and from that point on would receive—and be limited to spending—a set amount per state, all candidates could concentrate on the issues and campaigning, rather than spending such a huge amount of their time raising money. In the few days between the Iowa caucuses and the New Hampshire primary, you would expect the candidates to spend every working hour in New Hampshire. That is logical. The *Washington Post* had this item: "Rep. Richard Gephardt was in Washington last night, Sen. Paul Simon in New York, Sen. Albert Gore in Dallas. Each was pausing in his quest for votes to search for the other main commodity of politics: money."[7] At one point during the campaign, columnist Colman McCarthy noted: "Simon, more at ease with the flow of ideas than cash, is bearing up."[8] Candidates and donors tire of this process, and the public senses—accurately—that somehow they lose.

The $500,000 raised by the candidate could go for central office expenses, printing of literature and bumper stickers, and whatever the candidate and the staff determined. As soon as the candidate raised the $500,000, he or she would be eligible for $700,000 in Iowa (or whatever the agreed-upon figure would be) and a set amount in other states. Any candidates who received less than 10 percent in three succeeding states would no longer be eligible for funds, except that if a candidate passed that mark in a later state, he or she would once again be eligible.

Such a system would provide a much more level playing field and discourage the nonsubstantial candidate from entering simply to get the campaign funds. Raising that amount of money would not be easy, though not so difficult that any serious candidate would be unable to do it.

Readers may have other ideas for shortening the campaign or dealing with the money problem. I would welcome them. We are in a forest where no paths have been blazed in this country.

One of the nonissues of a presidential campaign that is elevated to an issue by the nonsophisticated is the question of taking money from political action committees, better known as PACs. They may be formed by businesses, labor unions, professional associations, or people interested in a particular cause. They collect money and give it to candidates in sums that are usually larger than individuals would donate, hoping to have a greater impact on the candidate. The presidential candidates who made themselves sound virtuous by declining had in past campaigns accepted PAC money. Or their campaigns arranged for money to go directly from corporations and labor unions, without even the thin cover of PACs, to state party organizations to assist them. Since PAC money amounts to only 2 to 4 percent of the total in presidential campaigns and ordinarily is available from the same source in individual contributions if the PAC money is not accepted, the candidate can sound virtuous while not harming his or her campaign.

I support legislation to do away with PACs that cause a much more serious problem at the House and Senate campaign level than at the presidential level. But doing away with PACs is not going to solve problems if we continue with the present campaign funding system. There is little difference between getting $5,000 from a corporate PAC or getting five $1,000 contributions from officers of the same corporation. The answer is public financing, through voluntary one-dollar checkoffs on federal income tax forms to pay for it, with strict limitations on expenditures.

We know that whatever reforms are enacted will have to be modified during the years to come. For every reform is followed—just as day follows night—with attempts to circumvent the reform.

United States senators were elected by the state legislative bodies rather than by the people until early in this century when the Seventeenth Amendment to the Constitution was adopted. The reform came about because of rumors, and sometimes more than rumors, of legislative bodies voting for candidates because of corruption. Illinois contributed to this reform when the Illinois legislature elected William Lorimer, the "Blond Boss" of Chicago's West Side, through a $100,000 slush fund raised by Chicago corporations, part of which went to bribe at least seven votes in the Illinois legislature. It stunned the nation that corporate money could be used to almost buy a seat in the United States Senate. The fact that a huge sum like $100,000 would be spent to elect a United States Senator also shocked the public. On July 13, 1912, the Senate refused to seat Lorimer by a 55–28 vote. That stimulated the reform of moving selection away from state legislative bodies directly to the people.

Many saw it as an opportunity to take away the influence of money in selecting senators, to create a situation where rich and poor alike would have an almost equal chance to be elected. Senator Jeff Davis of Arkansas insisted that "if the Senators were elected by direct vote of the people, the country would not witness the nauseating spectacle" of the Lorimer scandal. He concluded, "The times demand a different system, a different mechanism for selecting the members of this great body."[9] Senator Robert Owen of Oklahoma said, "I think it [is] better for all the people that there should be an end made to the election of Senators by the sinister commercial forces of the Republic."[10] How appropriate that a succeeding Oklahoma senator, David Boren, should be leading the fight for once again ending the power of "sinister commercial forces" by providing for public financing of campaigns.

The $100,000 spent to elect Lorimer is small indeed next to the $16.5 million spent to elect a senator from North Carolina in this decade, and the millions all of us have to spend who are elected to the Senate. Shifting the election of senators away from state legislative bodies was a sensible reform but reforms are never finalized. Once again we need a reform, public financing of campaigns at the congressional level and an improved public financing system for the presidential race.

Improve the financing mechanism for presidential nominations and you will: (1) get more good people to consider running; (2) provide greater equity among those seeking the office; (3) give candidates the opportunity to spend more time on the issues, less on fund-raising; and (4) elect a president more free from obligations that a president should not have.

There are other small changes that could improve the process.

One is that more states should enact laws like that of Texas, which has permitted both Lyndon Johnson and Lloyd Bentsen to run for national office while at the same time seeking reelection to the Senate. After Senator Dale Bumpers decided not to seek the presidency in 1988, I almost approached Senator George Mitchell of Maine to urge him to consider making the run. He would make a superior president. I did not do it because he faced a reelection race in Maine in 1988. He could not realistically consider a long-shot race for the presidency. If he could have sought both offices at the same time, I would have urged his candidacy. Under Texas law a vacancy created by the election of a president or vice president is temporarily filled by the governor, and then a special election is held as early as the third Saturday in January. Dick Gephardt *withdrew* his candidacy rather than *suspend* or continue at a more modest level, because under Missouri law he had to decide to run either for the House or the presidency. If Missouri law had permitted him to be a candidate both for the presidency and the House, my guess is that he would have continued both efforts, or at least not withdrawn. We could encourage more senators and many more House members to run if other state laws were changed to be similar to the laws of Texas.

The two parties will be forced to review changes in their conventions. The convention is now a big party rally, a most expensive rally, but not the place where the candidate is chosen. The convention makes the choice official in a circus atmosphere that foreign reporters and diplomats who attend find both great entertainment and a great puzzlement. "What is the point of all this?" they ask over and over. It is a process not dictated by reason but by tradition.

The convention is a grand reunion of people interested in politics and in most instances it cements support within a party around the candidate. It gives that party a lift in the national polls.

Forcing some reappraisal is the television camera. *Washington Post* television critic Tom Shales wrote after the Democratic convention: "What was going on was probably the last Democratic National Convention to get TV exposure this exhaustive, even though this year's was down from 1984's. . . . We were watching the dance of a dinosaur."[11] Despite the drama of a possible Jesse Jackson-Michael Dukakis confrontation, television ratings were low for the convention. Low ratings call for change, and when the focus of the television camera changes, so will the convention; precisely how, I do not know. As one who participates in several graduations each year, I've often thought, "I wonder if anyone has ever asked, 'Do these ridiculous hats really make sense?' " Instead, we continue to wear them, part of tradition. There ought to be at least a few people who ask, "In view of the current situation, where candidates are chosen before the convention, does the convention still make sense?" Maybe it does, but unlike graduation ceremonies where television ratings are not a factor, the conventions will change.

To the credit of the Dukakis staff and Democratic National Chairman Paul Kirk, the 1988 convention in Atlanta emerged almost a total success. On the last day of the convention, I encountered conservative television commentator John McLaughlin on the floor and asked him what he thought of the convention. "On a scale of one to ten, I'd give it a nine," he responded. That was a few hours before the Dukakis acceptance speech, and the moving final two hours had to elevate that evaluation to a nine-and-one-half. The Dukakis speech was the finest I have ever heard him give.

The Republican convention gave George Bush a chance to demonstrate both his skills and his weaknesses. His acceptance speech had a homey eloquence and lack of pretension that were impressive. But his selection of a vice presidential candidate was viewed by most political observers as neither well-handled nor wise. If you had taken a secret vote among Republican senators on who within their ranks would be most qualified to succeed to the presidency if something happened to the president, with no senator permitted to vote for himself or herself, Dan Quayle would not have received a single vote. Lloyd Bentsen would have received many in a similar vote on the Democratic side. If you were to ask Republican senators to vote in a secret ballot, and forget party considerations, who is more qualified to take over the presidency in an emergency, Bentsen or Quayle,

Bentsen would have won by a landslide. Reaction among Republican senators to the Quayle choice was devastating. I serve on the Education Subcommittee of the Senate with Quayle, and a Republican member of that subcommittee told me, "The only good thing about Quayle getting elected vice president is that we get him off the Education Subcommittee." Quayle became a political liability and quickly was assigned roles that assured minimum visibility. Comedian Jackie Mason commented, "The Bush people hid him better than the witness-protection program could."[12]

The Democratic convention gave most of those attending a genuine sense of unity and a sense that the ticket could win. It gave the runner-up, Jesse Jackson, a chance to have his day in the sun and to help in the healing process. Jesse grabbed the convention with his oratory and moved it emotionally. The tensions of the previous days diminished, and Mike's speech helped further ease those tensions. Talk about what Jesse wanted, what deal he got, escalated, but the *New York Times* got a quote from Jesse Jackson that perhaps best summed it up, "I want to be close enough to serve and far enough away to challenge."[13] The vague, indefinable feeling of goodwill prevailed at the convention, though there were some troubled waters ahead in the Dukakis-Jackson working relationship. On the floor after the Dukakis speech, as the delegates sang "America the Beautiful," the "Battle Hymn of the Republic," and "God Bless America," there was a genuine feeling of inspiration.

But it is hard to differ with Colorado's Senator Tim Wirth, "It's the last time for a convention like this. The whole thing is geared to television, and television is backing out, so something has to change."[14]

The Donald Regan book *For the Record,* with its harsh criticism of Ronald Reagan and the Reagan presidency, has caused many people to ask, "How could our system produce such a president?"

Altering the system can make it less likely that someone ill-equipped for the presidency will emerge. But ultimately in a free country, if the people pay too little attention to the issues and the background of the candidates, the results will be less than desirable.

A really fundamental reform is not likely to come soon. Former Senator Thomas Eagleton has suggested that a convention of 585 people should select each party's nominees and do away with the party caucuses, primaries, and convention. His suggestion: A caucus of the members of the House and Senate and governors, plus the party nominees for those offices who lost to the opposition party, so that all congressional districts and states would have the full complement. He adds: "Such a system would more often produce the best and wisest nominee for that particular presidential campaign."[15] Under his proposal, those making the selection would be people who know the strengths and weaknesses of the possible candidates much better than primary or caucus voters or convention delegates now do. The system he suggests would be closer to the process most democratic nations use and I believe would produce stronger presidents. It has the added advantage of rewarding candidates for Senate, House, and governorships who wage unsuccessful but important campaigns. Too often these candidates—often good people—are totally lost to the political process. But I do not expect to see this change in my lifetime.

A modification of the same idea came from a first-time delegate from Illinois, John White, who suggested that the members of the House and Senate and governors get together just prior to a national nominating convention and submit the names of four or five people they believe are qualified to be president. Then the convention would choose.

Political scientist James David Barber also favors a change, turning the choice over to government leaders within a party. The people who are now attending conventions are cheerleaders, he says, and "you do not let the cheerleaders pick the coach."[16]

Changes that are basic, like those suggested by Eagleton, White, and Barber, are so far from where we are now that they are not likely to evolve soon. The immediate changes that are achievable are to shorten the campaigns and improve the financing mechanism.

☆ **10** ☆

THE GENERAL ELECTION

I played a secondary role in the fall campaign.

Others will write in much greater detail about the general election. I campaigned briefly in twelve states, but primarily worked in Illinois after Congress adjourned, serving as state chair for Dukakis.

But the key phrase is "after Congress adjourned." The session dragged on and on, finally closing on October 22, 1988. Sessions that get closer than six weeks to an election become increasingly political and serve the public less well. In addition, for the majority in both the Senate and House who are Democrats, it meant that we could not be out campaigning for the ticket. Dukakis obviously needed all the help he could get.

What went wrong in the general election?

Bush went wrong.

Yes, he won, and if the only aim is to win the presidency no matter what the costs, then he can claim victory. But the costs were too high. He demeaned the presidency and the process in the way he conducted the campaign. When I learned that Roger Ailes served as his media expert, I told my friends that we were in for a dirty campaign. Ailes is the crown prince of negative campaigning. But I did not anticipate how bad it would get. Lee Atwater, a specialist in alley fights, joined his negative campaigning skills with those of Ailes. In any campaign there will be the unplanned, the slip of the tongue, like that made by a Dukakis press aide suggesting that Bush was carrying on an affair. Dukakis promptly fired her.

But it is a long way from a slip of the tongue to a multicolored slick printed brochure sent to Illinois voters charging: "Murderers, Rapists and Child-Molesters Are Voting for Dukakis." A Maryland piece was even worse. Yes, there were occasionally apologies from the Bush campaign, apologies that went almost unnoticed, but the poison entered the system.

I have been watching presidential campaigns most of my sixty years. This was the worst. So much of the tawdry entered the campaign that the media, preoccupied with polls, noticed only the worst abuses. Columnist James Reston noted: "Bush's loyalty to Ronald Reagan these past eight years was understandable and even admirable, but loyalty to his political manipulators is not admirable but intolerable. These win-at-any-cost hucksters are a disgrace to the democratic process, but the Vice President hired them and is running their trick plays."[1] Haynes Johnson wrote in the *Washington Post* that Bush has "run a shameful campaign of smears, lies and distortions. . . . Bush's campaign has appealed to fears and stirred racial prejudices, and I believe that he knows it."[2] It is difficult to come to any other conclusion. The Willie Horton ad had to be put together by cynical merchants of political flesh who felt that a racist appeal without the racist label would work. They ended up not only selling a candidate but said more about themselves than their malleable candidate. They emerged with the smell of the sewer about them, totally insensitive to the reality that self-restraint is necessary for a free system to work. The *Chicago Tribune* ran an editorial a few days before the election titled: "Charlatans Threaten Democracy." The editorial concluded: "We can no longer afford to abandon our heritage to the cynical wiles of the political soap salesmen."[3]

George Bush is now my president, and as a senator I will do my best to make his presidency a good one for the nation. I hope his great mistakes are behind him, not ahead of him. The danger is that someone who abuses the process to achieve public office may abuse the process while in office. Bad habits are not easily broken.

Dukakis responded to the negatives too slowly.

Speaker of the California Assembly Willie Brown says, "In this crazy business [of politics], a lie unanswered becomes the truth within twenty-four hours."[4] On Sunday before the election, *Chicago Tribune* national correspondent Jon Margolis appeared on a television program and commented, "Bush's ads were dishonorable, but Dukakis didn't answer him, and I don't find much sympathy for a chump."[5] How could a candidate go from seventeen points ahead after the Democratic convention to seventeen points down, according to an NBC poll, a few weeks before the election? By not vigorously responding to charges. After the campaign, Dukakis himself said, "I think one of the lessons of this campaign is that you have to respond quickly."[6] The Bush distortions should have been called that immediately, and then Dukakis could have gone on the offensive. On the Pledge of Allegiance issue, for example, a brief explanation should have been given of the United States Supreme Court decision on the case brought by the Jehovah's Witnesses, in which the Court said that no one can be compelled to say the Pledge of Allegiance. Then say that the real issue is not who says the Pledge of Allegiance most frequently, but who lives up to the spirit of the Pledge of Allegiance. We end with the words "with liberty and justice for all." Who really stands for that? And then answer that question vigorously.

The Atlanta convention ended on a strong note, with Dukakis seventeen points ahead of Bush in the polls. With that lead, the campaign lacked a sense of urgency in responding to the Bush commercials and attacks. That lack of a sense of urgency turned out to be politically fatal.

The liability of the high-comfort level after the convention, combined with Mike's natural reserve—lack of passion most journalists called it—could have been overcome, and in the final days of the campaign the race did tighten. But an unfortunate line in the acceptance speech dominated the thinking of those who put together the media and helped create the speeches: "This election is not about ideology. It's about competence." It is hard to argue with Bush's response in his acceptance speech: "Competence makes the trains run on time but doesn't know where they're going."

So when Bush attacked Dukakis as a liberal, instead of seizing the initiative, the charge went unanswered. Columnist Tom Wicker wrote, "Many failings have contributed to Michael Dukakis's lagging campaign for President, but one seems to be at the heart of the problem—the candidate's long, lame and basically unbelievable effort to deny that he and his party represent the great liberal tradition of the last half-century."[7] Another columnist observed, "We have seen him [Dukakis] . . . turning away from the best in his party's past. Dukakis and the Democrats have left the impression that they don't stand for anything." Then the writer criticized Bush in strong terms and concluded, "A plague on both their houses."[8] Until less than two weeks before the election the Republicans defined and distorted the word liberal. Then Dukakis called himself a liberal in the Franklin Roosevelt, Harry Truman, and John Kennedy tradition, but the ringing defense never came.

Mike Dukakis had a hard time conveying warmth.
Voters find it difficult to identify with a candidate whom they feel does not identify with them. As Mike himself said in speeches, he does not wear his feelings on his sleeve. He is a person who is self-disciplined and reserved. The former attribute would have helped him in the presidency, but it did not help him as a candidate.

"The problem with the Harry Truman and Thomas E. Dewey comparison many people make," a reporter told me a few days before the election, "is that Dukakis is too much like Dewey. Fortunately Bush is not like Truman, so that the result will not be too devastating. Bob Dole would have been more like Harry Truman. That would have been a landslide."

News magazines used the word "icy" occasionally to describe Dukakis. He did not come across that way privately, but until the last days of the campaign, that image prevailed. There were a few insights into the heart of Mike Dukakis, like the time he mentioned his father in his acceptance speech and for an instant started to choke up. But those insights into the emotional Dukakis were rare.

"Does he really care about me?" is a question the public asks of candidates and somehow senses in a variety of ways. Mike did not come across enough as a caring person, unfair as that public appraisal is to the private Mike Dukakis.

The campaign never clearly defined the message.
The competence vs. ideology thrust partially accounted for this. But a lack of a clear Dukakis message resulted in media—paid and unpaid—that too often confused voters rather than attracted them. The Bush message was irresponsible but clear. The Dukakis message was responsible but unclear.

The campaign needed an early declaration of independence.

Several weeks before the convention I sent Dukakis a letter with a series of suggestions, among them this idea for his acceptance speech:

> The issue of your independence is hard to magnify in its importance. You must make clear you are independent of everyone and yet want their support. For reasons that are not entirely fair, that applies particularly to the AFL-CIO and to Jesse Jackson. In your acceptance speech, you should make clear that you want the support of all organizations—including labor, farm, and business organizations—but you want these organizations and the American people to understand that you will be genuinely independent, that the question is not what some organization or pressure group wants but what is best for the nation.
>
> The same is true of individuals. You want the support of Al Gore, Jesse Jackson, Paul Simon, et al., and you will seek our counsel and advice, but everyone must understand that you will be the president, no one else. These things have to be framed carefully, but it is important to get the message out early.[9]

Independence from the AFL-CIO did not become that big an issue, but independence from Jesse Jackson evoked enough questioning that the role of Jackson caused awkwardness throughout the campaign. If the declaration of independence could have been carefully phrased in the acceptance speech, Jackson would have understood and then he could have been utilized all-out in the campaign without the hesitation that became all too obvious.

Staffing problems that plague every campaign also detracted from the effort.

Criticisms of "the Boston crowd" were abundant in every state I visited. Part of that is inevitable, because part of the duty of a campaign headquarters staff is to turn down requests and to monitor expenditures closely. But part of the problem was a need, as one critic told me, "of having a bricklayer or a plumber in the inner circle. The Boston crowd doesn't understand the real world enough." For example, it may be hard for someone in Boston to understand that the issue of gun control became a major issue in rural America. It should not have become a big issue but it did. And the response to it was both slow and anemic. The Boston crowd, great on understanding issues, were less able in understanding people. In my old congressional district in rural southern Illinois, gun control dominated the questions raised by those soliciting votes by phone banking.

Part of the staff problem I experienced, and every candidate experiences, has to do with those who are in an inner circle who are comfortable working with each other. They understandably feel that their efforts got the candidate to this point and feel confident they have the know-how to finish the task. Part of this failure to expand the inner circle is caused by a conscious or subconscious feeling that the closeness to the next president should not be shared with others, particularly others who might displace those now "next to the throne." This resulted in the sidelining of major players in the Democratic party whose counsel and aid would have been valuable.

Mike himself became more comfortable with the staff when John Sasso came back aboard. Dukakis never expressed negative feelings about others to me, but he had some unease about the operation. Simply having the candidate more comfortable helped in those final weeks. And after Sasso came back aboard, the campaign took on more vigor.

Immediately after the election, the inevitable chorus sounded forth from those who see an ideological shift as the answer to the Democratic party's problems of winning the White House. To see a shift from the party's traditional liberal base as the answer to the election is to read the results inaccurately, and if that advice is followed, the party will continue to lose. The way to win is to stand firm to our party's progressive traditions, not compromise or abandon them.

Pick a candidate who has a strong base of conviction and is able to project that to the public. Ronald Reagan did not win in 1980 because of his views but despite his views. Those who saw an easy victory for the Democrats if Reagan would be the GOP nominee failed to understand one key ingredient the American people look for in a leader: conviction. The public does not expect to agree with a candidate on every issue, but they want a leader with a strong sense of direction.

We will not win by abandoning the base of the party. Rather than running from our tradition, we have to define it ourselves in today's terms, but we have let the Republicans define what is liberal, what is progressive, what is the Democratic tradition.

In the last two weeks of the campaign, as Dukakis returned more to the Democratic traditional message, his campaign started to surge. It was already too late. But the return to the Democratic tradition made that surge possible and could have made victory possible, if it had started earlier.

The progressive message, properly conveyed, can carry in the South also. We cannot win the South by running to the right of the Republican candidate. "I could have sold Paul Simon easier than Michael Dukakis," the most conservative Democrat in the Senate, Richard Shelby of Alabama, told many of his colleagues. More than any region of the nation, the South is interested in better education, for example. A candidate who spells out a strong program to improve public education can build a strong base across the nation: in the cities, suburbs, and rural areas, in the South, North, and West. Combine a sound education appeal with a program for fiscal prudence and a balanced budget, and a candidate has the additions to the progressive formula that can carry the South. Add to that a sensitivity to small towns and rural America—the South is the most rural portion of the nation—and an appeal to those who are less fortunate economically, and a strong candidate will carry the South. Only one of the southern states has an average income that meets the national average, and that one state, Virginia, would join the others if it were not for the enclave around the District of Columbia with its relatively high income.

The messenger has to be able to sell himself or herself on television, but the message has to be in tune with the traditions of fighting for working men and women and for the less fortunate, for the traditional base of the Democratic party. If the candidate abandons the principles of the party, the people in the party will abandon the candidate.

One of the more conservative members of the Senate told me Dukakis lost for two reasons: He did not answer the Bush charges quickly enough, and he did not convey a warm personality. While other reasons can be added, those are the two principle reasons, and it is significant that Dukakis's place philosophically to the right or to the left is not regarded by most political leaders as a major factor in his defeat.

Having mentioned the things that went wrong with the 1988 general election, a great many things also went right. Dukakis did not win, but he conducted a campaign that did not pander, that told the truth, that did not distort, that no one could describe as shameful. That new grandchild of his will read about the campaign in the years to come with pride.

With a few breaks and a few different turns in the campaign road, journalists and scholars would be writing about the brilliant campaign he conducted. Public adulation and scorn are separated by only the smallest decisions.

The selection of Lloyd Bentsen turned out to be one of the right decisions, both because Bentsen is clearly prepared for the presidency and because the Bush choice of Dan Quayle struck so many in both parties as a weak choice. That became so apparent to everyone, even George Bush, that the half-hour election eve television special purchased by their campaign did not even mention Quayle. A Republican senator told me with a smile that he could only account for the Quayle selection by temporary insanity on the part of Bush. Most reactions by Republican Senators were not that extreme, but it is accurate to say that while Dan is personally popular as an individual with all senators, Republican and Democrats alike were appalled at the decision. Most Republican senators would agree with journalist James Reston: "There are two Senators from Indiana, and he picked the wrong one."[10] The other is Richard Lugar, highly respected.

Each of us who lost the nomination to Dukakis almost hourly encountered people who would say, "If only you were the candidate, we would be winning." I always answered, as I am sure others did, "Thanks. But if we all help, Mike can still win." But each of us probably secretly believes, "If I had been the candidate, it would have been different." And no one can prove us wrong!

I am immodest enough to believe that I could have handled the issues better, but none of us could have done a better job on the critical fund-raising side. Dukakis had a treasure, not just a treasurer, in Bob Farmer, his chief fund-raiser. And there were people around the nation, like businessman Andy Athens in Illinois, who devoted an incredible amount of time to seeing to it that Dukakis had the resources he needed.

There were superb staff people, like Steve Murphy in Illinois, and those who ran the Dukakis operation in Oregon and Washington. I met some marvelous staff and volunteers.

The campaign produced no speeches that are likely to be read by future generations of Americans because of their inspiration. In large part because of the Bush campaign, the nation did not have a massive dialogue on the issues. Instead we stumbled into election day with issues obscured and a feeling on the part of the electorate that 1988 did not display democracy at its best.

☆ 11 ☆

THE POLLS

My southern Illinois home is in an isolated, wooded, rural area where on many days we see more deer than people. It is fascinating to watch the deer and learn their habits. If you remain still and do not move, they will continue eating, or the young ones playing. If you are absolutely immobile, they will occasionally approach you. If they come upon you unexpectedly—or you come upon them unexpectedly—they usually freeze for a few moments, sometimes for a longer time, and do not move until you move. If you move toward them, they will run away quickly, gracefully. In order to survive, they have developed a keen sense of hearing. They have large ears, and they use them well. They may stop eating or walking at the call of a bird, which occasionally can be a danger signal. The slightest sound is detected.

We have developed too many political "leaders" with the deer habit. They listen for any sound, so concerned about possible danger to their careers that the slightest evidence of public opinion anywhere sends terror into their hearts. They may not have ears as large as mine, but their sound detecting apparatus is finely tuned. One of the major mechanisms they have for detecting any possible danger: the polls.

And people who are elected listening to the pollsters try to stay in office by listening to the pollsters. The net result is a virtual abdication of leadership.

Former Senator J. William Fulbright put it well:

162

Our elected representatives . . . study and analyze public at-
titudes by sophisticated new techniques, but their purpose has
little to do with leadership. . . . Their purpose, it seems, is to
discover what people want and fear and dislike, and then to
identify themselves with those sentiments. They seek to discover
which issues can be safely emphasized and which are more
prudently avoided. This approach to politics is the opposite of
leadership; it is followership, for purposes of self-advancement.[1]

This is not a phenomenon restricted to the presidential races. Far
from it. The presidential contests simply evolve from lower level
politics, and at all but the smallest local races, polling is playing
much too dominant a role.

All serious candidates for major offices around the nation commission polls. I do. But it is one thing to use polling to find out
where you stand relative to other candidates, to learn whether your
message on an issue has appeal. It is quite another to use polling to
determine what position to take on an issue—and that has become
all too prevalent.

I had a superb pollster, Paul Maslin. One of the things I like about
him is that he does not have apoplexy if I take some unpopular
stands. He does accurate polling, and I trust his judgment on most
things. Equally important, he recognizes the limited role polling
should take in a campaign. There are other national pollsters who
have a good sense of balance. Peter Hart is one of them. But excessive
reliance on the polls has produced too many leaders who are afraid
to lead. Like the deer, they simply stand and stare and remain frozen
until a poll is taken. A few letters frighten them.

At one point, Joe Biden said, "I can't tell where Joe Biden lets off
and Pat Caddell [his pollster] begins."[2] Probably an off-hand remark
taken out of context. But its truth applies to too many officeholders
and candidates. I can think of several to whom it applies with greater
validity than to Joe Biden. Political leaders should be able to separate
their own convictions from the soundings and advice of pollsters.

Harry Truman commented shortly after leaving the presidency, "I
wonder how far Moses would have gone if he'd taken a poll in
Egypt? . . . Where would the Reformation have gone if Martin
Luther had taken a poll? . . . Fortitude, honesty and belief in the
right makes epochs in the history of the world."[3] Polling is overrated
and much too dominant for candidates. Reporters pay far too much

attention to it. Not only does it dominate too many stories, the public gets polled on every conceivable subject. "Poll finds Infidelity a Lesser Evil Than Others in Picking a Candidate," is the headline for a front-page story, not in the *New York Post* or *National Enquirer*, but in the *New York Times*.[4]

Polling hurts in one other subtle way. Polling on an issue that is particularly controversial, showing deeply divided opinion, results in candidates providing fuzzy answers, making the issues less precise and the campaign more boring than it should be. All of us have been guilty of that.

Public opinion neither can nor should be ignored. A leader must have some sense of public opinion. But it should be used primarily to lead, not follow. Public opinion can tell politicians that people want leadership on the drug problem or on the arms race, but public opinion cannot ordinarily provide the *how* of leadership.

Public opinion polls show clearly that people want three things, by overwhelming majorities: more services, fewer taxes, and a balanced budget. We should not even pretend that we can provide all three at once.

The curiosity of a candidate and staff can lead to spending too much money on polling. In my 1984 senate race, we spent too much money on polling.

In the presidential race we did not, but if we had had ample funding, perhaps we would have. I hope not.

We spent a total of $237,000 on polling, a modest expenditure for a presidential campaign; some would say too modest. We had tentatively budgeted up to $115,000 for polling for Super Tuesday and $10,000 each for a poll in South Dakota and Minnesota, but we ended up doing none of these because of our changed political and financial status.

At least three candidates spent substantially more than these sums.

Leadership involves doing more than what may provide votes. Real leadership must risk losing votes. Polling tends to mute the voices that should call for change.

Senator Bill Bradley of New Jersey has provided leadership on the problem of third-world debt. That issue has required endless hours of work on his part on a difficulty that probably interests less than 2 percent of the population of New Jersey or any other state. It is extremely important to the future of our nation and other nations. Are votes available to him for digging into this issue? Hardly. The same time spent on something with more general appeal could help him immeasurably more. But leadership is not doing just what is comfortable or easy or has the quick payoff.

Two issues I've worked on have a long-term payoff for the nation but little immediate appeal: greater stress on foreign language instruction and more research to find an inexpensive means of converting salt water to fresh water. I mentioned both at one point or another in the campaign, but discussion of issues like these, or on third-world debt, gets no media coverage and stirs few voters.

Former Minnesota Senator Joseph Ball wrote that successful politicians "often march in parades, particularly the popular ones, but rarely do they lead them."[5]

The temptation to simply follow public opinion is neither a new phenomenon nor solely an American caprice. Almost two thousand years ago, the historian and biographer Plutarch wrote: "For this is indeed the true condition of men in public life, who, to gain the vain title of being the people's leaders and governors, are content to make themselves the slaves and followers of all the people's humors and caprices. . . . These men, steered, as I may say, by popular applause, though they bear the name of governors, are in reality the mere underlings of the multitude. . . . As Phocion answered King Antipater, who sought his approbation of some unworthy action, 'I cannot be your flatterer and your friend,' so these men should answer the people, 'I cannot govern and obey you.' "[6]

Britain's Winston Churchill noted: "Nothing is more dangerous than to live in the temperamental atmosphere of a Gallup poll, always taking one's pulse and taking one's political temperature. . . . There is only one duty, only one safe course, and that is to try to be right and not to fear to do or to say what you believe to be right."[7]

Finally, the polls are often wrong. More often than the pollsters like to admit, they miss their target. Even if, in theory, James Madison and those who founded our nation were wrong in warning us not to become too infatuated with public opinion, it is difficult to measure the accuracy of many polls. The final *Des Moines Register* poll for the Republican Iowa caucuses showed Dole leading with 37 percent, followed by Bush at 28 percent, Robertson 13 percent, and Kemp 11 percent. Robertson ended up running second. (Dole 37 percent, Robertson 25 percent, and Bush 19 percent.) Polling turned out to be in error in a major way. Polling was wrong on the presidential primary in Illinois. We know it from the results. Published polls erred in my 1984 senate race in Illinois, consistently suggesting that I would lose when I emerged the victor. But if polling suggests that a majority of people oppose or favor a certain policy, there is no pragmatic way of measuring whether the pollsters are accurate or not, so we assume they are accurate. In the midst of this campaign, pollster Louis Harris, who does no polling for candidates, said, "Nobody is blowing the whistle on good polling and bad polling. . . . A lot of polling is a wet finger to the wind."[8]

In the Michigan caucuses, the pollsters predicted a Dukakis win. "Dukakis Ready to Bury Gephardt in Michigan," read one newspaper headline based on a poll.[9] "Dukakis Machine Hums in Michigan," headed a story in the New York Times that included this sentence: "It is already clear that early, careful organization, coupled with good strategic and tactical decisions, has given Mr. Dukakis an edge here as it has in other states."[10] Jackson beat Dukakis, 53 percent to 29 percent.

Polls are like whiskey. They should be used with great caution, but some candidates end up being "pollaholics," totally dependent on them. "Pollaholics" may hide their habit from reporters and their families. But tucked away in drawers and in closets are polls that almost have become their lifeblood. You may not smell the polls on their breath, but like too much whiskey, you can tell it by their erratic behavior. They have become intoxicated by the polls.

We should not give those candidates major responsibilities.

☆ 12 ☆

THE FAMILIES

When a candidate runs, it is not only the candidate who is on the firing line, it is also his or her family. I am blessed with a family that has grown up liking public affairs and the political process.

All the candidates' families I met respectably represented their candidates, frequently doing a much better job than other designated surrogates. I noted that the representatives in Congress or senators or governors who appeared on behalf of candidates at dinners and other events often talked about themselves more than the candidates they were there to represent. But wives and children and mothers and brothers and sisters stuck to the subject at hand—the candidate.

I did not see that much of the spouses and other relatives of GOP candidates, but over the years I have worked with or known Barbara Bush, Elizabeth Dole, Joanne Kemp, and Elise DuPont. They are some distance from the traditional candidate's wife who simply smiles and is a clinging vine to her husband. (I did not get to work with or appear at events with either Pat Haig, the wife of Al Haig, or Dede Robertson, the wife of Pat Robertson.) Barbara Bush, for example, has provided leadership on the question of adult illiteracy—not a subject likely to erupt in headlines or gain sizable support for her husband's candidacy. "Liddy" Dole is an attorney and former cabinet member who came into Senate and House offices and pleasantly but firmly pounded her fist to win a point. It would be out of character for her simply to be a pleasant addition to a

167

photo session. Marilyn Quayle strikes many people as brighter and tougher than the vice president. "She's the one who ought to be the candidate for vice president," people on the campaign trail heard again and again. What can be said of these three can be said of the wives of all the candidates. The old mold has been broken. I saw much more of the Democratic families than the Republican families and uniformly they made a good impression. Relatives have good days and bad days, just as the candidates do, but they left an overall favorable feeling with audiences and people they met.

Mike Dukakis had his mother speaking for him, as did Dick Gephardt and Al Gore, and there were perhaps other mothers I did not encounter. Gephardt's mother, Mrs. Loreen Gephardt, in particular, seemed to be all over Iowa, outgoing and pleasant.

On most days our wives went in one direction and we went in another, covering as much ground as possible. Jeanne and I made it a point to spend at least one or two days a week campaigning together and with rare exceptions that happened. In that way, we could see each other, learn what was happening in another part of the country, and share the burdens and excitement of a campaign more fully. Despite the crowds and frenzied activity, in many ways campaigning for the presidency is a lonely job. When there can be some sharing, it is helpful to the candidate and to family life. Jeanne and I talked to each other on the phone each evening, with those rare exceptions when one would be on the West Coast and the other on the East Coast and the time difference meant one of us would have to be awakened. Part of my schedule each day: the phone number where I could reach Jeanne that night.[1]

I remember sharing the speakers' podium in North Dakota with Jane Gephardt, and I told the audience, "I have a small scandal I want to share with this audience. I've been seen in public more these days with Jane Gephardt than I have with Jeanne Simon." It was true!

Our wives encouraged us and aided us with their special perspectives. Kitty Dukakis and Jeanne Simon both have a lower boiling point than their husbands, and that helped to stir Mike and me from time to time. Jill Biden is a teacher and brought that perspective to Joe. Lee Hart showed special strength in Gary's reemergence as a candidate. Gary stated candidly he would not have reannounced without Lee. "It got down to how much she was willing to take," he said.[2] "Tipper" Gore knew the national issues but also has shown leadership on the cultural scene. Jackie Jackson matched Jesse's more bombastic style with quiet grace. Hattie Babbitt brought legal and other skills to Bruce's campaign. And Jane Gephardt is a really superior handshaker and meeter of people. She comes across as genuine.

Kitty Dukakis received attention early in the campaign with her public announcement that she had had a twenty-six-year dependence on prescription diet pills and had, with difficulty, broken the habit. The media paid less attention to her interest in the problems of refugees and her other work. I applauded when she responded to a question about redecorating the White House, "I have absolutely no interest in that area."[3] Wives of presidents can do more than that!

All of us who are candidates have some prejudices, and one of mine is that Jeanne would have made a superb wife of the President. She would have been visiting coal mines and Indian reservations and kept me in touch with the nation, as well as lobbying members of the House and Senate on the phone and in person, urging votes for and against various measures.

When I could not accept an invitation to speak to the Utah AFL-CIO convention, Jeanne filled in for me. When fund-raisers were held that I could not attend, frequently Jeanne went, whether that was Atlanta or Hartford or Portland, Oregon. She worked incredibly hard and covered almost as many miles as I did.

I would not have become a candidate without Jeanne's enthusiastic support. As we pondered the decision—and we didn't have much time for pondering—she said, "Go for it." That clinched my decision. A lawyer and former state legislator, she is as happy campaigning and fighting for causes in which she believes as she is in doing anything. Her pleasure in life seems to grow measurably with involvement in a political campaign or working for worthy causes. And she is good at it. When the wives had a forum at Drake University in Iowa, Jeanne opened by saying, "Today you didn't ask us to wear a white orchid, or pour tea, or give our husband's favorite recipe—and I thank you for that." She spoke for all the wives. Political leaders reflect this new attitude. The wives of candidates are treated seriously, not as ornaments.

Six months after I announced my candidacy, my daughter Sheila and Perry Knop, a Southern Illinois University graduate student and farmer, were married. For their honeymoon they invaded Iowa for four months and also visited New Hampshire, South Dakota, Wisconsin, and other states. They had been campaigning for me before their marriage but afterwards they became full-time volunteers and were extremely effective. Perry's agricultural background and political interests added to Sheila's lifetime interest in public policy. Sheila is twenty-seven and a lawyer. She handles herself well in public situations. One of these years she probably will become a candidate for public office.

I did not get to see Sheila when she spoke for me, but I did catch her on the ABC program *Good Morning America*. She appeared with Neil Bush, Jesse Jackson, Jr., and Robin Dole. Morton Dean started the questioning by asking Sheila, "What really bugs you about your father?" Sheila said with candor that the family "does not let Dad play the piano when anyone is around because his playing is so terrible, and when he hasn't found time to get a barber, sometimes he'll get scissors and do a temporary job on himself, which our family finds less than satisfactory." The others found no flaws in their fathers. I liked Sheila's candid answer better—even though it failed to recognize my great skills at the piano.

Our son Martin, twenty-four, is a professional photographer and became my right arm during the campaign. He traveled with me almost constantly. It gave the two of us a chance to spend more time together than for any similar period during his entire twenty-four years. And it gave him the opportunity to meet some of the nation's best photographers and to get an insight into a presidential campaign, both personally and with his camera. Several of his pictures made *Newsweek* and other publications, including the *New York Times Magazine* and the *Chicago Tribune Magazine*.

It was a rich experience for both of our children. When our family gets together we exchange stories about campaign experiences and characters. The process provided an abundance of both.

But a substantial family sacrifice is involved in all of the little things we lose that most families take for granted, like privacy, attending a movie occasionally, and knowing where your laundry is. There are no eight-hour days. Campaigning is an early-morning to late-night activity. Unless an entire family is willing to make this sacrifice, it would be difficult indeed for a candidate. For Sheila and

Martin, the campaign meant one more step into the limelight, into a life they had known and accepted since childhood because Jeanne and I had always been active politically. Our family traveled through the northern part of Illinois in my race for lieutenant governor in the summer of 1968. The shooting of Bobby Kennedy suddenly stunned the nation, and following his death almost all candidates suspended campaigning for a few days. Our family took this time to go north to Wisconsin for a brief vacation. Sheila was seven and Martin four. In Geneva, Wisconsin, we walked past a small shop stamping out whatever messages you wanted on sweatshirts. The children each wanted one that said, "Vote for My Daddy." In spirit, they have been wearing those sweatshirts since that time.

There are candidates for president with small children who have been successful, John F. Kennedy being a prime example. Frankly I would not have considered it if my children were small. At twenty-three and twenty-seven, my children were largely on their own. For Al Gore and Dick Gephardt, both with smaller children, making the decision to run had to be particularly difficult.

Other candidates' relatives helped in the presidential race from time to time. Al Gore's father, Senator Albert Gore, Sr., became one of the most familiar figures on the campaign trail, popular with people everywhere, as well as with the other candidates. Joe Biden's sister, Valerie Biden-Owens, did a particularly good job for him. John Dukakis, the twenty-nine-year-old son with Capitol Hill and acting experience and his wife Lisa, helped Mike, both before the convention and afterwards. Andrea and Kara Dukakis also were active and effective. Jesse Jackson, Jr., makes an excellent impression and appeared on television programs for his father. "The *real* Jesse Jackson," I call him in jest. Jesse, Sr., is obviously proud of him, as he should be. The other Jackson children also were active and presented their father to the Atlanta convention. Sheila and Martin got to know the children of the other candidates much better than I did. As a group they served the candidates and the process well.

My mother, in her early eighties, has helped in past campaigns and wanted to go to Iowa, but she has been having health problems and I discouraged her. My father was a Lutheran minister, so I suggested that instead of traveling, she should get on the phone and call Lutheran ministers. She set about her task in a vigorous and systematic way, calling literally hundreds of Lutheran ministers in Iowa and other states. As I traveled, I frequently ran into those my mother had called.

She and my brother, my neighbors, and my former neighbors all were interviewed by an untold number of reporters. In early December I received a letter from my mother with this paragraph: "The fellow from the *Los Angeles Times* was here for about two and a half hours today. Very nice guy. He asked more and different questions than any of the others. This is number 23— only five or six over the phone, the rest all came here."[4]

My brother, Reverend Arthur Simon, volunteered a week in Iowa, and spent several days in New Hampshire. My relatives in Wisconsin, particularly the Henry Simon family, helped. My brother-in-law, Bill Hurley, and his family helped. Jeanne's cousins, Tom and Marie McDermott, were magnificent. Other candidates had similar help.

There may be times in the lives of people when relatives are less than welcome. But a candidate needs all the help he or she can muster, and relatives are welcomed with open arms. Voters like to get acquainted with a relative of a candidate. Meeting a real live relative of the candidate is the next best thing to meeting the candidate. John Kennedy's relatives played a major role in his success in 1960, and Jimmy Carter's wife and children helped him significantly in 1976.

Part of the modest success my campaign achieved, despite the handicaps of a late entry and lack of funds, came because I had a family that strongly supported me and what I stand for. The day when the families of candidates do not discuss the issues is past. There are still a few around, like Model A Fords, to remind you of another era. But most wives and children of candidates today will do substantially more than look pleasant for photographers.

Not officially a part of the family, but almost part of the family, were members of the United States Secret Service. I declined to take advantage of their services initially and then in about a two-week period we received three death threats, one in Iowa, one in New Hampshire, and one in Texas. To my knowledge these were the only threats received during the entire campaign, but they concerned enough people that I felt the responsible thing was to accept Secret Service protection.

I did it somewhat reluctantly because I have from time to time seen problems arise between candidates and the Secret Service. Their presence literally means twenty-four-hour-a-day protection, with the lack of privacy that implies. But privacy was diminishing rapidly anyway.

They turned out to be a really fine group of men and women. It sounds trite to say, but it is true: Every American can be proud of the Secret Service.

When I plunged into the crowds and did other things to give them gray hair, they were tolerant of me. The aim of the candidate who enjoys campaigning—as I do—is to meet as many people as possible, to "press the flesh." If a candidate likes people and is willing to show it, that eventually comes across on television. But the job of the Secret Service is to provide as much protection as possible, and the crowd situations make that protection difficult. So there is something of an automatic conflict between the aims of the candidate and of the Secret Service.

They worked closely with me and with the local police wherever we were. If someone showed up at an event who had a history of mental problems or threatening people, the local police quickly notified the Secret Service. Occasionally I would be directed to take a different exit or our route to an event would suddenly be changed. Other than at a formal speech where they become obvious, the Secret Service in most situations are not visible to most people and would be virtually undetected except for their earpieces that keep them in touch with one another. If someone acts a bit surly or looks a little less than completely normal, and that is combined with a hand in a pocket that has a bulge, you will see the Secret Service (or as my daughter calls them, "the Secrets") move into action quickly and deftly. That hand gets lifted out of the pocket so rapidly the person involved usually is unaware of what has happened. Someone from a car in the next lane spotted me while we were stopped at a red light in Wisconsin. He got out to come over and shake my hand or talk to me. But the circumstances were unusual enough that he suddenly found himself surrounded by Secret Service personnel, thoroughly frightened I am sure.

A candidate is given a briefing about procedures and where there may be dangers. One of the things I learned is that most assassinations around the world take place from moving cars. That has not been our experience in the United States, but one of the reasons for our better record is the Secret Service with its careful planning for moving public officials and candidates from place to place.

One not-so-minor plus of having Secret Service protection is that they take over driving the car in which the candidate rides. Prior to their joining the campaign, the candidate frequently ends up in cars driven by volunteers, sometimes excited volunteers, sometimes so excited that they spend their time looking at and talking to the candidate rather than watching the road. My wife experienced one automobile accident in which the car was destroyed, though neither she nor the person driving was hurt. As I look back on the series of drivers I had, it is amazing that more candidates do not experience accidents.

Members of the Secret Service follow a candidate wherever the candidate goes. Their work requires real sacrifice and dedication, and I came away from the campaign with an already high opinion of the Secret Service elevated appreciably. As recently as 1944, Senator Harry Truman, a candidate for vice president, could drive his own car around Washington and have virtually no protection. After Truman became vice president, he had one Secret Service agent assigned to him. Times have changed in the United States, though in many other nations the type of protection we find necessary for our top officials is unknown.

Two hours after suspending my campaign and requesting that I no longer be given Secret Service protection, I went to a men's clothing store in Washington, D.C. I suddenly found myself buying sports shirts with no cameras following me, no reporters asking questions, no Secret Service around me.

It was an exhilarating feeling, like a bird must sense when suddenly freed from a cage.

☆ 13 ☆

THE STAFF

I am grateful to a host of people, many staff members and many more volunteers, who made my race as respectable as it became. But nothing is as distracting to a candidate, or can doom a candidacy more quickly, than staff problems. All candidates have them. You attempt to keep them to a minimum.

The person who is good at running a business, or good as a number two person in a campaign, or good at running a congressional office, or good in any number of other positions, may not be a good person to run a campaign. In the position of campaign manager you need someone who gets along well with people, can make fast decisions, who has a good business head, who is self-assured enough that he or she is eager to bring people into a campaign and not keep them out, who has a keen sensitivity to what needs to be done to win, and who has some sense of vision for the campaign, who views things in something more than a day-to-day light. On top of that, the campaign manager has to get along with the candidate. If you who read this suggest that no such combination of skills exists, you are correct. But the campaign manager has to come as close to that ideal as possible.

If staff members don't work out—and the candidate can never tell that in advance—you have to make a change quickly. In many other situations, you can gradually ease someone out of a position, but a candidate who wants to win does not have that luxury. I know of one excellent gubernatorial candidate in a major state (not Illinois) who

175

lost his race because he was reluctant to change campaign managers when circumstances required that it be done.

Whether it is selecting key staff people, or your media consultants, your pollster, your lawyer, or your accountant, a candidate should not do it on the basis of personal friendship. If you are about to have heart surgery, get the very best heart surgeon you can find. You may have a good friend who is a great veterinarian, but he or she is not the one to do your heart surgery. As president, you will have to make some tough decisions. A candidate should start by making them as you put your campaign together.

I had the good fortune of having people on my staff who really believed in the importance of our effort for the future of the nation. Floyd Fithian, Brian Lunde, Paul Sullivan, and Barbara Pape were among those who were key staff people at the top administrative level. Leslie Kerman headed our legal staff, a key component in a campaign where the smallest details of Federal Election Commission regulations become important. Former Congressman (and senatorial candidate in Pennsylvania) Bob Edgar headed my fund-raising effort for a much longer period than he had originally agreed to serve, and Amy Zisook succeeded him. Heading our press efforts were Terry Michael, David Carle, Jim Killpatrick, Lea Sinclair, and Pamela Huey, with our media person, David Axelrod, working closely with them. In naming a few who contributed significantly, I overlook scores whose names should be added who worked long hours and suffered through the emotional ups and downs of a presidential effort.

One problem that erupted severely restricted our efforts during the latter part of the campaign. I have already outlined (in chapter 3) that a few days before the New Hampshire primary, Leslie Kerman and Barbara Pape told me that we were over $500,000 in debt.

I had made explicitly clear that I wanted the campaign to be at a break-even point, with no deficit, if at any point I had to withdraw from the campaign. I assumed that mandate was being followed. People with good intent but poor business skills can go astray and they did.

After Jerry Sinclair looked over the books, he reported to me that some federal and state income taxes withheld had not been paid from the earliest days of the campaign, that unemployment compensation and workmen's compensation, required by the law, had not been paid, and that financially the campaign was in deep trouble—worse than I had been first told. We had a total indebtedness of approximately $1.3 million, with a small part of that to be covered by matching federal funds that would be coming in.

I immediately had to restructure the campaign so that we could continue the effort with fewer people and reduce the indebtedness at the same time we continued the campaign—essentially running the campaign with a substantial handicap. But I had no alternative.

If I were to advise a would-be candidate, that counsel would include getting a hard-headed CPA to work for you from the day you open your headquarters. Even with the best of intentions, keeping financial control is difficult, and if you do not have someone on top of things, you may end with a sizable deficit. John Glenn ended his 1984 campaign approximately $4 million in debt. To his credit and as a real indication of the character of John Glenn, he did not walk away from his debts. When you have people operating in fifty states in your name, it is extremely difficult to keep tight control. Get someone who can. What happens is that people who work for you authorize expenditures they have no right to authorize. They do it with the noblest of motives, believing some key expenditures can make the difference, but the candidate suddenly finds himself or herself facing unauthorized bills, debts created in the candidate's name.

By the time I withdrew as a candidate, our deficit had been reduced to approximately $600,000. Not good, but a much smaller deficit than most of the candidates ended with. Compounding the problem of a deficit for candidates is that there continue to be ongoing expenses. It takes money to raise money. Plus, the Federal Election Commission requires that an office remain open several months for them to do a painstaking audit. The presumption of every campaign is that a painstaking audit, where they spend several months working, will result in some fines for technical violations of the law and regulations no matter how careful you are. Every campaign experiences that. Protecting us somewhat, I had the good fortune to have an excellent attorney, Leslie Kerman.

The reason for the deficit was management that paid much more attention to the political side of things than to the financial, though some campaign deficit is a nearly universal experience of presidential campaigns. As of June 30, 1988, the only candidate without a debt was Pierre DuPont. By then my debt had lowered to $467,000 and continued to be lower than almost all of the candidates. By the end of 1988, thanks to the help of many people, my debt had been eliminated. For all of the candidates' staffs, the political side of a campaign is fascinating, exciting; the financial side much less so. It is understandable that paying much more attention to the political side dominates the attention of top staff people. Bob Edgar and his people—including Amy Zisook, Garry Wenske, May Mineta, and Skip Powers—did a solid job on the fund-raising side of things. In the early part of the campaign, with rare exceptions, we exceeded our modest fund-raising goals. When for a time the campaign appeared to be taking off in Iowa, we exceeded our fund-raising goals substantially. There is nothing like winning to help reach financial goals. But sufficient prudence on the spending side did not exist. Decision makers saw Dukakis and others outspending us, whether for staff in Texas or television in Iowa, and the need to try to keep up with the opposition became too overpowering.

I do not suggest that more sensible spending would have altered the end result. Some believe that but I doubt it. It could however have avoided the deficit and my dramatic curtailment of spending during the final weeks of the campaign.

We had other problems also. Some were relatively minor, like a volunteer housed in Wisconsin by host volunteers who allegedly ended up stealing some things from his hosts. But that was very much the exception to the marvelous experience we had with volunteers and people who took them into their homes.

Every campaign of any significant size has its internal wars. That's part of a campaign, particularly a campaign that relies heavily on volunteers, on believers if you will, and sometimes the line separating a believer and a zealot is a fine one indeed.

Often the people involved in staff turf wars may not recognize that is what they're doing. There is also a tendency of the top staff to rely on people with whom the staff members feel comfortable, who basically agree with them. Instead of diversity of ideas and viewpoints, the tendency in the real power base of a campaign (and every campaign has a small group of staff who really wield the power) is to associate with those who reinforce viewpoints, rather than with those who may differ.

In the first part of my campaign, that real power base rested on a small group of white males, all in their late fifties and early sixties. A reporter noted the tightness and monolithic nature of that circle early in the campaign: "Some of Mr. Simon's longtime backers . . . see [him] surrounded by a narrow group of advisers, people much like himself."[1] I gradually changed that, but change did not come easily. Females, blacks, and Hispanics were not part of that campaign inner circle initially. When I had to make changes at the top level of the campaign, instead of a small group of white males in their fifties and sixties it became a small group of white males in their late thirties and forties.

No matter what fancy organization chart you may draw up for your campaign, ultimately there will be approximately six to ten people who will make the key day-to-day decisions. Your campaign manager and his or her deputy are two of them. The person in charge of fund-raising and your accountant are two. Your lawyer probably will be one. Your press secretary and the person in charge of the field operation are two more. Depending on how you structure the campaign, those will be approximately the top key staff spots. Your media consultant and your pollster will complete the circle. The group should work together well, but not be too much like each other. Diversity of ideas and background is essential.

There develops in every campaign a suspicion of "others," whoever they may be. To be close to someone who may be the next president of the United States is heady stuff and—consciously or subconsciously—sometimes, as new people come in, there is the unexpressed fear that "they" might move in and supplant "me," whoever "me" is. The desire to be close to the throne, and keep others from getting too close, is part of every presidential struggle. There is also suspicion: Will he or she really be loyal to our candidate? Converts are viewed with skepticism and even cynicism, when they should be welcomed. When the Biden people came aboard in Iowa, the meshing at the Iowa level went reasonably smoothly, though even in Iowa there was a reluctance to bring local leaders (not just Biden people) into the key decision making. In New Hampshire, Mike Marshall did a much better job of that than was done in Iowa. But at the national level, we could have used the input of the Biden people much more than we did. Biden's chief Iowa public person, former Iowa State Senator Lowell Junkins, was eager to be used to bring in more Biden people from around the nation. I pushed for it but clearly there existed an unexpressed fear that the Biden people might take over. The result was the less than effective use of a valuable resource. It hurt us in Iowa and other states. And it hurt us financially.

A slightly different opportunity and problem arose when in the latter part of the campaign, one of the nation's most respected political operators, Charles T. Manatt, came aboard as the chair of our campaign. A former national chair of the Democratic party, his presence sent a signal to politicians around the nation that I should be considered seriously and it helped, specifically in his home base of California. But it is not easy for the full-time staff to work into the campaign someone who wants to help, who could contribute a great deal because of his experience. I asked him to work on some specific problems as they arose in the campaign, and he helped in many ways, making a valuable contribution. The simple use of his name added stature to our effort though he contributed far more than that. But he did not get worked into the scheme of things as fully and as effectively as both he and I would have liked on some of the key decisions. (Another former Democratic national chair, Fred Harris, once a senator from Oklahoma, also supported my candidacy.)

We had blacks on the staff, but with the exception of Mike Matthews who played a key role in the South, none at the very top level. Jesse Jackson's candidacy created part of the reason for that, in my campaign and in others. Prominent national blacks privately supported my candidacy but were reluctant to do so publicly because of the Jackson factor, though if I had picked up those extra few hundred votes to carry Iowa, that would have changed quickly and dramatically. I am particularly grateful to those few, like former U.S. Ambassador to Algeria Ulric Haynes, Jr., who played a key role in negotiating the release of U.S. hostages in Iran, who were willing to publicly support me. Much more typical were those who said they felt obliged to support Jackson initially and then would be with me. Some key national leaders in the black community urged me to become a candidate with that understanding. There were also some, like Dr. Joseph Lowery, head of the Southern Christian Leadership Conference, who publicly said that his "two favorite candidates" were Jesse Jackson and Paul Simon, a graceful way to solve the dilemma in which many found themselves. William "Bud" Blakey, who is counsel and staff director to one of my subcommittees in the

Senate, helped on a volunteer basis as did others, but it is not the same as having key blacks in the top echelon of the headquarters on a full-time basis, people who can be policy developers.

I regretted this for political reasons, because we could have done a better job in reaching the black community, even though I recognized that Jesse Jackson would win there overwhelmingly, just as Mike Dukakis carried the Greek-American community overwhelmingly. I regretted this lapse also because all of my life I have led on civil rights, on making opportunities for others. I became the first white subcommittee chair in the House, outside of the Subcommittee on Africa, to appoint a black staff director, and I came from a House district that was 3 percent black. In the Senate I am one of three Senators to have a black subcommittee staff director. And on the legislative front I have always pioneered. The presidential staff had enough blacks and other minorities in key spots to avoid criticism, but not enough to show leadership. The best example of leadership on this front in recent presidential races was Jimmy Carter's 1976 race. It can be argued that he had to because of being a southerner, but I believe it was much more than that. He wanted to show through his campaign staff what he believed. I was less than completely effective on that score, and the campaign suffered in small ways that are generally not immediately visible.

There is a subtle difference, but an important distinction, between accepting intellectually that there must be minority involvement in the staff and significantly reaching to where we should be. That intellectual acceptance goes beyond tokenism, but it lacks the "gut commitment" required. I have learned that where that gut commitment is lacking in key staff people, it takes considerable pushing on my part to get the kind of across-the-board involvement that I want.

What can be said of blacks can also be said of women and Hispanics and people with disabilities. Jumping into a campaign without advanced planning as I did resulted in the evolution of a staff without clear staffing goals. And it showed. When I had made my decision to run, I wanted to make it public so there would be no question, particularly with my late start. Once you announce the world descends on you, and what appear to be less important decisions on staffing are made by others. I would have been wiser to take an extra week before announcing, and plan our staff setup carefully.

In the Hispanic community, we had some prominent national leaders, including Representative Kika de la Garza, Chairman of the House Agriculture Committee; former Immigration and Naturalization Commissioner Leonel Castillo; and San Juan Mayor Baltasar Corrada. For a short time on our staff, we had Felix Sanchez, formerly a key aide to Senator Lloyd Bentsen of Texas, as well as an impressive young Hispanic who headed our Texas effort, Richard Raymond. Again, that high-level person in the headquarters inner circle did not exist.

Women gradually played an increasingly important role in the campaign, including finally in that inner circle, but we did not have someone on the staff who was a nationally recognized women's leader. At one point Bella Abzug of New York, Midge Miller of Wisconsin—both nationally recognized women leaders—and one or two others urged precisely that at a meeting in Des Moines. Had the campaign successfully gone beyond Wisconsin, I planned to ask Midge Miller to come aboard with the campaign full-time. A former Wisconsin legislator, she did a superb job enlisting volunteers and helping our campaign in other ways.

Because of my work through the years with the disabled community, I had excellent support there, but decisions on things as varied as headquarters, rally sites, and personnel sometimes did not reflect what I wanted. Judy Wagner of my Senate staff, one of the better informed people in the nation in this field, helped as a volunteer in the campaign and unquestionably played an important role in the support I did receive.

The other shortfall we had in personnel was in two key but related areas: issues and speech writing. The issues side of it is discussed in chapter 3. But, with issues also goes the need for effective speech writing. I rarely read a speech, but I certainly am not going to read one that is dull and mediocre, that does not reflect me, not only in substance but in style. It is particularly difficult writing for a writer. A speech writer has to be able to almost breathe with the candidate, to sense the candidate's style of speaking and thinking. Ted Sorensen did both superbly for John Kennedy, but not often do you find that happy combination. Peter Mahoney, formerly with Gary Hart, tried; and David Axelrod helped, and it is no reflection on either that some of what they gave me I used but generally what they produced did not quite fit me. Three people emerged, toward the end of the campaign, who sensed a little better than others what I needed: Jim Broadway, a former reporter and public affairs consultant; Jim Pyrros, a Detroit attorney and former Washington Capitol Hill staffer; and Robert Krueger of Texas, a former congressman and former ambassador. All three came up with good, strong, sensitive phrases or examples that I could use. Had the campaign continued I would have tested them more.

Early in the campaign I decided to make a major foreign policy address. I put together a few ideas, but before they could be refined and circulated, a rough draft went to several key figures around the nation, a draft I had neither seen nor authorized. I learned about it when I received a phone call from former Secretary of State Cyrus Vance, who suggested a series of changes that should be made. I took them over the phone, too embarrassed to tell him that I had no idea what he was talking about. When I saw the draft, I found something that was well-intentioned but a substantial distance from anything I would want to circulate, even in rough draft form. I made sure that did not happen again.

As I bare my soul on what went wrong, because it might be helpful to some future candidate who may read these words, the recitation of this chapter so far points out the shortcomings. But an incredible number of things also went well. We could not have gone from a virtual zero in any serious consideration to being the front-runner for a short period without most things going right. Most things went right. Much as I would like to say I am responsible for what went right, the strong staff and superb volunteers deserve most of the credit.

I had more volunteers in Iowa and New Hampshire than any other candidate. They came from Georgia and California, Oregon and Louisiana, from every corner of the nation. They were incredible, sleeping in barns, sometimes; walking through the snow to reach some isolated voter; doing all of the things that can influence voters—and then thanking me afterward for giving them the opportunity. Almost universally they enjoyed their experience.

In addition to excellent staff people who worked with the volunteers, Illinois Attorney General Neil Hartigan helped to organize the Bow Tie Brigade (a phrase first used by Mitchell Locin of the *Chicago Tribune*), volunteers from Illinois who went to Iowa and later in smaller numbers to New Hampshire and other states. Others sent letters. Much of our success in Iowa came because of Neil's leadership and those hundreds of volunteers. Jan Schakowsky, an activist in Illinois, organized substantial numbers of senior citizens who helped in these volunteer efforts.

Among the staff people who played key roles also were those who worked on the thankless job of scheduling, a key spot where you have to say "no" to people much more frequently than you can say "yes." When you say no, you must try to do it without alienating people. Scheduling also has to give the candidate time to reflect, to get a chance to see things in perspective, and my schedule omitted that far too much. I have no one to blame for that but myself.

I also quickly—though not quickly enough—learned that telephone calls had to be screened more thoroughly. At one point, I had accumulated almost six hundred "urgent" calls that should be made, plus the fund-raising calls that are so essential. For illustration, here are calls for me to return, passed along to me on one day in December by my personal secretary, Jackie Williams, one of the unsung heroes of the whole campaign:

Cliff Brody, a friend who has a newsletter on financial affairs.

Peggy Cohill, KMOX, St. Louis.

Mickey Brennan, Ironworkers, wants to explain their financial contribution policy.

Elizabeth Drew, writer for the *New Yorker.*

Richard Goodwin, former speechwriter for John F. Kennedy.

Tom Donovan, president of the Chicago Board of Trade.

Marcus Raskin, head of a Washington think-tank group.

John Sherman Cooper, former Republican senator from Kentucky.

Sylvia Corbin, one of my former staff members now living in Atlanta who wants to volunteer to help.

Stanley Gold, Los Angeles business leader and supporter.

Larry Saunders, Kentucky state senator.

Clayton Fritchey, retired journalist.

Bill Deutsch, head of the Illinois Petroleum Retailers.

Steve Yokich, United Auto Workers in Michigan.

My notes do not indicate whether these calls were made, and if they were made, how many people I reached.

These were calls I "should return." In addition, there are calls that I initiated on fund-raising, to political leaders, to reporters and columnists. These must fit into a day where every minute is scheduled. Many days there would be thirty minutes and occasionally an hour set aside for phone calls, but when we got behind schedule because of weather problems or the thousand and one other things that can delay a caravan, the easiest thing to scrap in the schedule is that half hour for phone calls.

Between the unavailability of those to whom I returned calls, and the squeeze in the schedule, I doubt that I reached half the people that day. There is something of a sigh of relief when you return a call and the person isn't there. You have the best of both worlds. You've returned the call but haven't taken much time to do it. Those not reached go on a list which I should follow through on, or for a member of my staff to call.

Another key group in a campaign are the advance people, a small group who develop special skills in knowing where to hold a meeting, how to attract a crowd, how to use the candidate's time most effectively, how to get the best shots for television, and dozens of other small details that make a campaign stop appear to be an effortless success.

Part of all of this is the fundamental question: How much time should a candidate spend running his own campaign? A candidate who pays too much attention to details is dead politically. You have to delegate authority, and then if you sense shortcomings in those to whom it is delegated, you make changes. Drawing the line is not easy, and every candidate in looking back sees where mistakes were made in both directions.

But key to a candidate's success is his staff and the volunteers. That I came as close as I did to winning the nomination is a tribute to their good work.

☆ 14 ☆

ADVICE TO THE PUBLIC

The political process for selecting candidates should be improved, but the finest process that minds can devise ultimately will fail if people do not take an interest. That interest is one of the encouraging things about those two early states, Iowa and New Hampshire. But even there, a candidate has the discouraging task of convincing some voters that their franchise is important, that they can make a difference. Cynicism toward all politicians still corrodes too much of the potential electorate.

How can citizens get more effectively involved in presidential politics? The real answers are not dramatic. Readers looking for new, simplistic answers that can suddenly change things will not find them in this list. But here are a few suggestions.

Get some experience campaigning.
Before you launch your efforts in the next presidential race, find a candidate for Congress or the state legislature or county clerk who has some appeal to you. Volunteer. You will soon be doing some uneventful, undramatic chores, but you will be learning the process. Don't expect to influence anyone until you have done your apprenticeship. That means stuffing envelopes, making phone calls, knocking on doors. In the midst of my first race for the U.S. House, a student from Southern Illinois University came into my campaign headquarters to volunteer. I happened to be there, and when I suggested that he could help in assembling a mailing that we were

trying to get out, he declined. He wanted to volunteer to help set foreign policy for me and give me his insights on world affairs. I pointed to Ralph McCoy, the head librarian at this university with 24,000 students, who at that point could be seen assembling and stuffing those envelopes for our mailing. I thought the example might inspire him. But it obviously turned him off. He wanted to influence policy but he did not have the willingness to do that basic work that eventually might make that possible. The late Senator Paul Douglas of Illinois once said: "There are many who profess their devotion to the common good. But the test is whether they are willing to ring the doorbells of an indifferent citizenry and to brave the opposition of entrenched greed."[1] Get some experience campaigning before the next presidential race, and you will be more valuable in that contest.

Pay more attention to what is happening.
The level of attention to issues, to the backgrounds of the candidates, to the problems that have not emerged as issues in a campaign suggest that we have a considerable distance to travel in our political sophistication. Watch television programs that provide information, not just entertainment. C-Span's coverage of the House and Senate and of many events is often worth watching. Ted Koppel's *Nightline* enriches evening programming immensely. Cable News Network not only provides the news but also some solid programs. The Sunday morning talk shows often are good. Where you see deficiencies in news coverage, ask for improvements. Read magazines and more than one newspaper. Be someone who develops leadership not simply because of your personal qualities but because you are more understanding of the issues and personalities than others.

Become reasonably familiar with one or two issues.
Pick one or two problems or issue areas that really interest you. Start reading everything you can find in those areas. Make sure you read both sides of a question so that you have a reasonably accurate perspective. Follow what your legislators are doing in the issue or issues you choose. Write to them. Go to meetings where you can ask questions. Then when the next presidential race is upon us, write the candidate or candidates. If it is a multicandidate field, try to attend a meeting where you can ask a question or two. Your familiarity with

one or two issues will make you a more contributing citizen and also assist you significantly in evaluating the presidential candidates. You are much less likely to be taken in by a slick line hastily memorized by a candidate.

Those three steps you can take immediately. Then, as the next presidential race approaches, there are more concrete things you can do to have an impact on this key office. Answering the question of why the candidate seeks office, what he or she wants to do, is difficult to determine. You cannot make the judgment simply by what the candidate says. You have to look at how he or she says it, what the record is. But determining this question of why the candidate seeks office is the most important and fundamental question. The British author, C. S. Lewis, writing in the time when the word "man" was used generically, said something of significance that applies to presidential candidates also: "In many men's lives . . . one of the most dominant elements is the desire to be inside the local Ring and the terror of being left outside. Unless you take measures to prevent it, this desire is going to be one of the chief motives of your life, from the first day on which you enter your profession until the day when you are too old to care. Of all passions the passion for the Inner Ring is most skillful in making a man who is not yet a very bad man do very bad things."[2] There is nothing more Inner Ring than the presidency. The public must weigh whether the candidate primarily seeks that position for the emotional satisfaction or because the candidate wants to do something for the nation.

Encourage someone to run you believe would make a good president.
There are hardly any genuine drafts for the presidency. But one of the questions that runs through the mind of a potential candidate: Will I do well enough so that I will not embarrass my family and myself? A candidate can never know that answer in advance with certainty. A few spontaneous letters from around the country may be interpreted as indications of support that has some breadth. Almost any senator or governor who receives one hundred spontaneous letters within a four-week period, urging him or her to run for the presidency, will begin to consider it. Look the field over carefully for the next presidential election in your party when you do not have an

incumbent president, and select someone you believe would make a great president. Then write to that person, and get three of your friends to do the same. I can virtually guarantee you that your letter will be read and reflected upon.

As you look for a candidate, also look for qualities that you want in a president. Is there a good balance between experience and ideas? Does he or she demonstrate qualities of thoughtfulness and courage? Is there a solid base of conviction, a sense of direction and purpose? Look at the potential candidate's record, not just the statements and press releases.

Does he or she have a sense of history? Is that combined with a solid inner core of stability and common sense? Does the candidate show a breadth of interest and intellectual curiosity? What does the candidate read—and does he or she read books, and if so what are they? Is there a demonstrated humanitarian instinct in the candidate? While domestic policies tend to dominate elections, the greater responsibility a president has is in foreign policy. Is there an understanding in this field? Does the candidate come across as genuine so that as president people would believe and support necessary programs when he or she appeals to them?

Contribute financially.

Money has been mentioned frequently in this book because it is so paramount. A small contribution from you, and getting some of your friends to contribute also, would be of significant help to a candidate for president. Contributions of less than $250 are matched by the federal government through the one dollar contribution you check off on your federal income tax form. The more candidates receive in contributions from average citizens, rather than those with major financial interests at stake, the more our government is likely to respond to the needs and hopes of those citizens.

Get an organization to which you belong to do a better job.

Most organizations are not as effective as they could be or should be in influencing presidential choice, and most that do try to influence wait until the general election. By then, the greatest choice already has been made. The field has narrowed from almost twenty serious candidates in both political parties to two. The more important choice by far is made in reducing the field. There is an awkwardness in an organization getting involved, because within the organization there will be divisions, and any organization can survive only a limited number of divisive fights without coming apart. But deftly handled it can be done with minimal harm.

In an earlier chapter I mentioned examples of organizations contributing now but they could do a better job.

One of this nation's largest organizations is the American Association of Retired Persons, more commonly called the AARP. Until recently, they have not (with rare exceptions) exercised their political muscle. It has been a sleeping giant, doing much good but generally not in the political arena. "A good, bland, non-controversial organization," one of my Senate colleagues has called it. This year the giant started to move. In its first real attempt to exercise political muscle, the AARP has learned that it had influence by helping focus attention on a major issue, long-term care, but it can do better.

What could they have done to be more effective without jeopardizing their organization? Suppose the AARP followed through by asking members of their national board to evaluate each candidate in both political parties on a scale of one to ten on four key questions: How strong is the candidate on long-term care for seniors? How strong is the candidate on other issues that affect older Americans? Is the candidate electable? Does he or she have the general background a president should have? Then the AARP could give the cumulative evaluation of their national board on these questions with the admonition that candidates should not be judged solely on one issue or one set of issues. This would not constitute an endorsement but would send a much clearer signal than is now communicated. If on a score of one to ten, Smith got an evaluation of 8.7 and Jones 4.3, it would be a much clearer signal to the AARP members than they now receive.

Organizations at a minimum should provide information about where the candidates stand on key issues, and most can do a more effective job than is now done.

Candidates should not be judged by the standards of one organization alone. But individuals and organizations can be more helpful in moving the nation toward effective leadership.

Getting the organization to which you belong to do a better job in evaluating presidential candidates would be a public service.

Write to friends in key states.

You may not live in Iowa or New Hampshire or another early key state, but you probably have friends in one or more of them. A personal letter to just two people you know in those states could make a difference. Or it may be to people affiliated with an organization to which you belong, or people in the same profession. A few days ago I received a copy of the alumni directory of Dana College in Nebraska. I could send a letter to alumni in Iowa and New Hampshire. There are any number of ways of getting the names of people to whom you can write in one of the early key states. Don't underestimate the value of those letters. If nothing else, ask the candidate's office for the names of as many people as you are willing to contact. The office would be happy to provide such a list.

Volunteer a weekend or more in a key state.

One of the most exhilarating things for a candidate is to be walking through the snows of Iowa or New Hampshire and suddenly spot a familiar face: Harry Barnes, a retired school teacher from Elgin, Illinois; Rhonda Abrams, a young lawyer from San Francisco; Gordon Allen, a retired farmer from Eldorado, Illinois; and many others. Did they do more than inspire the candidate? You bet they did. Without those volunteers, my close call in Iowa would have been anything but a close call. Knocking on doors in a strange state may not be your concept of an ideal vacation, but I have yet to meet one of those hundreds and hundreds of volunteers who hasn't expressed to me how much he or she enjoyed the experience. A great many have written thanking *me* for giving them the opportunity. How grateful I shall always be to these unheralded volunteers. If you not only volunteer, but also get others to volunteer, you multiply the impact of your efforts.

Write letters to the editor.

In almost all newspapers, the letters to the editor have a higher readership than do the editorials. In part it is because they are signed. They also tend to be briefer and more vigorous in their expression of opinion. The net result is a high readership. Take advantage of your opportunity to reach a sizable audience and an audience that tends to vote and be influential.

One word of caution: There is a tendency in campaigns to view things in terms that are too clear-cut, that your candidate is surrounded by virtue, and the opposition candidates are the personification of evil, or in terms almost that stark. Keep in mind that your arguments are usually more persuasive if you are reasonable. While today you may not be enamored with another candidate, that candidate could emerge as the nominee of your party. Don't position yourself so that you have to eat too much crow; don't create a situation where you are not believable if later you support another candidate.

Recently George McGovern said that a mistake had been made in referring to the Vietnam War as an immoral war by those opposing it. He said that by calling it immoral, by implication those who supported the war were labeled immoral, and that caused some of them to dig in and become rigid, rather than reexamine their position.

Too much righteous indignation is not persuasive, either for causes or candidates.

☆ **15** ☆

IN RETROSPECT

What did it all mean? Was it worth the effort, not only for me but for the thousands of others who got involved in my campaign?

Those of us who were candidates but not nominated are listed as losers. But we added some interest to the process, improved the dialogue of the campaign a little, talked about the things in which we believe, and in ways that cannot be measured precisely, added to the nation. After I suspended my campaign I would occasionally hear the three remaining Democratic candidates and then Michael Dukakis talking about things I had stressed, sometimes even using the same phrases. I would have done the same if I had succeeded rather than Dukakis. So there is a positive gain to the nation for our having been candidates. When I first announced, there were those who wrote that I would have no appeal to young people. But at Harvard, Yale, Brandeis, the University of Iowa, the University of New Hampshire, the University of Minnesota, Dartmouth, Luther College, Swarthmore, Drake University, Grinnell College, Simpson College, and a host of other schools, halls were overflowing, sometimes students literally hanging from the rafters and crowded around windows to listen in halls too crowded to enter. At the University of Wisconsin, I spoke to three or four times as many people outside the auditorium as were inside, people who could not get in. To those who get depressed about the future of this nation, let me take you to a college campus!

Making the race gave me a chance to know my fellow candidates and the people of the nation as I could do in no other way. A few newspapers around the nation have noted that I left not supporters but believers. The young student in Iowa who told me, "I got involved in politics because of you." What will that mean for her future and for the future of the nation? No one knows. But it provides satisfaction to a defeated candidate.

My colleagues in the Senate were graciously tolerant of my absences during the campaign. One of the questions I asked myself as I faced the possibility of running: Will it in any way impair my work in the Senate and my relationships with my colleagues? It has not. When they think I have a good idea they vote for it, and when they think I have a bad idea they oppose it, as before.

The *St. Louis Post-Dispatch* said approximately what several journals did after I departed the race: "Sen. Simon's message is one of growing importance. It is prospering in part because of the senator's character—his honesty and compassion. That's a lot for the Democratic Party and the country to be thankful for. Although Paul Simon didn't win, he left an important legacy of which he can be proud."[1] The wounds of defeat are helped to heal by words like that and by the many letters of encouragement people generously sent, like the Yale professor who wrote: "You gave this campaign humanity and decency and maturity."[2] An American citizen who emigrated from the Soviet Union thirteen years ago, attended a Democratic rally during the campaign "to observe American politics in the making." In an article about his experience he had these generous words: "Simon's appearance brought a welcome relief. He spoke with the ease of a politician who needn't worry about impressing the crowd and who knows how to be forceful without being shrill. In a deep, sonorous voice Simon talked about an American that is a little more humane, a trifle more rational, and in the process managed to convey that most coveted by men and women of his profession: the image of a person who really cares."[3]

More important for me than the words of praise, greatly appreciated as they are, are other things:

The thousands of students who got involved, many for the first time, some of whom will stay involved and a few of whom will eventually become candidates themselves. The contributions they will make cannot be calculated.

I saw this nation as you can in no other way: Our weaknesses and strengths; our racism and enthusiasm; our appalling lack of knowledge of the rest of the world, but campuses rich with ferment; our rural areas and small towns, like much of urban America, in decline, yet skyscrapers rising in those same cities and rural America fighting to rebuild; our rivers visibly and casually and indifferently polluted, just as highways are strewn with garbage, but people in New Hampshire and New Orleans concerned about the environment; our underclass, largely hidden, and ignored by most of America, but also an America becoming sensitive to at least one part of the underclass, the homeless.

When you sense little interest on the part of most citizens in the problems of desperate poverty of so many in our nation, when you despair because there is infinitely greater interest in the World Series than in world arms control, when you find too many of the nation's comfortable more interested in yachts than in quality urban education, when you start to give up on the system, then little things happen to lift you and give you hope.

You meet a ten-year-old boy in Centreville, Iowa (population 6,558) who is studying Japanese. You discover in a small New Hampshire community, a hall filled with people concerned about the arms race. In Alabama and California, you find volunteers who are willing to devote an incredible amount of time to tutoring those who cannot read and write.

And I think of Hamilton High School in Milwaukee. Knowing that I helped create a federal statute, Public Law 94–142, that mandates education opportunity for the nation's disabled youth, school officials there had a chorus of mentally retarded young people sing for me. Prior to the creation of that law, most retarded and otherwise handicapped young people were not being helped by our schools. The chorus recited in unison the preamble to the constitution, and then they sang, "This Is My Country." I glanced over at the twelve or fourteen reporters traveling with me, somewhat cynical viewers of the political process, and I did not detect a dry eye among them. Nor were my eyes dry.

If that legislation had not passed, probably half of those chorus members would be in institutions today.

Is our system perfect? By no means.

Despite that, can we accomplish some good? Those young people in that chorus are the answer. Government is not the enemy. It is simply a tool that can be used wisely or unwisely.

Years ago our family drove through South Dakota and visited Mt. Rushmore, but this time in South Dakota I talked to Indians from the Pine Ridge Reservation about their problems, a very different perspective. You learn the problems of "the Valley" in Texas and nuclear energy in New York and New Hampshire. You come to understand the opposition to oil derricks off the stunningly beautiful coast of northern California. You talk to a young man in Minnesota who had his arm completely cut off in a farm accident and then sewn back on and made useful, but the family faces an avalanche of medical and hospital bills they don't know how to meet. You talk to a family in New Hampshire where a parent suffers from Alzheimer's disease and other complications, and the family has received over $900,000 in medical and hospital and nursing home bills. Asian-Americans tell you their hopes and ambitions and the difficulties they encounter.

I also had fun. I saw Lorne MacArthur with whom I served in the Army, now a school principal in Waltham, Massachusetts. I saw college classmates and even high school classmates. Only a Rotary Club member can fully appreciate having one-hundred and twenty Rotarians in Waterloo, Iowa—mostly Republicans—singing the following to the tune of "R-O-T-A-R-Y, That Spells Rotary":

> B-O-W-T-I-E, that spells bow tie.
> B-O-W-T-I-E, Paul Simon is the guy.
> He's his own man, it's plain to see;
> He wears his tie with dignity.
> B-O-W-T-I-E, that spells bow tie.

Yes, there were days of physical exhaustion. But there were many more days of exhilaration, of having a good time, of recognizing that something as small as a handshake from a candidate can give pleasure to so many people.

And there was satisfaction in seeing the quality and the diversity of the support. A day or two after I announced my candidacy Norman Cousins, the distinguished author and leader, walked in and handed me a contribution of $1,000. Pianist Andre Watts sent a contribution of $500. Words of encouragement came along the way from people as diverse as entertainer Whoopi Goldberg, architect I. M. Pei, baseball manager Sparky Anderson, and political observer Walter Cronkite.

More important than the support and encouragement was the inner satisfaction of knowing that, however inadequately, I was addressing the real needs and potential of the nation. And I sensed people respond, not in large enough numbers to nominate me but perhaps in large enough numbers to help shape the future.

For all the defects of the present campaign system, it showed me the nation as I would never have known it otherwise. It did the same for George Bush and Michael Dukakis. George Bush will be a better president because he walked in corn fields in Iowa and talked with Hispanics in California and did all the things an American candidate for president is forced to do.

I saw an America attracted to the superficial, but I also saw an America with a warm heart and great resources that the right leadership can use to make this rich nation an infinitely richer nation, and make our world safer and better for future generations. I saw an America cheering and responding to slogans, but I also saw an America that can be thoughtful, that has a sense of community to which a leader can appeal. I saw an America yearning for leadership of compassion and vision and courage.

Running for president was a great experience. I doubt that I shall do it again, but I have no regrets for having run. On a scorecard where votes are tallied I am listed as a loser, but in every other way I came out a winner. My horizons have been broadened. I am a better senator and better citizen. And I believe my country is a little better for my experience.

Endnotes

Preface

1. Quoted by Robert F. Kennedy, *Robert Kennedy in His Own Words,* edited by Edwin O. Guthman and Jeffrey Shulman (New York: Bantam Press, 1988), p. 252.

Chapter 1. Prelude to a Candidacy

1. Letter to Paul Simon, signed by Representatives Fortney H. (Pete) Stark and Barbara Boxer, Richard Lehman, Norman Y. Mineta, and Don Edwards of California; William Lehman and Charles E. Bennett of Florida; Marcy Kaptur and John Seiberling of Ohio; Cardiss Collins of Illinois; Sam Gejdenson of Connecticut; Charles Rose of North Carolina; Wes Watkins of Oklahoma; Stephen J. Solarz of New York; and Robert W. Kastenmeier of Wisconsin, dated June 30, 1986.

2. "The best guy for prez: Illinois' own Paul Simon," by Richard Reeves, *Quad-City Times,* September 26, 1986.

3. "Simon Boomlet," by John McLaughlin, *National Review,* September 26, 1986.

Chapter 2. The Race (I)

1. Editorial, "Retro-Democrat," *Baltimore Sun,* May 26, 1987.

2. Editorial, "A Refreshing Democratic Entry," *St. Louis Post-Dispatch,* April 12, 1987.

3. Editorial, "Paul Simon: Principle, Ideas Before Image," *Peoria Journal-Star,* April 11, 1987.

4. "Can Paul Simon Make the Doubters Change Their Tune?," by Jon Margolis, *Chicago Tribune,* April 14, 1987.

5. After Biden withdrew from the race, physicians discovered two aneurisms in his head that required major and delicate surgery, and later found a serious blood clot. Biden credits his withdrawal from the race for saving his life. After seven months of medical care and rest, he has returned to the Senate fully restored to good health but perhaps a little more subdued, a little more serene.

6. "Simon Wins in Poll at Broadway Fair," by Greg Hinz, *Chicago Sunday Star,* September 8, 1987.

7. Poll published by Peter Hart in the *Chicago Tribune,* November 7, 1987.

8. "Simon Bears Watching in Democratic Race," by Carolyn Barta, *Dallas Morning News,* September 28, 1987.

9. "Sen. Simon's Stock Suddenly Soaring," by David Broder, *St. Louis Post-Dispatch,* November 10, 1987.

10. "Cuomo, Uncommitted, Says Simon 'Looks Strong,'" by Jeffrey Schmalz, *New York Times,* November 6, 1987.

11. Molly Ivins quoted in "Reporters Don't Write Off Simon's Long Shot Effort," *Chicago Sun-Times,* May 11, 1987.

12. "Making Mr. Right," by Andy Boehm, *Los Angeles Weekly,* June 5–11, 1987.

13. "The Candidate from Another Time," by Jack Beatty, *Los Angeles Times,* August 20, 1987.

14. "Pee Wee's Big Adventure," by Fred Barnes, *The New Republic,* October 5, 1987.

15. "Suddenly, He's Looking Good," by Christopher Simpson, *The Washington Times,* October 14, 1987.

16. "Events Kick Simon Candidacy Into Gear," by Keith Love, *Los Angeles Times,* October 10, 1987.

17. Jimmy Carter quoted in "Carter Says Simon Can Win Voters in the South," by Mitchell Locin, *Chicago Tribune,* October 5, 1987.

18. "Some of That Old-Time Religion," by Walter Shapiro, *Time,* November 16, 1987.

19. "Reign of Errors," by Jonathan Alter and Mickey Kaus, *Newsweek,* October 31, 1988, reprinted from an earlier undated edition of *Newsweek.*

20. "Could Dukakis Be Simon-ized?" by David Nyhan, *Boston Globe,* November 29, 1987.

21. "'Tortoise' Simon Overtakes Hares," *Chicago Sun-Times,* November 9, 1987.

22. "Sen. Simon's Stock Suddenly Soaring," by David Broder, *St. Louis Post-Dispatch,* November 10, 1987.

23. "Simon Is Drawing More Voters—and Criticism," by David Shribman, *Wall Street Journal,* November 13, 1987.

24. "Simon's Climbing, Say Several Polls," by Judy Keen, *USA Today,* November 23, 1987.

25. Quoted in "If Dems Split, Cuomo Will Run, Carter Says," by Steve Neal, *Chicago Sun-Times,* November 15, 1987.

26. "The Emerging Candidate: Who Is Senator Simon?" by Robin Toner, *New York Times,* December 9, 1987.

27. "Simon Offers a Government That Cares," by Robert Maynard, *Waukegan News-Sun,* December 17, 1987.

28. "U.S. Politics Meets the Honest Man," by George Neavoll, *Wichita Eagle-Beacon,* December 27, 1987.

29. Sen. Robert Dole quoted in "Choice Candidates and Funny Men," by Larry King, *USA Today,* May 23, 1987.

30. "Bush, Simon Images Compared by Bush," *Boston Globe,* November 8, 1987 quoting from *The Washington Times,* author not indicated.

31. "The Sprint," by Fred Barnes, *The New Republic,* February 8, 1988.

32. "Gary Hart: A Study in Narcissism," by Ellen Goodman, *Arlington Heights Daily Herald,* December 22, 1987.

33. "Shallow Sounds of Campaign '88," by Michael Kramer, *U.S. News & World Report,* December 28, 1987.

34. "Simon Attracts Large Crowds, Slips in Polls," by Keith Love, *Los Angeles Times,* February 4, 1988.

35. Editorial, "Our Views on the Candidates," *Des Moines Register,* January 31, 1988.

Chapter 3. The Race (II)

1. "New Hampshire Voters in Hibernation Until Iowa Caucuses," by Philip Lentz, *Chicago Tribune,* December 13, 1987.

2. "Simon Down, Jesse Up," *Chicago Sun-Times,* March 14, 1988.

3. "Jackson Jumps Ahead of Simon in Poll," *Peoria Journal-Star,* March 14, 1988.

4. "Simon Sagging on Eve of Vote in Home State," *Boston Globe,* March 14, 1988.

5. "Simon Gets New Life," by Wayne Woodlief, *Boston Herald,* March 16, 1988.

6. "Simon Cleans Duke's Clock," by Peter Lucas, *Boston Herald,* March 18, 1988.

7. Sub-head below "Bush, Simon Score Wins in Illinois Primary," by Paul West, *Baltimore Sun,* March 16, 1988.

8. "Simon Leads Pack in Illinois," by Thomas Oliphant, *Boston Globe,* March 16, 1988.

9. "Backyard-Voting Trend Continues," by Paul Taylor, *Washington Post,* March 16, 1988.

10. Editorial, "The Duke and the Baron," *The New Republic,* August 1, 1988.

Chapter 4. The Candidates

1. Marvin Kalb, *Candidates '88,* (Dover, Mass.: Auburn House, 1988), p. xix.

2. "Reunion in Dwarfville," by Martin F. Nolan, *Boston Globe,* January 17, 1988.

3. Alex Seith, quoted in "What Mike's Like," by Norm Oshrin, *Sterling Daily Gazette,* September 19, 1988.

4. Statement made March 10, 1988, quoted in "What's My Line?" *Washington Post,* April 27, 1988, author not indicated.

5. "Bush vs. Dukakis," by Harrison Rainie, *U.S. News & World Report,* May 2, 1988.

6. "Dukakis," by Larry Martz, *Newsweek,* July 25, 1988.

7. Quoted in "Letter from Washington," by Elizabeth Drew, *The New Yorker,* April 4, 1988.

8. Debate sponsored by the Democratic Leadership Council, Washington, D.C. The debate was held at Tulane University, New Orleans, November 2, 1987.

9. "Even as He Loses, Jackson Is Winning," by David Broder, *St. Louis Post-Dispatch,* May 2, 1988.

10. Ray Rollinson, letter to Paul Simon, March 14, 1988.

11. "Paul Simon," by Adam Hochschild, *Mother Jones,* January 1988.

12. Quoted in "Thoughts on the Business Life," no author indicated, *Forbes,* June 3, 1985.

Chapter 5. Dealing With The Issues

1. "Simon the Salesman Dealing in Retail Politics," by Mitchell Locin, *Chicago Tribune,* June 10, 1987.

2. Pam Huey memorandum, September 30, 1988.

3. "The Shrinking of the Candidates," by Steve Daley, *Chicago Tribune,* September 30, 1988.

4. "We're All Accomplices in the No-Issue Campaign," by Lawrence Grossman, *New York Times,* October 31, 1988.

5. Editorial, "Campaign Issues. What Issues?" *New York Times,* April 13, 1988.

6. "Voters Bored With Emphasis on Issues," by Robert Wagman, *Sterling-Rock Falls Daily Gazette*.

7. "If You Hope to be President . . . Ideas Just Get You Into Trouble," by William Schneider, *Los Angeles Times*, January 1, 1988.

8. Pat Robertson quoted in *Candidates '88*, by Marvin Kalb and Hendrik Hertzberg, (Dover, Mass: Auburn House, 1988), p. 148.

9. "Letter From Washington," by Elizabeth Drew, *The New Yorker*, August 15, 1988.

10. "Word to Dukakis: Be Bold," by William Greider, reprinted from *Rolling Stone*, *Chicago Sun-Times*, May 29, 1988.

11. "The Duke's Challenge," *Newsweek*, May 2, 1988.

12. Printed in *Congressional Quarterly*, July 23, 1988.

13. "Letter From Washington," by Elizabeth Drew, *The New Yorker*, April 4, 1988.

14. "How America Voted: Early and Often, and Mostly by the Old Rules," by R. W. Apple, Jr., *New York Times*, June 5, 1988.

15. Henry E. Brady and Richard Johnston, *Media and Momentum*, edited by Gary Orren and Nelson Poslby, (Chatham, N.J.: Chatham House, 1987), p. 184.

16. Editorial, "Gary Hart Calls It Quits," *St. Louis Post-Dispatch*, May 9, 1987.

17. "NPP Democrats Should Look to Simon," by Roland Perusse, *San Juan Star*, July 20, 1987.

18. "Does Simon Have a Pinocchio Problem?" by Michael Kramer, *U.S. News & World Report*, November 30, 1987.

19. Editorial, "Flim-flam," *Peoria Journal-Star*, December 3, 1987.

20. Editorial, "A Useful Debate," *Quincy Herald-Whig*, December 7, 1987.

21. David Yepsen quoted in "Iowa Poll: Simon, Bush Debate Losers," *Rockford Register-Star*, December 3, 1987.

22. Marvin Kalb and Hendrik Hertzberg, *Candidates '88*, (Dover, Mass.: Auburn House, 1988), pp. xix-xx.

23. Editorial, "Simonomics Now Adds Up Better Than It Did Before," *Philadelphia Inquirer*, January 11, 1988.

24. Quoted in "Simon Take Political Gamble With Economic Policy," by Mitchel Locin, *Chicago Tribune*, January 8, 1988.

25. "Journeys With Humphrey - Memoir of a Peace Mission That Failed," by Norman Cousins, *Saturday Review*, March 4, 1978.

26. Bonus Books, Inc., 1987.

27. Commentary by Dan Rather, CBS Radio News, May 11, 1988.

28. Address of Senator Edward M. Kennedy, John F. Kennedy School of Government, Harvard University, November 30, 1987.

29. "Jackson Seen as Caring but Lacking Experience," by E. J. Dionne, Jr., *New York Times,* December 1, 1987.

30. Senator Wendell Ford in conversation with Paul Simon, June 1988.

31. Quoted in "Pat Robertson: A Candidate of Contradictions," by Wayne King, *New York Times,* February 27, 1988.

32. Kalb and Hertzberg, p. 144.

33. "Robertson Says God Guides White House Bid," by T. R. Reid, *Washington Post,* February 15, 1988.

34. "Report from the Kemp Campaign," no author indicated, *Presidential Campaign Hotline,* February 5, 1988.

35. Kalb and Hertzberg, p. 155.

36. "Lutheran Long Shot: Paul Simon," by Daniel Cattau, *The Lutheran,* August 1987.

37. *Baltimore Sun,* August 16, 1988.

38. "Competence Liberalism," by George Will, *Washington Post,* July 22, 1988.

39. *Collected Works of Abraham Lincoln,* ed. by Roy P. Basler, (New Brunswick, N.J.: Rutgers University Press, 1953), Vol. I, pp. 111–112.

40. Associated Press story by Doug Richardson, No. 1538, dateline Indianapolis, July 14, 1987.

41. "Gary Hart Attack: Media Scrutiny, Democratic Foes," by Maralee Schwartz and Eleanor Randolph, *Washington Post,* January 29, 1988.

42. "Letter From Washington," by Elizabeth Drew, *The New Yorker,* August 15, 1988.

43. Debate sponsored by the Democratic Leadership Council, Washington, D.C., Tulane University, New Orleans, November 2, 1987.

44. *New York Times,* February 16, 1988.

45. *Washington Post,* February 19, 1988.

Chapter 6. The Debates

1. Marvin Kalb and Hendrik Hertzberg, *Candidates '88,* (Dover, Mass.: Auburn House, 1988), p. xvi.

2. Kalb and Hertzberg, p. xvii.

3. Eddie Mahe, Jr., quoted in "In Search of George Bush," by Randall Rothenberg, *New York Times Magazine,* March 6, 1988.

4. Larry Speakes, *Speaking Out,* (New York: Charles Scribner's Sons, 1988), pp. 85–86.

5. From the program "Firing Line," broadcast by PBS, July 1, 1987.

6. Ibid.

7. "America's Future: A Presidential Debate," NBC, December 1, 1987.

8. Paul Maslin memorandum to the Simon campaign, October 16, 1987.

9. Quoted in "Front-Runner Hart Stumbles as Lackluster Iowa Debater," by Larry Eichel, *Detroit Free Press,* January 17, 1988.

10. "America's Future: A Presidential Debate," NBC, December 1, 1987.

11. Democratic National Committee debate transcript from debate held October 7, 1987.

12. "Two-Gun Al Duels Tough Gunfighters," by Roger Simon (no relative), October 11, 1987.

13. Kalb and Hertzberger, pp. 172–173.

14. "Is Anybody Listening?" by James A. Barnes, *National Journal,* February 1, 1988. The debate coaches making the judgments were Jack Kay, University of Nebraska; Gregg Walker, Oregon State University; Michael Pfau, Augustana College, South Dakota; and Thomas J. Hynes, University of Louisville.

15. Quoted in "My Campaign Failed—But the System Works," by Bruce Babbitt, *Washington Post,* February 21, 1988.

16. *Time,* October 1988.

Chapter 7. Should Iowa and New Hampshire Be So Dominant?

1. *Washington Post,* January 17, 1988.

2. "I'm Giving Up Iowa and New Hampshire," by Raymond R. Coffey, *Chicago Sun-Times,* December 28, 1987.

3. "Super Tuesday Has Turned Out to Be a Super Flop," by Richard Reeves, *Philadelphia Inquirer,* March 9, 1988.

4. "Not-So-Casual Simon Draws Pair at Casual Cafe," by John Carlson, *Des Moines Register,* May 5, 1987.

5. "NBC Nightly News," May 15, 1988.

6. *St. Louis Post-Dispatch,* May 8, 1988.

7. "The Phantom Poll Booth: Think You Know Who Really Won the Iowa Democratic Caucuses? Think Again," by William Saletan, *American Politics,* June 1988, Vol. 3, No. 6.

8. "Little Big Men," *Newsweek,* November 21, 1988, no author indicated.

9. "Dukakis's Strategy Plays to Strengths," by David S. Broder and Maralee Schwartz, *Washington Post,* April 24, 1988.

Chapter 8. The Media

1. *Washington Post,* June 5, 1988, box on page 4 about TV talk shows.

2. Quoted in "Gary Hart, The Elusive Front-Runner," by E. J. Dionne, Jr., *New York Times Magazine,* May 3, 1987.

3. "Bite-Sized Policies: The Trivialization of Leadership," Sen. Gary Hart, Peter Strauss Lecture, Yale School of Management, November 11, 1987, mimeographed and unpublished.

4. Ibid.

5. "Answering Hart and Kennedy," by Tom Winship, *Journalism Review*, May 1988.

6. Craig R. Whitney, letter to Paul Simon, May 5, 1987.

7. Paul Simon, letter to Craig Whitney, June 3, 1987.

8. *Congressional Record,* April 26, 1988, p. S 4734.

9. J. Leonard Reinsch, *Getting Elected,* (New York: Hippocrene Books, 1988), p. 17.

10. "TV's Role in '88: The Medium Is the Election," by Michael Oreskes, *New York Times,* October 30, 1988.

11. Edward Kennedy speech, November 30, 1987, at Harvard's Kennedy School of Government, excerpts in *Washington Journalism Review,* May 1988.

12. Conversation with Paul Simon, May 31, 1988.

13. Hart lecture.

14. *Newsweek,* May 2, 1988.

15. Story originally published in a book by Paul Simon, *The Glass House,* (New York: Crossroad/Continuum, 1984), pp. 120–121.

16. "Democrats Face the Texas Primary," by Richard Ryan, *Texas Observer,* November 6, 1987.

17. "Simon Was 'Rare' at the Roast," by Donald Kaul, *Joliet Herald-News,* June 25, 1987.

18. "Taking a 'Simon Says' Approach to Sen. Simon," by Garry Wills, *Chicago Sun-Times,* September 14, 1987.

19. "Warm-Hearted Candidate," no author indicated, *The Economist,* August 1, 1987.

20. "Some of That Old-Time Religion," by Walter Shapiro, *Time,* November 16, 1987.

21. "Stumping With Simon," by Dan McCullough, *Naperville City Star,* March 17, 1988.

22. "Class Like Simon's Always in Style," by Mike Royko, *Telegraph-Herald,* (Dubuque, Iowa), May 15, 1987.

23. "Simon Leads Us Into Anti-Image Era," by Jeff Greenfield, *Moline Dispatch,* May 21, 1987.

24. Royko column.

25. Vic Fingerhut quoted in "Pee Wee's Big Adventure," by Fred Barnes, *The New Republic,* October 5, 1987.

26. Letter to Paul Simon from Florence Garrett, Hunt Hill, Bridgewater, Connecticut, January 9, 1988.

27. "Let Surrogate Candidates Smile for TV," by Michael J. O'Neill, *New York Times,* April 9, 1988.

28. William J. Small, *Political Power and the Press,* (New York: W. W. Norton, 1972), p. 81.

29. "Skins vs. Shirts," by Mark Shields, *Washington Post,* February 12, 1988.

30. "Simon, In Tight Contest, Returns to Basic Appeal," by Robin Toner, *New York Times,* January 29, 1988.

31. "What's the Primary Message?" by Henry E. Brady and Richard Johnston, *Media and Momentum,* edited by Gary R. Orren and Nelson W. Polsby (Chatham House: Chatham, N.J., 1987), p. 184.

32. "Babbitt Blasts Simon Proposals," United Press International, *Kankakee Daily Journal,* January 6, 1988.

33. "Report from the Simon Campaign," by Terry Michael, *President Campaign Hotline,* January 20, 1988.

34. "Doubt Is Cast on Simon Role as Foreign Correspondent," by Chris Black, *Boston Globe,* January 3, 1988.

35. Quoted in an article by Monica Langley in the *Wall Street Journal,* quoted in "Take 2," by Carl Sessions Stepp, *Washington Journalism Review,* July/August 1988.

36. Oreskes article.

Chapter 9. The Process

1. Richard Gaines and Michael Segal, *Dukakis, the Man Who Would Be President,* (New York: Avon Books, 1987), p. 311.

2. Quoted in "Bumpers Decides Against a 1988 President Bid," by Richard L. Berke, *New York Times,* March 22, 1987.

3. Two books that deal with the financial problems in much greater detail are *Financing the 1984 Election,* by Herbert E. Alexander and Brian Haggerty (Lexington Books), and *The Best Congress Money Can Buy,* by Philip Stern (Pantheon).

4. "Jackson's Bid for Funds Is on a Roll," by Thomas B. Rosensteil, *Los Angeles Times* Service, *Boston Sunday Globe,* March 27, 1988.

5. "Let Political Pros Dethrone King Money," by Thomas Eagleton, *St. Louis Post-Dispatch,* July 24, 1988.

6. "The Curse of Campaign Fund Raising," by John Frederick Martin, *New York Times,* July 11, 1988.

7. "Trying to Cash in on Iowa," by Charles R. Babcock and Maralee Schwartz, *Washington Post,* February 11, 1988.

8. "Simon and the Liberal Appeal," by Colman McCarthy, *Washington Post,* September 13, 1987.

9. Quoted in "Illinois and the Four Progressive-Era Amendments to the United States Constitution," by John D. Buenker, *Illinois Historical Journal,* Vol. 80, No. 4, Winter 1987.

10. Ibid.

11. "Dukakis's Grand Finale," by Tom Shales, *Washington Post,* July 22, 1988.

12. Quoted in "Even Wild Dogs Couldn't Keep Them Away," by H. John Schwartz, *Newsweek,* November 21, 1988.

13. "Dukakis Sets out to Parlay Unity into Fall Victory," by Michael Oreskes, *New York Times,* July 23, 1988.

14. "Poor Ratings May Kill 4-Day Conventions," by Helen Dewar and Lloyd Grove, *Washington Post,* July 22, 1988.

15. Eagleton article.

16. "Pick Candidates by Peer Review," by James David Barber, *New York Times,* April 10, 1988.

Chapter 10. The General Election

1. "Bush's Choices: Quayle, Hucksters," by James Reston, *New York Times,* October 26, 1988.

2. "Where Is This Year's Truman?" by Haynes Johnson, *Washington Post,* October 28, 1988.

3. Editorial, "Charlatans Threaten Democracy," *Chicago Tribune,* October 30, 1988.

4. Quoted in "Willie Brown Sees Dukakis Errors," by R. W. Apple, Jr., *New York Times,* October 31, 1988.

5. City Desk, NBC-Chicago, November 6, 1988.

6. Quoted in "Wistful Dukakis Sees No Bush Mandate," by Robin Toner, *New York Times,* November 10, 1988.

7. "Dukakis's Great Denial," by Tom Wicker, *New York Times,* October 28, 1988.

8. Johnson article.

9. Paul Simon letter to Michael Dukakis, July 6, 1988.

10. Reston article.

Chapter 11. The Polls

1. "The Legislator As Educator," by J. William Fulbright, *Foreign Affairs,* Spring 1979, p. 722.

2. Quoted in "Such Empty Generational Politics," by Charles Krauthammer, *Washington Post,* October 2, 1987.

3. Harry S Truman quoted in a letter to the editor, "Basing an Opinion

on Polls Is Irresponsible," by Dr. Richard L. Hill, Littleton, New Hampshire, *Manchester Union Leader*, August 12, 1987.

4. "Poll Finds Infidelity a Lesser Evil Than Others in Picking a Candidate," *New York Times*, May 6, 1987.

5. Ferdinand Lundberg, *Scoundrels All*, (New York: Lyle Stuart, 1968), p. 88.

6. Dryden translation of Plutarch's *The Lives of Noble Grecians and Romans*, from *Great Books of the Western World*, (Chicago: Encyclopedia Britannica, 1952), Vol. 14, pp. 648–49.

7. Quoted in "How Former Presidents Have Used the Polls," no author indicated, *National Journal*, August 19, 1978, p. 1314.

8. "Pollster Decries Polls for Presidential Race," by Daniel R. Browning, *St. Louis Post-Dispatch*, April 8, 1988.

9. "Dukakis Ready to Bury Gephardt in Michigan," by Gene Grabowski, *The Washington Times*, March 25, 1988.

10. "Dukakis Machine Hums in Michigan," by R. W. Apple, Jr., *New York Times*, March 24, 1988.

Chapter 12. The Families

1. Jeanne has written her own experiences of the campaign in a book *Codename: Scarlett* (Continuum), which will be published in May 1989.

2. Quoted in "Standing by Her Man," by Ellen Goodman, *Boston Globe*, January 12, 1988.

3. Quoted in "Kitty Dukakis," by Bob Grogin, *Los Angeles Times* Service, *Chicago Sun-Times*, June 15, 1988.

4. Ruth L. Simon, letter to Paul Simon, December 7, 1987.

Chapter 13. The Staff

1. "Backers Fear Inexperience May Hobble Simon's Campaign," by Bill Lambrecht reporter for the *St. Louis Post-Dispatch*, in *The Washington Times*, May 26, 1987.

Chapter 14. Advice to the Public

1. Paul H. Douglas speech at Macon Junior College, Macon, Georgia, from the papers of Virginia DeSimone, Paul Douglas's personal assistant.

2. C. S. Lewis, *The Inner Ring*, the memorial oration at King's College, the University London, 1944, in *The Weight of Glory*, (New York: The Macmillan Company, 1949), pp. 58–61.

Chapter 15. In Retrospect

1. Editorial, "Paul Simon's Contribution," *St. Louis Post-Dispatch,*
April 11, 1988.

2. Letter from Paul Gewirtz to Paul Simon, April 11, 1988.

3. "Democracy in the Hands of the People," by Dmitri N. Shalin, *St.
Louis Post-Dispatch,* February 26, 1988.